T0253940

Mostly Codeless Game Development

New School Game Engines

Robert Ciesla

Apress®

Mostly Codeless Game Development: New School Game Engines

Robert Ciesla
Helsinki, Finland

ISBN-13 (pbk): 978-1-4842-2969-9   ISBN-13 (electronic): 978-1-4842-2970-5
DOI 10.1007/978-1-4842-2970-5

Library of Congress Control Number: 2017948735

Cover image designed by Freepik

Managing Director: Welmoed Spahr
Editorial Director: Todd Green
Acquisitions Editor: Pramila Balan
Development Editor: Matthew Moodie
Technical Reviewer: Nakul Verma
Coordinating Editor: Prachi Mehta
Copy Editor: Kim Wimpsett
Compositor: SPi Global
Indexer: SPi Global
Artist: SPi Global

Distributed to the book trade worldwide by Springer Science+Business Media New York, 233 Spring Street, 6th Floor, New York, NY 10013. Phone 1-800-SPRINGER, fax (201) 348-4505, e-mail orders-ny@springer-sbm.com, or visit www.springeronline.com. Apress Media, LLC is a California LLC and the sole member (owner) is Springer Science + Business Media Finance Inc (SSBM Finance Inc). SSBM Finance Inc is a Delaware corporation.

For information on translations, please e-mail rights@apress.com, or visit www.apress.com/rights-permissions.

Apress titles may be purchased in bulk for academic, corporate, or promotional use. eBook versions and licenses are also available for most titles. For more information, reference our Print and eBook Bulk Sales web page at www.apress.com/bulk-sales.

Any source code or other supplementary material referenced by the author in this book is available to readers on GitHub via the book's product page, located at www.apress.com/9781484229699. For more detailed information, please visit www.apress.com/source-code.

Printed on acid-free paper

This book is dedicated to Dennis Ritchie (1941–2011),
the creator of the C programming language

and

my friend Tuomas Mäkelä.

Contents at a Glance

Contents

About the Author

Robert Ciesla is a freelance writer from Helsinki, Finland. He earned a bachelor of arts degree in journalism and has a knack for writing urban fiction and directing short films. Robert has worked on many video games on several platforms since being a kid in the mid-1990s. His latest venture is Soiree Games, a burgeoning games company specializing in products with a socially aware slant. Robert's personal web site is at robertciesla.com.

About the Technical Reviewer

Nakul Verma is a professional game developer and currently works as a senior unity developer at Aquimo Sports Pvt Ltd. He has worked in a variety of game genres using multiple technologies. Specifically, he has worked on casual puzzle games, an endless runner, an endless casual game, card games (rummy on Cocos2d-JS and an African game), and a physics simulation sample and is currently working independently on his own game that will be hitting stores soon. He is proficient in game technologies such as Unity, Cocos2d-x/JS, Construct, and Allegro. Gaming has always been one of his favorite hobbies along with sports, music, and break dancing. His favorite game genres are first-person shooters, platformers, and puzzlers. When he is not making or playing games, he is working out, break dancing, or messing around with some gadget.

He earned a bachelor of technology degree from PEC University of Technology in the field of electronics and electrical communication.

Acknowledgments

I'd like to thank the entire Apress editorial team for their support and constructive criticism. Their input greatly helped shape my vision for this book for the better. As Robocop once so eloquently put it, thank you for your cooperation.

Introduction

Why would anyone get into the video game industry? I'll give you two pretty good reasons.

- As of 2017, the global games market was estimated to be worth more than $100 billion.

- It won't stop at $100 billion.

From the rectangles on the TV that used to excite people in the 1970s to the painstakingly drawn pixel art of the 1980s and the 1990s to the 3D revolution of the 2000s, video games have been increasingly influencing the aesthetic enterprises around them. Now, in 2017, we have truly reached the Golden Age of the Video Game. The line between cutting edge and retro has never been this blurry. It's hip again to be pixelated. Unlike those early millennial times, a gigantic software team is no longer a must-have prerequisite for success. Thanks to some new tools and digital delivery systems, the one-person operation is back.

Not only do we have the technical know-how to produce nearly movie-quality game experiences, but some very powerful pieces of game making–software are becoming both numerous and widely available. In addition to having top-notch hardware support, this type of software is finally becoming accessible to all. There are tools for every budget and every skill level. And the end results can be more impressive than the audiovisuals in Hollywood. Finally, after 40 years or so, making game creation software is a truly viable option for investors and programmers alike. This is where we, the small-time entrepreneurs, cash in. This is it.

But as great as all of these tools are, this book is not about productivity software per se; it's more about every future game visionary out there. This book is about you, my friend, and together we will take *your* ideas from *your* consciousness to all those little screens in the world. Video games are no longer a mere industry. They are a culture, and you're part of it. Now more than ever.

—Robert Ciesla
CEO, Soiree Games

CHAPTER 1

■ ■ ■

Getting Ready!

Before you felt the urge to create your own games, you probably were a consumer of games for quite some time. You've played a lot of them over the years, and you have intuitive ideas of what appeals to gamers like you.

Prior to getting serious about game development, you should consciously seek factors that make a game great. The biggest overall successes in entertainment software history all share common traits. To a degree, you are wise to emulate them. Let's take look at these titles, shall we?

- *Tetris for mobile devices by Alexey Pajitnov & EA*: More than 100 million copies sold. It was originally released in 1984 for the Electronika 60, a then-hip computer from the Soviet Union.

- *Wii Sports by Nintendo*: More than 82 million copies sold.

- *Minecraft by Mojang*: More than 70 million copies sold.

- *Grand Theft Auto V (GTA V) by Rockstar Games*: More than 52 million copies sold.

- *Super Mario Bros by Nintendo*: More than 40 million copies sold.

Now let's take a look at the indie contestants.

- *Minecraft by Mojang*: More than 70 million copies sold

- *Super Meat Boy by Team Meat*: More than 40 million copies sold

- *Fez by Polytron Corporation*: More than 40 million copies sold

- *World of Goo by 2D Boy*: More than 40 million copies sold

- *Bastion by Supergiant Games*: More than 3 million copies sold

What do all of these titles have in common? They're multiplatform. In some cases, they're very, very multiplatform. One of them, *Wii Sports*, came bundled with a cool new system—see if you can get on that bandwagon! These ten games are intuitive to grasp and control, offering a smooth gaming experience. There are also memorable main characters with highly merchandisable gimmicks—Italian plumbers, anyone? And there's a lot of

© Robert Ciesla 2017
R. Ciesla, *Mostly Codeless Game Development*, DOI 10.1007/978-1-4842-2970-5_1

violence, in the case of *GTA V* (and many hit games that didn't quite make the list), which is a gangbanger simulation of the highest caliber. For some reason, the people of this planet really, really enjoy their extreme violence.

So, the following features are what sells:

- *Flawless game mechanics*: The player doesn't have to struggle with controls or grasping the idea of the franchise. The basics are simple, and they work at all times.

- *Lasting challenge*: The game is virtually unbeatable (like *Tetris* and *Wii Sports*) and/or provides tons of replayability.

- *Deployment for multiple platforms*: Keep those Windows-only games to a minimum.

- *Memorable, merchandisable characters*.

- *Conflict and violence*. In general, this planet loves it. In games, it certainly helps.

Now, as a small developer, it's likely you will need to wear many hats. Let's take a look at these roles in the video game industry next. Working with modern video game–making software, it's unlikely you will need to ever dwell very deep into more complex areas of programming, but it's still a good idea to get acquainted with some common industry job titles.

Who Does What in the Video Game Industry

Many of the following development team roles are increasingly becoming specialized as video games rival blockbuster movies in their armies of creative people working on them.

Producer

Responsible for keeping the whole project together, a video game producer benefits from both hands-on experience in as many related fields as possible and a sense of overall vision. The number of a producer's creative responsibilities varies within development teams. In some cases, a producer solely works as management, solving conflicts and keeping a team going.

This may be an unnecessary post in smaller projects, however. A tiny operation obviously doesn't benefit much from a hired producer.

Some typical producer duties include the following:

- Building and maintaining a functional team

- Contracting out work and delegating responsibilities

- Media relations

Designer

Video game designers come up with the conceptual part of a product. Good game design is timeless. Think of chess: it was designed in the sixth century and is still going strong. Creating balanced game dynamics and a low enough learning curve are the designer's job. Also, as sprawling 3D games are all the rage, level designers are very much in demand. Modern level designers usually work with dedicated software, sometimes provided by the programmers in the team.

Programmer

Programmers handle perhaps the most diverse bunch of duties within game production. There are numerous specialized programming fields needed in creating a competitive product. In the early days of the 1980s, being a programmer meant you were the sole person behind a title. Not so much in modern times, although there are exceptions (*Minecraft*, for one, is a one-person operation). Being a programmer can mean these things and much more.

- *Game core creator*: This is what people usually mean by programmer. The game core creator is responsible for game mechanics, main visuals, and player controls.

- *Artificial intelligence developer*: This person is responsible for making smart enemies within a game.

- *Problem solver*: If you're really good, you may be hired as a mercenary programmer to solve a development team's issues within a project.

- *Physics expert*: This person is responsible for creating realistic maps/levels for games with a set of artificial laws of physics governing the game world.

- *Networking specialist*: Many games are run online these days as multiplayer war zones. This creates a whole host of challenges to a project.

Usually, being a good programmer requires a strong sense of logic and/or mathematics. The importance of math is somewhat exaggerated in most programming literature, but it always helps. Some fields of programming work, such as physics, simply do require strong math skills.

Many programmers have a "pet language," which is one they are most comfortable with. Make sure yours is one of the more useful ones, such as C++ or Java.

Visual Artist

Video games used to mostly feature simple on-screen shapes for visuals. Since the advent of 3D graphics in the mid-to-late 1980s, visual artists span an increasingly large group of subfields. These include the following:

- *2D artist*: This includes duties such as presentation and, in the case of 2D games, in-game visuals.

- *3D artist/3D modeler*: These artists create 3D objects with software such as Blender or Maya.

- *3D animator*: This may in many cases be the job of the modeler also. An animator works with the 3D objects created by the modeler and crafts fetching animated sequences, such as a 3D human walking, running, or fighting.

- *Texture artist*: In essence, 3D objects need a coat of digital paint on them to make them look less bland and more realistic, which is the duty of the texture artist.

- *Environmental artist*: Most 3D games need compelling vistas to make them draw the players in.

- *Conceptual artist*: Especially bigger projects benefit from unified art direction. Concept drawings on whatever media help with this goal.

Sound Designer/Musician

If you are an experienced musician, you can in theory make it as a video game composer. Earlier on, as in the 1980s, computer musicians were required to create their compositions pretty much using programming skills. As of late, as long as the output is in digital form, your audio work can be quickly incorporated into a video game project.

Sound designers may or may not also be musicians. What they need is the ability to create audio usable in a video game context, meaning mostly sound effects and atmospheres.

Tester

Testing is a very important phase in a video game's life. If you are a one-person developer, you should put considerable effort into testing your products thoroughly before release.

There are roughly two stages of game testing: alpha (in-house) and beta. Beta testing refers to the public at large volunteering to spot issues in your game. Beta testing can be either by invitation only or in public.

Game testing is actually a rather grueling line of work. Therefore, getting beta volunteers for a company with no industry status can be difficult. Here are some steps you may want to consider if you are in this position:

- Have an attractive company web site with a clearly marked beta testing page.

- Be timely and considerate in your communications. Do not advertise the position until you have a product ready to be tested.

- Proudly announce your projects in all of your social media accounts.

- Utilize sites dedicated to discovering beta testers, such as Betahound.com.

As fun as it sounds, game testing is not for everybody. Your testers need to have attention to detail (e.g., STEM major students) and the ability to work under serious stress. Emphasize and look for these qualities in your future beta testers.

Writer/Copywriter

Here are some of the types of work a writer may be doing in a video game project:

- Character dialogue. This may or may not refer to fixing lousy dialogue some programmer came up with.

- Tutorial prompts.

- Copywriting (i.e., advertising text, usually provided by freelancers).

Common Pitfalls for New Developers

Make sure you read the following common pitfalls and know them absolutely by heart before you start work on your first serious game. The indie game industry is one of great hopes and disappointments. But if life gets in the way, you weren't ready in the first place.

The Motivational Hole

The developer loses interest in his or her product and keeps the number of levels to a minimum. Usually this means the product should be considered commercially unviable.

Make sure you can realize your game before you start work on it. Don't try to make a four-dimensional game with an infinite number of artificial intelligences dancing perfect polka, unless you are sure you can do just that. Don't waste time. Stay different but realistic. Also, leave multiplayer to the big houses. It eats months of one's resources and is hardly a striking feature anymore.

Having said all that, do not rush out a product. There is probably no electronic arts (EA) executive behind your back with a cattle prod, gently reminding you there's a deadline in two days. You are the boss. Your ultimate and only concern should be a high-quality product shipping out when it's ready. Look back on the list of hit games. Your game, too, needs to provide a lasting challenge.

If you get stuck, take breaks. Stop thinking altogether every now and then to reboot your brain. Some people, especially the academics and theorists, tell you every game should re-innovate something. They're just being grandiose. It must be all that grant money. Turn on the radio. Do you hear that? Mediocre sells most. Let innovation come to you if you can, but know that it's not necessary. Your first release doesn't have to be groundbreaking. Aim for a good overall product.

The Ugly Date Syndrome

The developer uses subpar (audio)visuals for the product and hopes no one notices.

For many entrepreneurs, getting some unique and high-quality graphics is a pain. Unless one takes the decidedly lo-fi route, a good game needs to look presentable. Would you go out in a stained old tracksuit from 1975? As is the case in realms of human interaction, appearances matter quite a bit. Also, while the user can switch off the audio, they cannot do so with the graphics.

If you're sure you need cartoony or otherwise competitive graphics of the traditional kind, befriend some graphic artists. If you can afford it, pay them. If not, promise them exposure. Be nice and talk them into it with numbers; show the artists magnificent ways to boost their portfolios. Visit Behance.net and other online portfolios to find what you need. Never stop at one potential artist. Send dozens of e-mails if need be.

You can also make games without graphics, bypassing the possibility for this pitfall altogether. Think abstract action games, where the graphics are generated in-game. Digital photography is an awesome way to create atmosphere for visual novels.

The reason there are not many titles available to list with the Ugly Date Syndrome is simply that most developers take the illness seriously. Well, I could mention *Superman 64* for the Nintendo 64 here, as well as *Gods and Generals for Windows*, a truly atrocious display of indifference for the graphical abilities of the PC.

But no, *Minecraft* doesn't fit the list: it does have a clumsy aesthetic, but it works while being charmingly retro. Legions of bearded hipsters agree: that's part of a game's overall appeal.

The Wrong Game Engine Issue

The developer chooses a game engine not really suited to his or her grand idea (and notices this after weeks or months of work).

The most important choice you make as an indie games entrepreneur is the choice of game engine. Look for the engine that best suits the genre of your project. Make sure other developers working in the same genre have used the same tools you have your eyes on.

Don't take any game engine developers' promises as gospel. The engine you're interested in must work with your concept today. Don't wait for this or that version (that may or may not come out in the future). If an important platform isn't being deployed to the moment you purchase the engine, forget it. If that important feature that makes or breaks your game isn't there, neither should your money. While freeware engines often have a passionate community around them, they may not be getting very many donations to spur them on into the future.

The Prequel Syndrome

The developer ignores all criticism and forges ahead in an intellectual vacuum. The result is what happened with a well-known sci-fi movie prequel trilogy (with laser swords in it).

Not all criticism is intended to help you. But not all criticism is trolling. You need to consider just one thing: is the criticism constructive? If the answer is yes, you must toughen up and start thinking of ways to incorporating the input into your project to some degree. Good ideas give your game wings.

There are many ways a developer can receive feedback. Start with Steam Greenlight Concepts and IndieDB to name just two. Get a few presentable screenshots of your game in there. Spam these links to your friends. Create awareness. When you have something truly exciting to show the world, create a trailer video of your game. A video is the best way to promote your product. It's cheap and cross-platform, reaching way beyond desktop computers, all the way to pretty much any mobile device out there. Besides Steam and IndieDB, host your video on big video sites, such as YouTube and Vimeo. Ask for feedback in your videos and messages to potential customers.

The last stage before release is to get in touch with the press. Approach the publications geographically closest to your operation first. This way you may draw some feelings of camaraderie from the journalists and thus keep you going. Then take on the world. You need a good video trailer of your game at this stage with ideally a lot of views.

The No Testing Needed Approach

The developer hopes his or her own skill level is the perfect measuring stick of that of the overall population's.

The thing is, you may not share the reaction times and brain power of the good customers at large. In case of more cerebral games, keep your puzzles logical and at least somewhat intuitive. Try to keep the difficulty level even throughout all of your games, apart from the slight upward curve everyone expects. There's nothing like an overtly difficult level 4 to make people frustrated enough to stop playing your game altogether. Take the horrible nest level in the mega-hit *Alien: Isolation* from 2014. Loading a saved game every three seconds or so isn't very entertaining, no matter how great the rest of the game is.

Consider releasing a demo or a free beta of your blockbuster with built-in feedback capabilities. At a minimum, play your games with someone other than your tortoise and/or goldfish.

Perfectionism Quest

The developer continues to hone his or her product indefinitely, never wrapping up the development process. Eventually the project is shelved indefinitely.

As an indie, you rarely have deadlines etched on any stones. This can be problematic when it comes to actually delivering a product. Perfectionism Quest is simply the antithesis of The Motivational Hole. You can always allocate too many—or not enough—time on a product and sabotage it in the process.

If you are called a "perfectionist" by people who know you well, you may benefit from taking this scenario seriously. Once your product meets these minimum requirements for going on sale, any further work on it is simply unnecessary.

- Competitive audiovisuals

- Working game mechanics

- A lasting challenge

- A completed testing phase

No developer can release a perfect product, especially as their first release. Remember, updating software products is trivial in these times. You can and should always be prepared to release frequent updates to your game—and/or make a sequel!

A Programmer's Mind

The developer's head is full of exciting new concepts for video games. Why should only the original project take all their resources? They can work on a little something on the side too!

While it's great to have a flourishing creative mind, sometimes you just have to resist the urge to start another game project when the original is not complete. In a worst-case scenario, working on multiple projects confuses the developer so that eventually they can't really tell which is the one game they should be focusing on. This is all to the detriment of the developer's list of completed titles.

Draw the line between your learning phase and your first serious game. While learning the ropes of video game making, you obviously shouldn't try to turn every tutorial file into a finished product. However, in the context of creating your very first serious game, you should resist the urge to start work on games B, C, and D. If you a drawn to experimenting with certain new elements, why not incorporate them into your original project?

Let's say your first release will be a top-down racer game. Suddenly you feel like some on-screen violence. Should you start a tank-based shooting game on the side? No. Just add a few bonus weapons into your original racing game to satisfy your needs for projectile weapons—and get back to work.

In Closing

You should now have an idea about which factors contribute to a marketable video game. You are also aware of the main types of job assignments in the industry as well as the most common pitfalls facing indie developers. The next chapter deals with some historical game creation tools, giving you an idea of how the industry has developed over the decades.

CHAPTER 2

Game Engine Museum

History is a gallery of pictures in which there are few originals and many copies.

—Alexis de Tocqueville

Modern game engines are far from being the only ones. Far, far in the history of mankind, some noble individuals attempted to bring the same ease of creating games to more technically limited systems, such as the Commodore 64 and other 8-bit wonders. You'll now take a look at some of these archaic pieces of software, presented in this chapter in chronological order.

To qualify for this chapter of the book, a software package must include all the tools needed to create at least a relatively presentable game. Also, the end result must be a game that is playable without any additional software installed on the end user's computer.

The Quill (1983) by Gilsoft

Interactive fiction (i.e., text-based adventures) was a big thing in the late 1970s and early 1980s. As it happens, almost all major 8-bit platforms had a conversion of The Quill by Graeme Yeandle, a renowned game developer in his own right. Being a hit product and having text as the only element to work with, the software was eventually localized into Swedish, French, and other languages. Not just a tool for the general public to fool around with, The Quill was chosen as a main development tool by many a commercial game developer. Some 450 commercial titles were created with the system before the genre of interactive fiction fizzled out.

Pinball Construction Set (1983) by Electronic Arts

While perhaps a simplistic framework by today's standards, Pinball Construction Set (PCS) does qualify as a bona fide game engine (see Figure 2-1). Even though the scope of what types of games could be achieved with it is obviously limited, what it did it did well. In addition, you could distribute your pinball tables as stand-alone releases without relying on the editor software. Also, PCS was probably the first video game creation software with markedly realistic physics.

© Robert Ciesla 2017
R. Ciesla, *Mostly Codeless Game Development*, DOI 10.1007/978-1-4842-2970-5_2

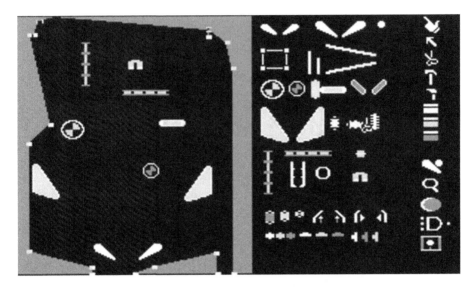

Figure 2-1. *Pinball Construction Set had a spartan but functional interface*

Originally released on the Apple 2, PCS found its way to the IBM PC, Commodore 64, and Atari 8-bit computers. Created by former Apple employer Bill Budge, the concept of the program was simply to allow users to create their dream pinball machine on a desktop computer. You did this by dropping elements of such a machine on a vestigial representation of a stripped-down coin-hogger. A variety of bumpers, flippers, and other such gadgets were at one's disposal. In 1983 the intuitive user interface was very well received and contributed quite a bit to the software's popularity.

Adventure Construction Set (1984) by Electronic Arts

In 1984, just two years into the business, Electronic Arts (EA) was but a thirsty little games house. It was during the 8-bit era's apex when EA released a revolutionary piece of software called Adventure Construction Set, commonly known simply as ACS (see Figure 2-2). The second in the series of EA construction sets, ACS was an ambitious undertaking by Stuart Smith. The product went on to influence countless game developers, especially in the role-playing game (RPG) genre. ACS did quite a bit to build EA into the behemoth it is today with its $7 billion in assets.

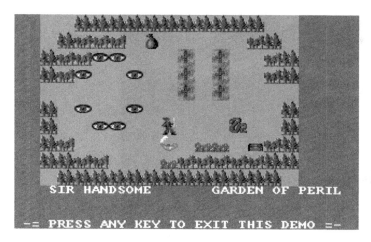

Figure 2-2. *An Adventure Construction Set demo game on an Amiga computer*

EA's contributions to early game-making magic are split into several categories of assets, including *world map, creatures,* and *pictures.* You can assemble relatively large tile-based adventures in whatever genre of RPG you're into, whether it's fantasy or sci-fi, thanks to the customizable resources. If for some reason you get tired of crafting your masterpiece and can't wait to finish the damn thing, Mr. Smith provided a feature called *auto-construct.* By specifying a few parameters, you could delegate your unfinished RPG game's fate to your computer and get a ready game in an instant. Ideally, game engine developers of the future will revisit ACS for this time-saving and amazing feature alone!

Although not visually exciting, ACS can output some rather engrossing RPG entertainment. Its legacy is clearly seen in several current game engines, such as the entire *RPG Maker* series.

Garry Kitchen's GameMaker (1985) by Activision

Not to be confused with Mark Overmars' Gamemaker, Garry Kitchen's GameMaker (GKGM) was a set of tools that provided a programming-free way of crafting a multitude of games for several platforms (see Figure 2-3). Although the bulk of Mr. Kitchen's expertise clearly went into the Commodore 64 version, his GameMaker was released also for the IBM PC and the Apple 2.

Figure 2-3. *Garry Kitchen's GameMaker game running on a Commodore 64*

GKGM was split into several specialized tools, each assigned to a unique task. In addition to the main editor program that worked in an uncomplicated variety of the BASIC language, you had SceneMaker, SpriteMaker, MusicMaker, and SoundMaker to create all the various assets for your projects. The software definitely took advantage of the then-impressive audiovisual capabilities of the Commodore 64. Clever use of the provided audio editors, in particular, resulted in commercial-quality sound. This component was sadly lacking from the IBM PC and Apple versions of the software, as they did not natively include the means to produce impressive audio.

Garry Kitchen's GameMaker is honestly an impressive piece of software. Fans of the retro aesthetic could do a lot worse than load up a copy on their (emulated) Commodore 64 and get busy making their own little titles. Also, the software provided a delightful alternative for chiptune composers to work their old-school musical magic with.

Shoot-'Em-Up Construction Kit (1987) by Sensible Software

Shoot-'Em-Up Construction Kit (SEUCK) is a notorious yet legendary piece of software for the Commodore 64, Amiga, and Atari ST computers (see Figure 2-4). In theory, you could create near-commercial-quality games with remarkable ease. Trouble was, all of them had the same mechanics. There were no upgrades for your ship, dragon, or plane. You shot at things. Things shot at you. You could have either a constantly scrolling playfield or one where the player pushed the screen forward. You had the option to change the title screen, and that was it.

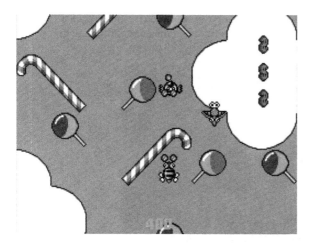

Figure 2-4. *A SEUCK game running on an Amiga computer*

Like some famous screwball once said, "If you gaze long enough into an abyss, the abyss also gazes into you." In the case of the typical SEUCK game, it's a lone score meter in a horrible font staring deep into the player's soul, accompanied by some grating sound effects and searing pangs of existential suffering.

While working in SEUCK is quite effortless, the games created with it are often a painful experience. Game reviewers at the time used the expression *SEUCK-like* as a seriously derogatory term when reviewing simplistic shoot-'em-up games that began flooding their offices in the mid-1980s. Also, the 16-bit version of the software was actually more sluggish and its output less presentable than the one from its 8-bit counterpart. No mean feat.

Ideally, game engine developers have learned one lesson from SEUCK: don't force a monotonous game mechanic to the users of your product, even if it's not a multipurpose tool per se. No game engine should enable the absolutely most clichéd way of doing things and nothing more. And no, you don't get any slack even if your product was released in 1987.

However, SEUCK deserves some kudos for being absolutely a beginner's tool. There was nothing wrong with the user interface. Drawing and animating sprites with the program was quite enjoyable. In addition, the software still has a dedicated fan base that has worked on some visual enhancements for the product, decades after its release. There are even some annual competitions out there with categories such as "most original SEUCK game" among others. SEUCK may be quite basic, but it's certainly not forgotten.

Arcade Game Construction Kit (1988) by Broderbund Software

A brainchild of one Mike Livesay, Arcade Game Construction Kit (AGCK) provided Commodore 64 owners with the tools to make polished, if simplistic, action games (see Figure 2-5). Coming on four mighty floppy disks, the software included all the relevant tools to create perfectly adequate visuals, audio, and levels. However, you were limited to nonscrolling games. You did have the option of using a technique called *flick screen*, which changed the room whenever you were at the edge of the screen.

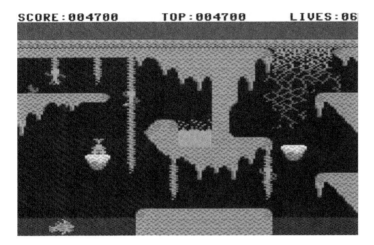

Figure 2-5. *The Arcade Game Construction Kit was great for creating platform titles*

The software was bundled with several games demonstrating the capabilities of the system. While hardly top tier, they were decent and workable into something commercially viable at the time.

AGCK was a rather ambitious piece of work and much loved by hobbyists at the time. Mr. Livesay did very well considering the limitations of the hardware—and the fact that most Commodore users didn't have the luxury of working on the machine with a mouse. Decent joystick-based interfaces are never easy to create.

STOS BASIC (1988)/AMOS BASIC (1990) by Mandarin Software

Written in part by Francois Lionet of Clickteam Fusion fame, AMOS and STOS are basically two versions of the same programming framework for two different platforms (see Figure 2-6). Also aboard the project was one Richard Vanner of The Games Creators fame, who has since worked on *GameGuru*, for one.

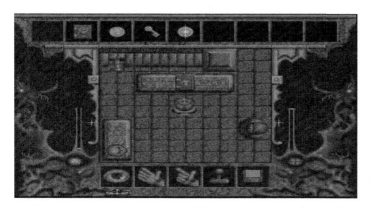

Figure 2-6. *Valhalla by Vulcan Software, a commercial Amiga game made with AMOS*

As you may have guessed, STOS ran on Atari STs and AMOS on the Commodore Amigas. The extra two years spent on perfecting AMOS meant the Amiga version had several improvements, mainly in support for the unique audiovisual hardware found in the Amigas. The work put into STOS and AMOS did probably influence later Clickteam products, such as *The Games Factory* and the wildly successful *Fusion* series.

While they were marketed as beginner's game-making software, neither STOS nor AMOS allowed casual users to create titles with commercial viability without spending dozens of hours knee-deep in BASIC programming—and add-ons. Most often, games produced with these systems performed shoddily with a low frames per second (fps) rate. The key was either keeping your projects as elementary as possible or investing in additional Mandarin Software products. The STOS/AMOS compiler accelerated programs written with the base software considerably.

Several core editions of Mandarin Software were available. In addition to the standard AMOS, there was an Easy AMOS for beginners as well as a more feature-rich AMOS Professional. The Atari side of things got expansions, too, with a slightly different focus. STOS Maestro attempted to rectify the ST's poor audio capabilities by adding support of sampled sound playback to STOS projects. Mandarin also released STOS Maestro Plus, which featured a hardware audio-sampler cartridge. 3D add-ons were released for both STOS and AMOS in 1992 to lukewarm reception.

Allegro (1990) by Shawn Hargreaves and the Allegro Developers

Not a game engine per se, Allegro (an acronym for Atari Low-level Game Routines) is an API for game development in C or C++ (`www.liballeg.org`). Starting its life on the Atari ST, the software library has been ported to more current platforms. Many games programmers have benefitted from giving Allegro a go, but mastering the framework is a learning experience for most. There's a reason why as of 2017 Allegro is 27 years old and still going relatively strong.

Although the API is very capable of most types of video games, it hasn't been used by many big franchises. One of the only exceptions is *Icy Tower,* the long-running hit game by Swedish developers Free Lunch Design. *Icy Tower 2* hit mobile devices in late 2012.

3D Construction Kit (1991) by Domark

The publishers made some grandiose claims with their 3D Construction Kit (3DCK), but the software didn't really deliver on them (see Figure 2-7). 3DCK came with an awkward VHS tape explaining all the wonderful things you could do with it, which only served to twist the knife. Although 3D was still in an embryonic stage in 1991, game mechanics are a timeless affair. 3DCK simply offered very little to do. You hovered around sparse landscapes. You could either collide with objects or shoot at them; at most, you could get shot back a few times. The software was fine as a rudimentary house-planning tool, but it offered very little else.

Figure 2-7. *The Atari ST version of the 3D Construction Kit demo game*

3DCK was released on pretty much every home computer platform of 1991. Based on a filled-polygon engine called Freescape, the tool ran slower than an octogenarian with rigor mortis. The 8-bit crowd would completely choke on the engine, presenting an average screen update rate of a couple of frames per second. The frame rate was only marginally better on 16-bit platforms. The much hyped built-in scripting language, Freescape Command Language (FCL), allowed for a decent degree of customization for the barren proceedings. But not even that could save such a product of limited possibilities. Again, the included VHS tape didn't help at all.

RSD Game-Maker (1991) by Recreational Software Designs

Not to be confused with Garry Kitchen's GameMaker, the RSD Game-Maker (RSDGM) is a charming little suite of tools for the early 1990s PC (see Figure 2-8). Working in a homely custom resolution of 312×196 (except for the menus, which were at a then-standard 320×200), RSDGM tools (and games) had a specific aesthetic about them. They were surely an acquired taste, as not everyone is a fan of blocky visuals and garish colors. Apparently, the creators (i.e. the Stone family) were!

Figure 2-8. *The alluring title screen of Blinky 2 on a 1990s PC*

A lot of the games produced with the software had an unpolished look to them and were mostly enjoyed by kids. This doesn't mean RSDGM didn't have its share of hit franchises.

Probably one of the biggest such hit series on the RSDGM is *Blinky*, which depicts the various escapades of a dinosaur-like creature. Created (and probably voiced, too) by Jeremy Lamar, the side-scrolling platformer got a decent amount of exposure in its heyday in the 1990s thanks to distribution on the AOL platform.

RSDGM was entirely codeless, relying on a mouse-driven user interface at all times. This was one of the main reasons for its worldwide popularity, in addition to the support offered for the latest hardware of the early 1990s, such as early sound cards and GPUs.

Although official support for the engine was dropped in 1995, the community behind RSDGM was rather active until the turn of the millennium. The engine in its entirety had its source code released to the public in 2014.

Zillions of Games (1998) by Zillions Development Corp.

An exotic contender, Zillions of Games (ZOG) works solely in the realm of board games (www.zillions-of-games.com). As the name hints, you do get an awful lot of board games out of it. The software operates on a scripting language, ZRF, in which one specifies the board, the rules, the pieces, and other properties of each project. Not exactly beginner-friendly, but it does get the job done.

ZOG only works with games running on the perfect information principle. This refers to games where all of the proceedings can be monitored by all of the participants (i.e., there are no unknown game elements for anyone). Despite its name, zillions of board games have not quite surfaced yet. Still, some 2,500 games have been made with it. Clearly, a serious fan base exists for the product.

Interestingly, the software is apparently still supported by the developers, making this a pretty successful endeavor. Also, a free expansion, Axiom, is available for all legitimate customers. With this add-on, developers can modify some deeper characteristics of the artificial intelligence.

■ ■ ■

## CHAPTER 3

A Game Maker's Lexicon: Level 1

Before moving into the territory of game-making software, you should have a grasp of the basic terms of the trade. By understanding the meanings behind these concepts, you can make a more useful comparison of the software packages available. Also, you'll get more out of game-related forums and conversations.

Some of the concepts mentioned next will be relevant for all video games, while others will have no bearing on your project whatsoever. It all depends on your choice of game type. For example, I've yet to hear of a text-based adventure that benefits from a visual effect called *anisotropic filtering*. Read on, and feel free to skip all the concepts you are already familiar with.

General Terminology

Next, we'll go through some select terms of the video game trade followed by a gentle primer on programming.

4X

In a video game context, *4X* refers to a strategy game genre popularized by the likes of *SimCity* and *Civilization*. It refers to the core elements of the genre: eXplore, eXpand, eXploit, and eXterminate.

AAA

This is a high-budget video game with usually a large team behind it. Think *Star Wars* games or the *Call of Duty* series. As a beginner/indie developer, you probably won't be participating in making AAA titles right away (not that you ever need to).

© Robert Ciesla 2017
R. Ciesla, *Mostly Codeless Game Development*, DOI 10.1007/978-1-4842-2970-5_3

Algorithm

This refers to the series of steps needed to solve a problem. A finished game, in short, is one big algorithm, or rather a collection of hundreds or thousands of them. You solve all kinds of problems with all kinds of steps, such as implementing user control, graphics, audio, and so on. Usually, an algorithm refers to smaller problems.

Application Programming Interface (API)

An API is a collection of tools for the creation of a specific type of software. There are many game-related APIs out there. The most important ones in this context are perhaps Microsoft's *DirectX* and Khronos Group's *OpenGL* (see Table 1-1). Most game engines presented in this book support DirectX, although there are exceptions.

As a new-school indie developer, you rarely need to go very deep with these technologies, but knowing their basics doesn't hurt.

How well a game runs on these two APIs depends on the underlying video card in a system. Most video card manufacturers have full DirectX support in their products. Unfortunately, the same doesn't always apply on the OpenGL side of things. See Table 3-1 for a comparison.

Table 3-1. *DirectX and OpenGL Comparison*

API	License	Supported Platforms	Main Benefits
DirectX	Proprietary; license included with every legal copy of Windows	Windows, Xbox	Best video card hardware support
OpenGL	Open standard with some patented parts	Windows, macOS, iOS, Linux, modern PlayStation and Nintendo consoles	Faster visual output; supports all major platforms apart from Xbox

Each revision of these suites of development tools contains improvements in their multimedia capabilities, such as more detailed 3D graphics and video playback. The first version of Microsoft's DirectX came out in 1995, while OpenGL 1.0 made its debut all the way back in 1992.

Bits, Bytes, and Binary

Computers and digital devices think in binary notation. This means all information is stored as 0s and 1s. All kinds of data can be created this way. Compact discs (remember those?) use binary data to store audio. Digital video cameras use binary to store video and audio. Computers use binary to store and manipulate many kinds of data. The Internet is a bunch of digital devices stuck together, all generating and interpreting binary.

We, the people, aren't too fond of binary code. Some of us are, sure, but for the vast majority it will be translated into something much more meaningful for us to enjoy, such as a nice graphical view of the system. So, have no fear. We do not deal in actual binary in the video game business.

A computer system has many layers to it. The highest layer is known as a *graphical user interface* (GUI). It's here where keyboards, mice, and visual representation of information come into play and make all the difference. This is the only layer a player needs when gaming. It's from the GUI that the programmers work their magic, too. We no longer need to type in obscure commands to get things done.

The lowest layer in any digital device is binary code. Actions in the GUI level are translated to binary for the computer to work with. Again, we don't need to know how to create any kind of program in binary. Instead, we'll use a nice graphical user interface for that, or any other, purpose.

Now, let's recap.

- A *bit* is the smallest amount of data a computer can access. It is either a 0 or a 1. Every file on any type of computer, on the deepest level, consists of sequences of these two bits.

- A *byte* is a collection of eight bits. It may signify things like, "What is the next displayed letter going to be? Is it a *W* or a *C*?"

- Example time. Here's a random bit: 1. Here's a random byte: 10010101.

The meaning of our two examples depends on the context. Take our random bit friend (1) and use it in a video game context. You can bet your left eyebrow games use single bits, too, and not just huge chunks of data. A single bit could donate the answer to the question: "Is the door open?" Usually 1 means yes; usually 0 means no. If you have a door in your game, in particular one that can open, this would make sense. This would all happen out of sight. See, even as a game maker, you wouldn't necessarily notice you just dedicated a single bit to this door-business. But your computer would. It knows things.

It may be through the webcam or maybe just the keyboard, but the fact of the matter is, your computer *is* observing you.

Chiptune

This is a type of video game music that first emerged in the 1980s. Typically chiptunes were synthesized in-computer with audio hardware unique to each system, instead of being recorded from an analog, external source. As the indie game boom came about in the late 2000s, chiptunes became hip again. There are several free programs for making this type of music, called *trackers,* including Milkytracker and OpenMTP, available for most popular platforms.

DLC/Microtransactions

DLC stands for *downloadable content.* In the age of high-speed Internet, developers came up with a concept to make considerable profit out of their product even after the initial sale. DLC refers to any extra content to a game, such as new maps, characters, or customization options.

A related term, *microtransaction,* refers to smaller in-game purchases of cosmetic or game-enhancing virtual items.

FPS

This refers to both "frames per second" and "first-person shooter."

Usually lowercase, fps is the rate at which a monitor displays consecutive images called *frames*. These days, 60 fps is considered smooth output. Some game designers even go for the magical 100 fps. A 3D game usually looks rather dreadful and jittery at anything below 30 fps. Usually, the frame rate on any machine is mostly derived from the oomph in its video card. More on this later.

FPS in a game type context refers to the ubiquitous genre of shooting things as seen from the killer's point of view. These kinds of games are a dime a dozen. For one, there's a huge franchise called *Call of Duty* out there. We can all thank *Doom* from 1993 for this. In my most humble opinion, the *Half-Life* saga by Valve Software was the last truly interesting FPS.

MMOG/MMORPG

MMOG stands for "massively multiplayer online game." It refers to any video game played *en masse* on the Internet. These games have anything between a few dozen to more than a thousand players participating simultaneously. This genre includes titles like *League of Legends* and *Eve Online.*

MMORPG simply stands for "massively multiplayer online role-playing game," thus referring to a more specific type of video game genre.

Particles (i.e., Particle Effects)

A *particle* refers usually to a type of non-resource-intensive graphical object, such as a drop of water, a snowflake, a spark, or some part of an explosion. Each particle has a set of attributes, such as life span, direction, and possibly gravitational pull. Particles are cheap and effective. For one, most of the time they lack an artificial intelligence, making them fast to execute even in a low-end system. Thanks to this, particles are usually used in large numbers without much of a slowdown for the system.

Most explosions, injury-related displays of blood, smoke, and other effects are created with particles these days, as they rarely need to be hand-drawn anymore. The public seems to prefer it this way. This is a matter of taste, of course. Particles can be used in both 2D and 3D games. You'd think developers would make sure each particle conforms to a rigorous scientific simulation of physics. Meh, most of the time particle speed and direction are randomized. Still, it looks good.

Ping

Depicted usually in milliseconds, *ping* refers to the lag in network connections. This is a central concept in multiplayer games and Internet use in general. The smaller the ping, the less delay there is in interacting in a network. Player connections with a ping of less than 30 ms or so is considered a playable network.

Pixel

A *pixel* is the smallest graphical unit on a display screen. This translates to a tiny colored dot. Everything you see on your display device consists of pixels.

Polygon

A *polygon* in a computer graphics context refers to a triangular geometric shape. This shape, for reasons we need not get into now, is the fastest type of elementary shape a computer can draw. All 3D graphics consist of polygons. The fewer polygons there are, the less complex the object, and the fewer resources it needs to run smoothly. You can create any object with a polygon, including circles, arches, cars, and people.

A 3D video game would look wonderful if all objects in it would be highly detailed and consist of, say, tens of thousands of polygons each. Unfortunately, there is always a trade-off between detail and speed. The more polygons per object, the more detail, but the slower the output.

Thankfully, not all objects need to be high in polygons. Objects far away in the distance in a scene get away with being quite low in the polygonal count.

Now, a "low-poly" object means one with a modest amount of detail (think of a single distant skyscraper), while a "high-poly" object (think of a realistic human face) can withstand scrutiny up-close and personal and still look presentable (see Figure 3-1). Some 3D developers choose a low-poly look for their whole games for aesthetic reasons or to seriously lower their games' hardware requirements.

Figure 3-1. *A low-poly object depicting the amazing aesthetics of a handsome gentleman. Also, a high-poly fox.*

Pong

Pong was the first mass-produced sports video game. Introduced in 1972, Pong featured two paddles on the side of the screen, bouncing a square "ball" between them. It was written by Allan Alcorn.

Primitive

This is a rectangle, a circle, or a square (or maybe even a triangle). As you may have gathered, primitives in computer graphics mean simple two-dimensional shapes. They have their uses (see "Particles") and are quickly drawn by even the slowest of video cards.

Resolution

Resolution depicts the amount of pixels available at once on a display, in other words, the screen size. Some common resolutions include Full HD (1920 pixels wide, 1080 pixels high) and 720p (1280 pixels wide, 720 pixels high). The larger the resolution in a game is, the less jagged the edges are and the more viewing room there is, but this comes with a strain on the video card. Find a good compromise between screen size and computational demands on the average system.

Your basic retro game runs fine in the classic resolution of 1024×768 or less. A game's worth is not in its resolution. The original Atari 2600 systems ran at a modest 40×192 pixels, and that system lived from 1977 to 1992.

Also, *resolution* often refers to the size and detail level of graphics in 3D games. Higher-resolution textures are impressive and more detailed but require more resources from the system.

Shader

A *shader* is simply a program-within-a-program that makes the computer draw something interesting on the display screen. Shader programs are usually executed directly on the video card, instead of your computer. This allows for offloading of some pretty complex tasks onto those powerful video cards of today. Video cards from, say, 2000 and onward are actually very much like miniature computers. As such, they are still under-used.

A common shader may, for example, change the entire game to black and white or to sepia. Shaders can also create psychedelic backdrops or realistic mountain vistas. You name it. There are hardly any limits to how a shader can change the visuals in a game. Of course, the more complex the shader is, the more resources it'll take from the system.

Most shaders are written in GLSL or HLSL, which are programming languages designed for this use. So, in addition to whatever language the game itself is written in, you'll find snippets of GLSL (or a similar language) here and there.

The first mention and use of a shader is from 1988 by the good people of Pixar.

Shovelware

Not related to Steam in any way whatsoever, this term simply refers to low-quality software or bundles of said type of software. The term originates in the 1990s CD-ROM craze, when large quantities of some rather atrocious programs were getting shoved onto the new-at-the-time medium. A single disc could indeed hold hundreds of oftentimes dire pieces of software.

Sprite

Simply put, a *sprite* is a small and usually moving graphical representation of something in a game's universe (see Figure 3-2). This term is usually used in a 2D context. In a car game, each car is a sprite from a developer's perspective. In a space-themed game, the ships and asteroids are sprites.

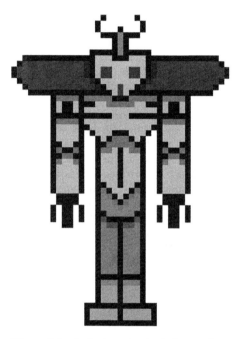

Figure 3-2. *A single sprite depicting a robot*

Instead of making changes to the entire screen, which is not necessary most of the time, you work on a sprite level to keep the momentum of the game going in order to save a system's resources. Most of the time our little sprites don't take a lot of video card memory. A much sillier approach would be to draw the tens of millions of various possible states in a game with full-screen visuals only.

The term *sprite* originates from the mid-1970s. It was made popular by Atari with its 2600 console, and it has been in use ever since. Who are we to complain?

Steam

This generally refers to a major online software distribution service owned by Valve Corporation, the creators of the *Half Life* franchise. While specializing in Windows games, it also serves Mac and Linux customers, as well as providing other types of content. In 2015, Steam provided 15 percent of the global PC game sales for the year. The service holds roughly 130 million registered user accounts.

Rendering and Prerendering

To render means to draw something using automated computer software dedicated to that function. *To render* a scene refers to the process of drawing all the various objects, lights, and shadows included in one area of a level or map. Before rendering, programmers and 3D artists tell the computer where all the objects are to be located, what they look like, and what they're up to. This is usually done with separate graphics tools, such as Blender or Maya 3D.

Rendering can be in real time, meaning all of the position and other data associated with the various objects is calculated on the spot, as you move your character around. This can of course be resource intensive with complicated scenes, but it's common in a video game context as it provides the greatest degree of flexibility in the overall visual experience. Real-time rendering puts the user in the greatest amount of control. Plus ultra-powerful video cards take care of this type of rendering.

Prerendering, on the other hand, refers to the process of generating (usually) complicated and life-like images *before* the user has any interaction with them. An example of a video game with mostly prerendered graphics includes the *Myst* series by Ubisoft. Prerendered games extract very little resources from a system but provide the user with quite a rigid visual experience, as all paths to be taken are predecided on by the game team, and not the player *per se*. There's no rotating the view usually, and no bobbing your character's head around with the mouse. You simply choose various paths the programmers have laid out before you and watch the animation unfold.

Not only is prerendering stale in the interaction and immersion departments, it's also the least space-saving method of providing a game. Early full-motion video (FMV) games were often delivered on many, many compact discs or even DVDs. *Plumbers Don't Wear Ties*, anyone? For the love of video games, don't look it up. Thank goodness those times are over.

Understandably, prerendering is mostly used in digital cinema (and related fields) where user interaction is nonexistent.

Resources

This term refers to the total number of assets a computer system has at its disposal. The computer consists of several different components, which combined form its overall processing ability. These components include the central processing unit (CPU), random access memory (RAM), video card, and hard drive (or drives).

Modern game software is probably the most resource-hungry type of program available, aside from high-definition video processing. When designing games, you want to make sure you require only the minimum resources from the buyer's hardware. Cut down on eye candy whenever you can without looking amateurish. Either do it well or don't do it at all.

Sandbox Game

This is a genre of video game where the player enjoys considerable freedom in his or her in-game activities. Instead of offering a rigid gameplay framework, players are pretty much free to do whatever they want in any order (within the confines of the game's universe). Think *The Sims* or *Grand Theft Auto* series.

Skybox

A *skybox* refers to a method of mapping four or more 2D images to form a coherent, realistic view of a sky, and possibly some unreachable objects, such as distant buildings, over the player in a 3D environment.

Vertical Sync (V-sync)

This is a technique to avoid screen tearing, which is an unpleasant separation of the parts of a display screen. Screen tearing sometimes occurs when a system is moving large amounts of visual data around, such as complicated 3D scenes, and the hardware isn't really keeping up.

While screen tearing is never pleasant, vertical syncing in some games can seriously slow things down. Some video cards just don't get along with certain games. If your update is slow, try switching off the v-sync.

WASD

This is probably the most preferred control method of video game characters on a computer keyboard in many types of games. It simply refers to W for up, A for left, S for down, and D for right.

The Fundamentals of Programming

Now it's time to up the ante, if ever so slightly. Let's proceed to take a look at the very basics of the fascinating subject of programming, shall we?

Programming Language

A programming language is a formal constructed language designed to communicate instructions to a computer. Programming languages can be used to create programs, such as games, or to otherwise control the behavior of a computer system on a deeper level. In other words, when you're programming, you are telling your computer to perform some very specific tasks, instead of just "open Firefox" and so on. Different programming languages usually have a different set of unique commands and syntax and are largely not interchangeable with one and other.

The software that runs a programming language is called a *programming environment* or an *integrated development environment* (IDE). A lot of this type of software is free these days, and quite a few support more than one programming language.

The game engines discussed in this book are all far more than rudimentary IDEs. Most of them feature extensive built-in tools to help a developer reach his or her vision in a quicker fashion. If you want to experiment with a more barren IDE, perhaps trying out various programming languages, Eclipse would be the most popular choice. It is available free of charge, after all.

There are dozens of various programming languages in the world today. New ones keep appearing on a sporadic basis. A lot of them are designed for many a useful purpose such as, indeed, making games. However, some languages are nothing but excessively brainy programmers' attempts at levity. Take brainfuck, for example. Commands are issued in plus signs and other unintuitive markings. How about Ziim, which only accepts arrow symbols pasted all over the screen?

These days it's uncommon for a programmer to create a game from the ground up all the way to a finished product just by typing in obscure commands, although this was the de facto method of game making in the past (think the 1970s and early-to-mid 1980s). Nowadays such an approach would simply be too time-consuming and rarely result in anything more than tic-tac-toe. There's no need to reinvent the wheel.

So, ever since the 1980s, developers have used dedicated development tools to create games. These tools include map, graphics, and audio editors, among other such utilities. Most of these were meant for the design team's internal use only. There were exceptions, but serious game-making tools for the public started appearing in the 1990s. In recent years the trend has, luckily, escalated. Creating a visually complicated modern video game from the ground up would be a form of insanity. That's where the game-making tools come in. But before we get to the game engines of the day, let's explore the theory of programming a little further.

How to Talk to Your Computer

There are three stages a software project must go through to end up as an executable file. Often all steps but the first are automated.

1. Source code (or project file) in a programming language (or game engine file format)

2. Assembler code

3. Machine code

You start with the programming language or game engine environment of your choice. You type a listing and/or use a mouse-driven IDE to create your project. Some of the game engines in this book are visual in nature and require no coding whatsoever. The product of this stage (i.e., the source code) is then turned into *assembler code* by specialized software known as a *compiler*. All game engines feature a built-in compiler of varying quality, by definition. At this level the code is still understandable by a lot of programmers.

The assembler code is then turned into *machine code*. Now all but the most nihilistic eggheads run away. Machine code is not compatible with most biological lifeforms. Finally, this horrific machine code is executed by your computer, and your potential customers get a game they can launch at their leisure.

High-Level vs. Low-Level Languages

A *high-level programming language* is usually the most intelligible kind to human beings and far removed from the clunky and often incomprehensible machine code. The focus of high-level languages is on usability and the ability to deploy to several platforms. Examples of high-level languages include Java, C++, and Python.

A *low-level programming language* forsakes much of the ease of use and cross-platform support for performance. Examples of low-level languages include the various versions of Assembler. The lowest-level language that exists is the dreaded machine code.

Compiled vs. Interpreted Languages

A distinction in implementation can be made with all programming languages. That is, they are either *compiled* or *interpreted*. In general, the lower the language level, the more likely they are using a compiled approach. This usually provides the best level of performance and security for most applications. Assembler code is almost universally delivered in a compiled form, as is C and C++, among many others.

An *interpreted language,* on the other hand, doesn't compile the source code into machine language prior to running the program. It merely interprets the code on the fly. Interpreted languages usually result in less efficient software and may not be optimal for audiovisually rich video game delivery. Interpreted languages also present some security concerns in the online environment as malicious code can be injected mid-execution.

Some languages, such as Java, are somewhere in the middle of the spectrum, as they use both compiled and interpreted components.

Control Flow: Nonstructured vs. Procedural Programming

As I have established, the syntax between programming languages varies considerably. However, there are some key elements that are shared by them all. *Control flow statements* are used to control the direction of code execution. With these statements you can stop the linear flow of the program and run parts of it at will. The most traditional form of control flow includes the use of user-defined labels (or computer-defined line numbers) and a GOTO command.

A well-implemented control flow is a must in serious programming projects. In the early days of coding a so-called *nonstructured* approach was popular. Nonstructured languages like BASIC used control flow commands (like the aforementioned GOTO) to navigate a code listing. This linear style of programming often resulted in *spaghetti code*, a term referring to confusing and inefficient code. It fell out of popularity as less linear and thus more robust approaches were developed. Virtually all modern programming languages are based on a more advanced paradigm, called *procedural programming*. This approach uses procedures to implement easily readable and, to an extent, reusable code.

Read more on these and other important programming elements in detail in Chapter 10, "A Game Maker's Lexicon: Level 2."

Procedures

A *procedure* (known in modern parlance as *method*) is basically a small program within a program that executes any type of task, from playing a sound effect to closing a program to displaying the number of player 1's lives. Procedures can be called as many times as needed, whenever needed. When a procedure is done executing its tasks, it returns control to the main portion of the program. Using procedures is a much more effective way of programming than the old-fashioned linear (i.e., nonstructured) style.

Although newer languages do support the older approach, it's actually considered a bad practice to use traditional control flow statements as it does cause cluttered code. Instead, it's a solid idea to use procedures to perform tasks whenever possible.

A Few Lines of Code

Now, just like you can communicate the same ideas with more than one human language, you can also do so in computer languages. You issue commands, in a specific syntax, to achieve whatever results are needed. You'll next take a gander at the act of putting the same five words on the screen in three different programming languages. These will be presented in order of increasing complexity, as shown in Listings 3-1, 3-2, and 3-3.

Listing 3-1 shows a rudimentary program written with the Commodore 64 BASIC language from 1982. Notice the use of line numbers and a control statement, GOTO.

Listing 3-1. Written with the Commodore 64 BASIC language from 1982

```
10 PRINT "Your favorite movie is Zardoz"
20 GOTO 10
```

Listing 3-2 shows the same program in generic C++ code. The print command is called printf in this language.

Listing 3-2. Same Program in Generic C++

```
#include <stdio.h>
int main(void) {
        printf("Your favorite movie is Zardoz");
}
```

Listing 3-3 shows the same program in the pre-Windows Assembler language on the PC. Don't worry, game developing in 2017 is nothing like this.

Listing 3-3. Same Program in Pre-Windows Assembler Language

```
main            proc
mov             ah, 9
mov             dx, offset hello
int             21h
retn
hello db        'Your favorite movie is Zardoz$'
main            endp
end             main
```

Variable

A *variable* is an arbitrary, often user-defined, label for a storage location of meaningful data. Manual declaration of variable types is not needed in many of the game engines featured in this book. However, you should understand how they work as they are a fundamental concept in any kind of software development.

The most common examples of variables in a game context include object coordinates, typically designated as x and y. These simply refer to an object's position on-screen. Other game-related variables might include the score count, the number of enemies destroyed, and the amount of time left.

The tiny example in Listing 3-4 might shed some light on how most variables work. Now, all variables need a name, which you pick (presented here in bold), and a variable type, which determines the allowed contents of data in that variable (i.e., whether it's a bunch of text or numbers).

Listing 3-4. Two Variables, first_name and player_one_lives, as Defined in C++

```
char first_name[] = "Peter";
int player_one_lives=3;
```

Here, first_name is a type char variable, which tells the computer this variable can consist of alphanumeric data only. You cannot, for example, perform arithmetic operations with variables of this type.

The int before the second variable is short for "integer," as in a type of number, which lets the programming environment know the variable must consist of numbers only. Arithmetic operations are fine between integers. If one tried forcing letters into the variable player_one_lives, you'd get an error. Don't confuse computers. They are terrible at guessing.

Variables are declared differently in different programming languages. In many types of BASIC, for example, you don't need to declare the variable type. It is done automatically based on what information you input. For example, the statement MYVARIABLE1="HAHA" assigns alphanumeric data, while MYVARIABLE2=3.14 assigns numeric (i.e., integer) data into the respective variables.

Now, let's recap.

- A variable is a small amount of RAM, named by the programmer, for storing meaningful data (number of player 1's lives, etc.).

- Variables need both a type (number/integer, text, etc.) and a unique identifier (e.g., player_one_lives).

Object-Oriented Programming (OOP)

This is not a buzzword, and every budding game producer should get acquainted with it. First introduced in 1983 with the C++ language, the OOP methodology is now a programming staple. I'll now go through some of the basic concepts in OOP as they pretty much apply to most, if not all, modern software design. Most current programming languages and game engines are object-oriented in nature.

OOP builds on the aforementioned procedural programming paradigm. In procedural programming, data (i.e., information) and procedures (i.e., the actors on that information) are kept separate. In OOP, they come together in the form of objects. This allows for more complex programs with less code. Well-designed OOP projects offer more reusability than those created with the procedural approach.

An object-oriented program doesn't automatically provide any wonderful graphics or rousing soundtracks for a game. All that is to be added later by additional, increasingly complex programming and the integration of audiovisual data. Before you get to the part where realistic 3D jets fly all over the screen, you have to organize the data. This goes for every game. At the very core of every program there's the data organization process. It needs to be logical so that other team members, possibly joining your team at a later time, understand what's going on.

Classes and Objects (i.e., Classes and Instances)

Object-oriented programming refers to an approach where the organization of meaningful data is the first priority. Now, there are two fundamental concepts in any OOP-based language: *classes* and *objects*. Think of classes as the blueprints for any logical structures in a project. There are objects and classes in any OOP-based program. All objects receive the same basic features of their respective classes. When an object is created based on a class blueprint, we refer to this act as *instantiating* a class. An object is therefore an instance of a class.

Now, say you are working on a program with cars in it. You probably should have a class called `Cars`. That would only make sense. Why would you call it anything else? Within this class, some basic properties (i.e., variables) are defined to be included with every car based on this class. For the sake of brevity, let's keep this list short. We'll have two properties: top speed and color. The `Cars` class contains instructions to keep the top speed at 100 mph for all automobiles. Also, for some unknown reason, the color is to be green for all of the automobiles by default.

Inheritance

Now, say you want a more luxurious line of automobiles. Let's make a new class for them. But wait, there's no need to create a new class from scratch. You can just make a subclass from the `Cars` class and call it something else, say, a `SportsCars` class. All the data programmed into the original `Cars` class is now in your new class, just like that. But for these faster cars, you'll upgrade the top speed to 150 mph. You'll let that be the only difference between your two classes.

This is known as *inheritance*. To reiterate, the original `Cars` class is now a superclass to the `SportsCars` class. The new `SportsCars` class is a subclass of the `Cars` class. Through inheritance, a programmer can reuse large amounts of class data to spawn new types of objects.

Methods

A *method* is simply a procedure in an OOP context. Methods therefore refer to actions invoked from within an object. Such actions might include displaying or manipulating the various properties of your automobiles.

And there you have the basic building blocks of OOP thinking. You include only meaningful data in classes. You organize the data so that both computers and people can make good sense of it. You reuse data where possible. It's a beautiful paradigm.

Abstraction and Encapsulation

Data is compartmentalized in the OOP paradigm; information is shared on a "need-to-know" basis. Not all information needs to be displayed to the end user (i.e., gamer) or even all members of a programming team. This approach translates to two more core concepts central to OOP: abstraction and encapsulation.

Abstraction refers to the approach of providing users with only pertinent information. In a game-related context, this might mean things such as the score count and the number of lives for player 1. There simply isn't a need to provide the gamer with exact numeric x and/or y coordinates of his or her spacecraft. The coordinates of this spacecraft can be simply represented by visual means.

Encapsulation works on a deeper level. It refers to the process of combining relevant data sets of variables (i.e., properties), methods (i.e., procedures), and other definitions into a class. A class can contain either *public* or *private* data. Private resources, unlike public data, are not accessible from actors outside of a class. For one, this prevents rookie members of a development team from messing up a project. The components (i.e., classes) in a program are more or less interconnected. By protecting the contents of a class, all other classes dependent on said construct are less likely to end up broken. The keywords of *public* and *private* in an OOP context are commonly known as *access modifiers*.

Let's focus on our little example of the automobile factory and imagine the powers that be decide to only ever manufacture green automobiles. Therefore, the variable (i.e., property) called color can be safely set to private as this will never need to be anything else. It simply doesn't need to get altered, ever.

Now, just for the sake of being tangible, let's take a look at some actual object-oriented code in Java with the automotive concept at its core. Listing 3-5 defines a class, two attributes, and a single method. Can you tell which element is which? A lot of modern game-making software doesn't require much of this, but learning some essentials never hurts.

Listing 3-5. Cars Class in Java

```
class Cars {
public:
        int top_speed="100";
        int Top_Speed_Query() { return top_speed; }
private:
        string color="green";
}
```

Next, Listing 3-6 defines the SportsCars class for the more luxurious vehicles. This is a new, derived class from the Cars class.

Listing 3-6. SportsCars Class

```
class SportsCars: public Cars {
public:
        int top_speed="150";
        int Top_Speed_Query() { return top_speed; }
}
```

Now, let's reiterate.

- OOP is an approach where the organization of meaningful data is the first priority within a software development project. Inheritable data sets, called *classes*, are at the core of this system.

- In OOP parlance, variables are referred to as *properties*, and procedures are referred to as *methods*.

- Classes are encapsulated sets of data that can contain both private and public data assets.

Common Programming Languages: A Primer

To further enhance your developer parlance, let's take a look at some historical and current programming languages. They all vary in complexity, power, and purpose.

BASIC

Created all the way back in 1964, BASIC stands for Beginner's All-purpose Symbolic Instruction Code. The language was devised to teach computer use for those not studying mathematics or computer science. Most computer manufacturers have implemented their own form of BASIC on their hardware. These variations include Atari BASIC, Commodore BASIC, and Q-BASIC for IBM-compatible PCs. Often, as was the case with the Commodore 64, BASIC was included in the computer's hardware, being available immediately after the computer was switched on.

Even in the past few years, some new variations of BASIC have been developed. The most modern variation of the language is probably Microsoft's Visual Basic.

A great beginner's language, BASIC in its variations may not be the ideal language for serious video game development, being somewhat clumsy and lacking in performance. Nonetheless, it is the most widespread programming language in the history of the personal computer, and it did wonders to educate people in all matters computer. And for this we may thank John G. Kemeny (1926–1992) and Thomas E. Kurtz from Dartmouth College.

C

Perhaps the most influential programming language of all time, C is a so-called procedural language. This means a program written in C consists of various subprograms (i.e., procedures) that are executed when necessary, making for efficient, reusable code. A simple example of a procedure in a C-based game would be one that displays, say, player 1's name.

C was developed by Dennis Ritchie (1941–2011) sometime between 1969 and 1973 while working at AT&T Bell Labs.

C++

Devised in 1978, C++ is one of the most powerful multipurpose programming languages out there. Known mostly for its high-performance output, this is the language for many a serious computer scientist and video game developer, as well as many hobbyists.

C++ added object-oriented programming into the C-language command set. A very influential language, C++ has left its traces on Java and C#, to name just two. The world of programming owns a big thank-you to the Dane behind C++, Bjarne Stroustrup.

C#

Pronounced "C sharp," this is a new language influenced strongly by, yes, C++. Introduced in 2000 by Microsoft, C# was designed to cater to a wide array of applications including those ending up on the Web. Like C++, the language is object-oriented in nature. Projects coded in C++, however, may run quite a bit faster than those created in C# and tend to be smaller in size. What the new language has in its favor is simplified operation; memory allocation is automated in C#, for one. The language is fast becoming a staple among many a budding programmer, as it is increasingly popular in colleges the world over.

Java

Java is a popular general-purpose computer programming language. Many other languages, in game creation use as well, are off-shoots of it. It is therefore recommended that a budding developer get acquainted with Java basics *post haste*. If there's one language worth mastering, it's Java. The first version of the language was introduced by Sun Microsystems in 1995, as envisioned by James Gosling.

JavaScript

Dating back to 1995, JavaScript was designed to extend the functionality of web browsers. The language helped usher in an era of more accessible and snazzy web sites. Still very popular as a general-purpose web site language, JavaScript has since seen other uses. Several game development frameworks for the language have been released for creating some rather impressive browser-based games. HTML5, the new *de facto* web standard released in 2014, works beautifully in tandem with JavaScript to create rich media apps and games for mobile devices, too. In fact, many of the game engines discussed in this book deploy to HTML5.

While there are a few similarities, JavaScript is similar to Java mostly in name only; the two are not interchangeable.

ActionScript

ActionScript is used in conjunction with Flash, the (dying) Internet-related content standard. The language was created in 2000 to make Flash presentations more complex and interactive. Originally devised by Macromedia, ActionScript is now under Adobe's auspices. A derivative of the C language, ActionScript also closely resembles JavaScript, which itself was greatly influenced by Java, which, in turn, was influenced by C++.

We're no longer in Kansas, people.

GML

Game Making Language (GML) is a Java-based programming language used in the popular GameMaker series of software suites. While not producing the fastest output of all time, it does have a nice set of graphics-related built-in commands. Also, both the Windows and macOS versions share the syntax. GML was developed by the venerable Dutchman Mark Overmars in 1999.

Python

Python is a language used by the likes of the Ren'Py visual novel game engine. The Python language is user-friendly while being relatively powerful. Python puts a priority on a more minimalist approach to coding than most languages. The language was devised by another Dutchman named Guido van Rossum back in 1989.

Lua

Lua is a fast scripting language, used by the Game Guru game engine among others. Lua is also well-suited for a wide variety of mobile systems, including Android and iOS devices. Based on the C language, *lua* means "moon" in Portuguese, just so you know. Also, they don't want you to spell it in all caps. See Listing 3-7.

Listing 3-7. A Simple Program in Lua

```
io.write('It's Lua, not LUA\n')
```

Some Words About Optimization

Before I get to the game engines, you should heed some universal advice on the important topic of optimization. It's a good practice to stay aware of this practice during all stages of your game development journey.

A programmer should require the very minimum of resources (RAM, hard drive space, CPU power, and so on) from the user's system in order to present a playable game. Optimizing a game means keeping all code-related speed bottlenecks, as well as all file sizes, to a minimum. This means rigorously testing different approaches to problems and sticking with the solution that uses the least amount of system resources. Sloppy coding equals unhappy customers. Spend as much time optimizing a game as you spent developing it.

Common optimization techniques include the following:

- *Keeping the code as simple as possible*: Don't go all fancy and convoluted if you can avoid it. Use simple data structures. Don't get clumsy or lazy either with dozens of lines of unnecessary code. Computers like chomping on straightforward data. The fewer lines of code needed to solve a problem, the faster the end result usually is.

- *Removing redundant resources from the project*: It's not uncommon to have (especially budding) programmers keep all kinds of junk files in their projects, just bloating the project file size. So, if you have a video file or an audio track that is never used in the game, take it out to save memory and keep the game file size as small as possible. Take out all the crap well before you forget about it.

- *Keeping individual file sizes within reasonable limits*: This goes for audiovisual materials and thus the final executable. If your game has a 20-minute soundtrack file in it, don't keep it in there uncompressed. Use MP3 or some other compressed file format, for heaven's sake. There's always a trade-off between file size and quality. At first it may seem daunting to fiddle with all the quality settings, but in time you'll find these optimal figures with ease. If you have the choice between a 400MB game and a 1.4GB game, take the smaller one, please. Remember, smaller game file size means fewer minutes spent downloading and getting it to run in general.

- *Proper optimization of sprite animation*: Keep the number of frames at a minimum. The more frames an animation has, the bigger the file size. For example, instead of using duplicate frames to create a slower animation, adjust the sprite animation speed in code instead.

In Closing

The choice of programming language used affects the end results greatly. Java, while popular, is slow compared to languages such as C++ and some of its derivatives. However, in these modern times, the effects of this choice are kept at a minimum, unless your game deals with thousands of instances on-screen at once. Most games are graphics-intensive and utilize the video card more so than the CPU. Also, none of the tools presented in this book requires extensive programming experience.

What a time to be alive.

Finishing this chapter, you should be able to answer the following questions:

- What is a variable?

- When are particles generally used?

- What are access modifiers?

CHAPTER 4

■ ■ ■

Commercial Game Engines

A *game engine* is simply a set of tools that allows for rapid development of video games. By incorporating (ideally original) audiovisual resources and game logic, even a single developer can come up with impressive results in a relatively short span of time. Many game engines use a fully graphical interface and require very little, if any, programming to get things moving. Most game engines are dedicated to either 2D or 3D development, although with the newer ones (e.g., Unity), the line is getting quite blurry.

Now, a *game library* is a very different affair compared to a game engine. Sometimes called *game programming libraries*, these are large sets of code meant to be accessed from a more traditional programming environment. Game libraries offer a lot of power and functionality, often more so than your average game engine. For beginners they may not be the best option because of the complexity involved in leveraging that power. A lot of heavy lifting in the form of intricate coding is involved. One needs to learn the essentials of some popular programming language, such as Java or C++, to get anything out of game libraries. Most game engines also incorporate some kind of scripting language for that extra custom control many developers will start to eventually crave. GameMaker has GML for scripting purposes, GameGuru has Lua, and so on.

From a developer's point of view, game engine software is usually split into four components. There's the resource view for managing audiovisual assets, a map designer, tools for game logic, and a scripting module. These may not be presented as separate modules; rather, some engines use the approach of a more unified design. Scripting support and editing, for one, may be incorporated into several places throughout the engine interface, from the map designer to each in-game object.

Deep underneath the developer view there's a lot more going on. Game engines take care of such things as physics simulation, object collision detection, graphics rendering (i.e., the act of drawing things on-screen), and other crucial functionality needed to create a video game. Game engines offer not only a user-friendly take on games development but a considerable degree of reusability of project components.

In many cases, using freeware game engines gets you only so far. Their developers are less likely to provide frequent updates, for one. Also, usually the most visually impressive cutting-edge technology is kept strictly in the commercial software sector.

We'll start the game engine review with some older versions of GameMaker (GM), since either they are still being sold or they have just not yet been released as open source. These versions of GM provide the perfect programming environment for the budding video games entrepreneur, teaching all the basics needed to get into games creation. They are simple to use yet powerful enough to demonstrate all the important

R. Ciesla, *Mostly Codeless Game Development*, DOI 10.1007/978-1-4842-2970-5_4

41

video game mechanics. And yes, many current video game companies are still using these tools to make a lot of money.

Before You Embark

There are very few, if any, video game development software applications built around a Create Game button. Games created with such a system wouldn't make anyone proud anyway. You must put in the hours, whatever genre or software package you're working with. The good news is, most game engines share a considerable number of concepts. Programming languages do vary, sure, but programming logic less so. Despite the growing number of beginner-friendly tools, serious video game development is hard work.

Eventually, you might steer away from the one-person "team" approach altogether. This is a big business with many opportunities. You might discover your own niche in the field, whether it's 2D graphic artist, general-purpose coder, or voice actor. Wherever your professional life takes you, the many, many hours spent on crafting your more or less successful titles will be a time fondly remembered—and well spent. Hands-on experience with the mechanics of game making is valuable experience for anyone in the industry.

The game-making tools are numerous, but this book is not about cramming all those (even more numerous) tutorials into one book. That would serve no purpose. The point is to help you pick the best development tools for your personal growth as a game designer to get you moving into the right direction. The primary purpose of this book is simply to empower you as a budding independent games developer, and that's exactly what I'll do. By at least now you should be putting on your favorite eyewear as we dwell ever deeper into game development (see Figure 4-1).

Figure 4-1. A pair of glasses. You might be needing them. (© https://www.flickr.com/photos/mayeesherr/, used under CC-BY-2.0)

Your First Game Engine

It can be daunting to pick a starting point if you have no previous experience creating video games or programming. All the terminology and seeming complexities involved can be intimidating. Still, you are reading this book because you want to learn the fine craft of video game development. Let's help you get started right now.

GameMaker Studio is the current best-selling product of YoYo Games. While it has its issues, the software is popular for a reason and quite flexible in many respects. There's a free version available for download for the Windows platform. Also, for Mac users without access to Windows, an older and slightly compromised version of the software GameMaker 7 can still be downloaded for free to learn the ropes. The principles of use are virtually identical in all versions of GameMaker.

There are several good reasons to pick this piece of software as a starting point for your games programming career.

- It allows you to quickly experiment with all major video game mechanics (collisions, enemy path-finding, difficulty levels, etc.).

- It will teach you some universal programming skills through its scripting language, GML.

- Finally, its output is very much commercially viable.

You can download GameMaker Studio (the nonprofessional version) for free from www.yoyogames.com/get. You can download GameMaker 7 for the Mac for free from https://web.archive.org/web/20130831034342/http://yoyogames.com/legacy.

Your First Game

The following tutorial is for you if you have no experience making games. In it, you'll create a very basic video game. The process shouldn't take more than 30 minutes. It's important you do this step by step instead of loading a tutorial file.

This tutorial will demonstrate the basic concepts I went through in Chapter 3, such as using variables and the basics of object-oriented development. While all the software applications presented in this book are different in their approaches, they all share these universal characteristics.

Now, before running GameMaker (GM), please familiarize yourself with the following mechanics common to all versions of the software.

GM Classes and Objects

Remember classes from Chapter 1 of the book? In general, objects derive the same basic features from their respective classes. A SportsCars class uses the regular Cars class for most of its functionality and so on. Well, in GameMaker, classes double as objects. There is no separation between the two. Object properties and behavior in GameMaker are derived from other objects. You won't find many mentions of the word *class* within GameMaker. But that doesn't mean it doesn't use them!

Events

Each object in GameMaker is controlled using a series of events, all available within any object. Table 4-1 describes some of the most important events in GM.

Table 4-1. *Typical GameMaker Object Events and Their Associated Actions*

Event Name	When the Event Is Triggered	Typical Associated Actions
Create	When the object is created	Set object starting position
Destroy	When the object is removed	Play (explosion) sound effects
Step	The time between the create and destroy events of the object	Manipulate and monitor object position on-screen
Draw	The time between the create and destroy events of the object (for visual actions)	Draw object sprite, incorporate particle effects
Collision	When objects collide on-screen	Destroy object (or objects)
Outside Room	When an object crosses the room edges	Destroy object (or objects)

Actions

Actions are simply the specific methods (i.e., procedures) within a GM object's events, such as "set variable x to 20" or "play sound effect number 2." You can either type actions with GML, GameMaker's internal programming language, or drag and drop the actions in their desired events (at least when it comes to simple projects and tasks).

The drag-and-drop functions in GameMaker do not cover the entirety of the software's capabilities. After you've grasped the basics, it's much easier to just add an action called "execute script" within an event and manually code what needs to be done. You can, again, make a more simplistic game entirely with the drag-and-drop interface.

Table 4-2 describes some typical drag-and-drop actions in GM.

Table 4-2. *Some Specific GameMaker Actions and Their Uses*

Action Name	Purpose	Example
Vertical speed	Set an object's vertical speed	Move enemy left.
Horizontal speed	Set an object's horizontal speed	Move player bullet up.
Create instance	Add more objects to the screen	Create missiles when the player presses left mouse button.
Different room	Change the room	End the game and enter a "game over" screen.
Execute code	Incorporate manual GML-code	Use GML to display some advanced particle effects unavailable when dragging and dropping.
Destroy instance	Remove objects from screen	Destroy enemy object when hit with player's bullets. Also remove involved player's bullet object.
Set variable	Manipulate data in a variable	Increase variable score by 200.
End game	Exit the game program	Exit to Windows after player selects Quit in the main menu.

Now, ladies and gentlemen, it's time to fire up your GameMaker. First, you'll create some more or less rudimentary graphical resources. You'll be operating in the GameMaker Studio IDE (see Figure 4-2).

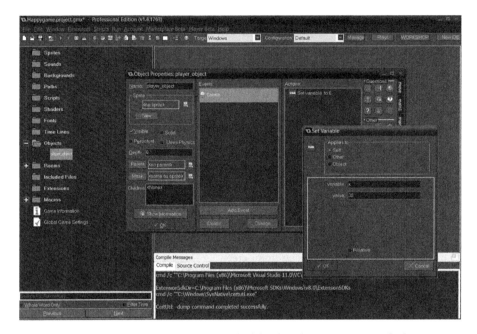

Figure 4-2. *The GameMaker Studio IDE. On the left side is the Resource Tree which is an organizer for all assets in your game.*

1. **In this tutorial you need to have only three sprites.** They are an enemy, the player, and a general-purpose ammunition sprite. Let's draw them all with the built-in sprite editor. Repeat the following steps for each of the three images.

    - Find the Sprites section on the left side of the display. Right-click it and select Create New Sprite.

    - Now, click Edit Sprite. Click the white icon labeled "Create a new sprite."

    - You now get to specify the sprite dimensions. The default of 32×32 pixels is fine. Click OK.

    - Click the pencil icon, labeled "Edit the image." You are now in the sprite-drawing mode.

    - Zoom in on the empty image a few times from the View menu.

    - On the left, there are a bunch of drawing tools. Experiment with them. You are now plotting pixels that will comprise the sprite when you're happy with it. Draw a happy face or a rocket. Or go crazy with the shapes and colors. Use your imagination.

        - A mask in the context of sprites is simply the *sprite collision area*. You select this with the Modify Mask button in the sprite properties window. The different choices for the sprite mask are "precise," "rectangular," "ellipse," and "diamond."

46

The sprite mask should correspond to the overall shape of the sprite. A square object works best with a rectangular mask, for obvious reasons.

While the "precise" setting is the most accurate by far, having large amounts of in-game sprites use this mask type may cause an overall slowdown, as it uses slightly more CPU processing power. Use the other mask shapes if you can.

Now you should have three different sprites in your library. If you are looking for some sprites created externally, you can simply use the Load Sprite button in the sprite properties window to import them into the project. Experiment with downloading sprite graphics from online resources and transferring them into GameMaker.

- Pro Tip: Try http://opengameart.org for all your copyright-free graphical needs.

2. **Next, you'll create a playground (also known as a *map*, *level*, or *room*) to experiment in. You can later add objects into a room simply by locating the *objects*-panel in the room view, selecting an object, and left-clicking at the desired location for said object.**

- Right-click Rooms and select Create Room or choose this option from the Resources menu.

- Click the Settings tab. Here there are some important options for you to use:

  - Width and Height set the room's size in pixels. For this tutorial, stay with a width of 1024 and a height of 768 pixels.

  - Speed sets the update frequency (per second) of the room. You will want to keep this at 60 for most rooms. This ensures the smoothest update on visuals.

  - Exit the room editor.

3. **Now it's time to create a player object. This is the object the player will be controlling.**

- Right-click the Objects category on the far left of the screen. Select Create New Object. Name it **player_object**. Select a visual representation for the object using the Sprite-section, which is right under the name field. You should have a choice of three different sprites if you followed the tutorial.

  - **You'll now set the player's initial position on-screen.** Click Add Event. Select a **Create** event.

- Find the **Set Variable** action from the right. It's listed under the control-section.

- Drag the Set Variable action onto the Actions-section of the Create event.

  - A new window will open. Enter the letter **X** into the "variable" input prompt.

  - For "value," enter **30**.

- Drag another Set Variable action onto the same part of the Create event.

  - A new window will open. Enter the letter **Y** into the "variable" input prompt.

  - For this "value," enter **700**.

- The `player_object` is now starting the room at 30 pixels from the left and 700 pixels down from the top. Remember, the Create event only deals with the moment the object is first created.

- **Next, you'll add some keyboard controls.** Click Add Event. Select the Key Press event.

  - Select <left> from the menu. This refers to the left arrow key on the keyboard.

- Drag yet another Set Variable action, this time onto the Press <left> event.

  - Enter **hspeed** into the "variable" input prompt. *hspeed* is a built-in variable which controls horizontal speed in GameMaker.

  - For this "value," enter **-4**.

- Click Add Event. Select the Key Press event again. Now, select <right> from the menu.

  - Drag yet another Set Variable action, this time onto the Press <right> event.

  - Enter **hspeed** into the "variable" input prompt.

  - For this "value," enter **4**.

4. **You will now create your mighty opponent.**

   - Again, right-click Objects. Select Create New Object. Name it **enemy_object**. You'll now set up the enemy's initial position. Associate a sprite for the object.

     - Add a **Create** event. Drag an action called Speed Horizontal onto the Create-event. Input **1** as its value.

     - Add variables called **X** and **Y**. Assign **800** in X and **30** in Y.

- **You'll make some safeguards for not losing sight of the enemy.**

  - Add a **Step** event.

  - Find the **Execute Code** action in the control-section of actions.

  - Drag this into the Step event.

  - A GML code window will open. Enter the following code:

    - `if x<0 x=room_width;`

    - `if x>room_width x=0;`

5. **It's time for an enemy bullet object.**

   - Yes, you know the drill by now! Create another new object, and call it **enemy_bullet**.

   - Associate a sprite for the object. Add a Create event on the object.

   - Activate the *move* group of actions. Drag the *Speed Vertical* action to the Create event. Input a **7** as the object's vertical speed. This means the bullet will fall down seven pixels each frame.

   - **Let's get some collision detection going on between these bullets and the player.**

   - Click Add Event and then pick **Collision**. Choose the player (`player_object`). The game now detects collisions between the enemy bullet and the player.

     - Let's make the player die if he or she hits an enemy. Click the main1 group of actions.

     - Drag an action called Destroy Instance onto the collision event (it looks like a trash can).

     - You'll then be presented with three options. Choose "other." This means the action will affect the object colliding with the current object (i.e., the player object colliding with the enemy bullet object, not vice versa).

     - If you had picked "self," you would be destroying the enemy bullet instead upon this collision. Actually, let's do that too. Drag another action called Destroy Instance onto the collision event. This time choose "self." *Voilà*. Now the enemy bullet is also destroyed upon impact with the player.

   - **Next you'll make sure all enemy bullets not visible on-screen are destroyed to save resources.**

   - Click Add Event and Other. Choose the **Outside Room** action.

   - Drag a Destroy Instance action into this event. Make sure it's set to *self*.

6. **Now you'll make the enemy fire his or her bullets at specific intervals using an Alarm event.**

- Open enemy_object.

- Add an event called **Alarm**. Select Alarm 0 from the menu that appears.

- Find the Set Alarm action from the submenu called *main 2* within the object. Drag this into both the Create event and the Alarm 0 event inside of enemy_object. Enter a value of **30** into "number of steps" in both cases.

  - This will trigger the alarm event every half a second, as the room speed was set to 60 in the room settings.

- Now, drag a **Create Instance** action into the Alarm 0 actions. You'll find it in the *main 1* -submenu within the object.

- Select the enemy_bullet object for this action.

- Click "relative." This option will use the X and Y coordinates relative to enemy_object when a new instance of enemy_bullet is created.

7. **Now, you'll make some bullets for you, player 1.**

- Create another new object, called **player_bullet**.

- Locate the object **enemy_bullet** from the GameMaker Resource Tree and right click on it. Select Duplicate to make a copy of the object. Rename it to **player_bullet**.

  - Hold on! Instead of a 7 as the object's vertical speed, input **-7**. This means the bullet will go up seven pixels per frame. Also, change the collision-event in the new object to monitor collisions against enemy_object, instead of player_object.

Now, for the grand finale of our little tutorial, use the techniques presented previously to create the following additional mechanics for the game:

- Pressing the spacebar will fire a player_bullet from a relative position to player_object.

- Moving player_object out of one side of the screen will make it appear on the other side.

- The enemy changes direction every six seconds (hint: use GameMaker's alarms).

Oh, and, did you remember to add both the player and the enemy into the room? If not, now's the perfect time to do so. There you have it! Your first functional bare-bones video game with all the basic mechanics in place. It may not ever equal *Tetris* in popularity, but your journey has begun. Congratulations.

Game Engine Reviews

Now, on to the tools of the trade. There are many commercial game engines. Here I cover engines geared for both 2D and 3D development. Unless stated otherwise, each game engine runs on Windows PCs only. The software is not presented in any particular order. All prices are approximate. The engines are rated on a scale of one to five in the following categories:

Commercial Potential

- Are there any notable games created with the system?

- Does the system allow export to more than one current platform?

Usability

- Is the engine intuitive to use?

- Is the user interface uncluttered and logical?

Audiovisuals

- Does the engine provide adequate technologies to create modern visual output?

- Do the engine's audio features allow a good degree of flexibility in formats?

Support

- Does the engine have busy forums?

- Do the engine developers respond swiftly to technical and other queries?

Overall

- This is the bottom-line grade based on the four previous factors as well as various intangibles.

GameMaker Studio Professional 1.4 by YoYo Games

www.yoyogames.com/

Price (Q1 2017): $147
GameMaker Studio Professional 1.4 is for creating any types of games.
The software can deploy on the following systems:

- Windows

- macOS

- Linux (Ubuntu)

- HTML5 (browser)

- iOS

- Android

- Tizen (Samsung)

The first GameMaker was envisioned by Mark Overmars and released in 1999 to much acclaim. Some seven revisions later, GameMaker Studio is the next generation in the GameMaker series of tools. The program offers much: there's seven deployable platforms and a track record of dozens of commercially successful games made with the engine. The performance is fine across the board, but some issues persist.

Commercial Potential: 4/5

Here are some notable games created with the system:

- *Undertale* by Toby Fox (2015)

- *Risk of Rain* by Chucklefish Games (2013)

- *Spelunky Remake* by Mossmouth (2013)

Usability: 3/5

Let's not kid ourselves: the GameMaker interface is quite lousy. You're greeted with tiny icons that have changed little since the first version of the software. Don't let that fool you. Using the engine becomes intuitive in no time.

Deployment for anything other than Windows can get clunky in GameMaker Studio. The other platforms all need tons of settings adjustments to start working. As your projects get more complex, the compilation time will increase considerably (shader users, I'm looking at you). Also, GameMaker Studio seems to struggle with application loading times. Unless you optimize your games by keeping the amount of in-game resources and shaders to a minimum, expect to spend up to five minutes waiting for your game to load. I'm not kidding. It's not an attractive proposal for the average gamer or developer.

Audiovisuals: 4/5

GameMaker Studio seems to have a sturdy 2D visual engine. It is based on the venerable version 8.1 after all. Most such projects zip along on even below average hardware.

Complicated projects in particular benefit from a setting called YYC. Many of the platforms on offer support this YoYo Compiler, which speeds up the game experience considerably in some scenarios. This used to be a separately purchased module; thank goodness it now comes standard. Projects with more than a few hundred moving objects in particular seem to thrive on this setting. Keep it on for all projects; it rarely hurts.

Since version 1.3, GameMaker Studio has supported shaders. This opened up a lot of opportunities for modern and funky screen manipulation. Think film grain or lens distortion effects. However, shaders slow down a project's launching time considerably. Try to keep them to a minimum in GameMaker Studio.

While the software supports 3D models, I found this functionality quite lacking. There's hardly any in-interface support for these features. Think of GameMaker Studio as a 2D engine with some 3D possibilities. Yet, if you're ambitious, you might carve a 3D space opera with this one. Who knows?

Like the classic editions of GameMaker, the vertical syncing in GameMaker Studio slows things down drastically and should be kept off at all times. YoYo Games and vertical sync are sworn enemies.

A handy companion tool for any version of GameMaker is Particle Designer 2 by Alert Games (see Figure 4-3). It's freeware and allows you to design and preview beautiful particles in real time. Simply create your particle and then export the data, which is automatically saved in GameMaker format via clipboard or copy and paste. All GameMaker versions that support particles will work with Particle Designer 2.

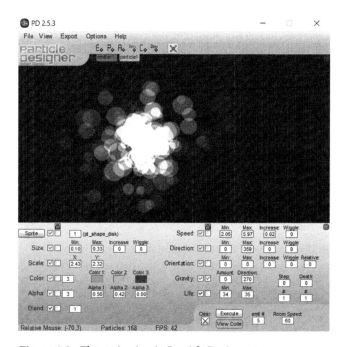

Figure 4-3. *The main view in Particle Designer 2*

You can download Particle Designer 2 from www.alertgames.net/old/index. php?page=software.

Support: 4/5

YoYo Games has a good track record in support. The forums are also densely populated. You'll find a wealth of tutorials both from within the software and from the community at large.

There's also a store called GameMaker: Marketplace that sells thousands of high-quality resources (https://marketplace.yoyogames.com). From extra sprites and backgrounds to full code libraries, you'll find what you need right there. The marketplace also has a fine selection of free assets.

Overall: 4/5

Mark Overmars did a big favor to the game engine industry with his monumentally influential work on GameMaker. Even the older GameMaker versions (versions 7, 8, and 8.1) are still loved around the world. In fact, they've been used to make highly successful commercial games in recent years, including *Gunpoint* (2013), *Hotline Miami* (2012), and its sequel *Hotline Miami 2: Wrong Number* (2015). Obviously this is a successful franchise in the game engine world. The powerful scripting language GML in particular is why pretty much any version of the GameMaker software is ideal for the beginning video game entrepreneur. What GameMaker Studio brings to the table is mainly multiplatform deployment and shader support.

While GameMaker veterans are right at home, GameMaker Studio may seem daunting at first for the novice as the interface is still somewhat clumsy. However, the engine is easy to use and becomes intuitive after a mere half-hour of using it. The end results can be impressive and will compete with many of the most successful titles out there.

Here are the GameMaker Studio minimum system requirements:

- Windows XP

- 512MB RAM

- DirectX 9.0c-compliant card with 128MB onboard RAM

- 200MB available space

GameMaker Tips

These techniques apply to all versions of GameMaker:

- *Learn to use the alarm events*: Assign them to all things that don't need to be set every single frame. The Step event is not your friend, as anything in it is executed every frame. If an object needs to change direction every now and then, do it with an Alarm event instead.

- *Make sure you remove all objects that leave the room and don't come back*: You don't want thousands of bullets that were once shot and will never hit anything again sucking out all the resources from the player's system. Simply add an Outside Room event to such an object and put a "Destroy the instance" action in it. Remember, objects exist even if they leave the view. They are not automatically destroyed.

- *You shouldn't execute scripts within the main action scenes, where all the hubbub takes place*: This might slow your game down. Scripts are fine, as long as you run them before or after the main action rooms. So, use the Execute Code action in these rooms instead of the Execute Script one. This is known as programming *inline*. So, let's not "call scripts." Let's keep it inline, people, with Execute Code instead.

- *Keep the drawing event clear of anything not related to graphics operations*: Don't calculate anything not directly related to drawing things on the screen. Doing that may slow your game down. For calculating anything and for all variable-related affairs, use the Alarm (and possibly the Step) event instead.

- *Disable the Draw Background Color setting in the room options*: This amounts to one less drawing event in the room, but only if your backdrop covers the whole screen. Otherwise, you get a mess.

- *Don't use views unless you absolutely must*: One such scenario might be split-screen two-player action. Having said that, how about having two players on-screen sharing a single view instead, with the players' coordinates determining the room position?

- *Do not ever use the synchronization setting in GameMaker*: Disable it at all times. Some atrocious speed reductions may otherwise occur. Several different video cards show this behavior.

- *Make sure you keep the room speed at 60 fps at all times*: Do not artificially slow things down by altering the room speed; do it by other means if necessary. This approach provides the smoothest output. Also, any setting other than 60 fps may result in severe screen tearing, and the only way to fix that is the dreaded vertical sync.

- *Keep the amount of objects on-screen at sane levels*: Use the Test Instance Count action for this purpose before creating any series of objects. This means a few dozen enemies, bullets, and other categories of objects at most.

- *Settle for the smallest passable resolution for your game*: Even with optimization, GameMaker isn't really great in the higher resolutions. This goes for any game engine, but classic GameMaker versions (7, 8, 8.1) seem to be really sensitive to this logic. Hey, you love retro, don't you?

- *Utilize surfaces*: They are tedious at first, but they provide much, much better performance than objects with sprites in GameMaker 7. Surfaces are data written directly to the video card memory. Some examples of good surface use are moving logos, backdrops, and related detail, and even some massive enemies that don't require precise collision detection. Use these lines of GML to define each surface:

```
surface_name = surface_create(x_size, y_size);
surface_set_target(surface_name);
<Draw your graphics here with draw_sprite,
draw_background or draw a primitive>
surface_reset_target();
```

   Congratulations. You now have a new surface to use! Use it with the `draw_surface(surface_name, x, y)` command. As always, keep this in the Draw event.

- *Keep your audio at 44.100Hz and 16 bits*: Other sampling rates or 24-bit samples may not play at all. Don't bother with Ogg, which may or may not work. Stick to MP3 for background music.

   Colliding objects with surfaces is possible. Instead of using collision masks, you use coordinates. X and Y, we love you.

- *Particles can collide, too*: Assign to a bullet object, or any projectile, a collision mask by choosing a sprite of roughly the same size as the particle stream you're about to implement. Then, put a particle emitter in its Draw action. This will overwrite the sprite in the object with a bunch of particles but keep the collision mask. Great for plasma-like weapons, fire, smoke, etc.

GameMaker 7 (Free) for the Mac

The free Mac OS X (Intel only) version of GameMaker 7 "is still available for download (see Figure 4-4). This version has no particle support and may have other serious limitations. The last update for the software was version 7.5.12 in 2010, which resulted in a relatively stable program. As GameMaker 7 for Mac is a relatively competent engine for budding Mac developers, YoYo Games should release the full version of this software as freeware. It shouldn't hurt the sales of its main products in any way.

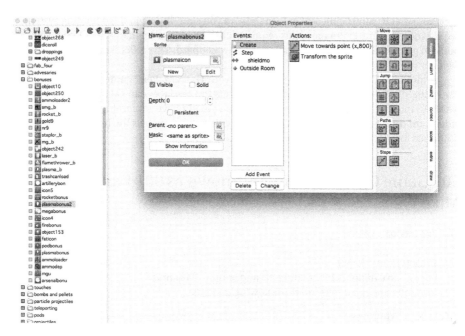

Figure 4-4. *The IDE from GameMaker 7 for Mac*

Even though it will never get another update, the full Mac version of GameMaker 7 is a solid and speedy alternative for Mac indie developers learning the ropes. It's a little gem, actually, if you can find it or were lucky enough to purchase it when it was still sold.

GameMaker 7 provides adequate tools for creating most types of 2D games. You can create platformers and shoot-'em-ups with ease. You're only limited by your own artistic abilities and the other artists in your team. Particle effects are implemented well in the full version of GameMaker 7 for Mac. While 3D is supported, it is rudimentary at best and hardly cutting edge. Simpler, Mario Kart–like driving games are a doozy on this suite, however. The 2D performance on offer is fine. You would have to run games made with these on a very low-spec Mac to have sluggish screen update. I'm talking pre-2004 hardware. Anything newer and the game will stay at an enjoyable speed, unless you layer dozens of backgrounds with hundreds of particles at the same time and forsake optimization completely. GameMaker 7 doesn't need a spectacular battle station from the developing point of view. A 2011 Mac mini with OS X Lion and an average graphics card runs GameMaker 7 quite admirably.

The games GameMaker 7 for Mac exports run well on Mac OS X 10.6 (Snow Leopard), but they do so even better on newer versions of macOS. From Lion onward, GameMaker 7 works wonderfully. No doubt this is because of Apple updating its OpenGL support to version 3.2—from the ancient version 2.1 in Snow Leopard.

Most audiovisual formats are supported by the software. There has been some talk about the macOS version not supporting the MP3 format to a full degree, but this seems to be an unfounded claim.

Note that if using GameMaker 7, make sure you state "Lion" in the operating system requirements. In my estimation, this requirement provides more than a 10 percent speed boost to graphical operations compared to Snow Leopard. This reflects on the developer well.

Additionally, if you use a lot of surfaces in your GameMaker 7 game, state "video card with 512MB of memory" in the requirements too. Surfaces can eat a lot of video card RAM. All those error messages you may be getting might have something to do with your video card running out of memory. Integrated video chips, such as the Intel GMA, are notorious for having low amounts of RAM at their disposal.

001 Game Creator (formerly known as 001 Engine) by Mike Weir

www.engine001.com/

Price (Q1 2017): $98
001 Game Creator is for creating 2D and simple 3D games.
The software can deploy on the following systems:

- Windows

- Android

- iOS

- HTML5

001 Game Creator (001GC) is a multipurpose tool for the beginner entrepreneur. The team boasts no programming is necessary with their engine—and for once they're right. Sporting an RPG Maker–like history and design, 001GC is capable of several different genres.

Commercial Potential: 3/5

There are no notable games created with this system. While the potential for commercial titles is there, this engine is mostly used by hobbyists.

Usability: 4/5

The interface in 001GC feels somewhat dated, which is typical for engines that have been in development since the 1990s (see Figure 4-5). Everything works: the sprite editor is simple enough to use and animate your characters with, adding events is simple, and the testing abilities are pretty much lightning fast. There's even a built-in device simulator of all your typical smartphones and tablets in case you're deploying on these devices. Of course, you're better off testing on actual mobile devices via Wi-Fi, which is an option in 001GC too.

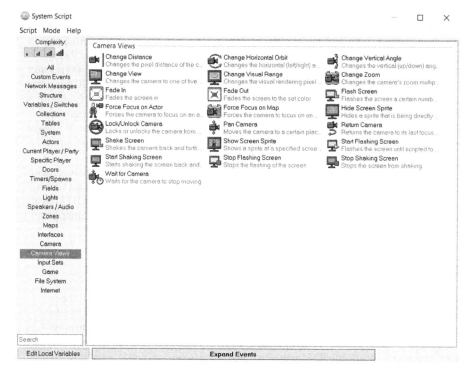

Figure 4-5. *Some events from the 001 Game Creator script editor*

Newcomers to the engine are greeted with a handy selection of demo games. These include the mandatory space shooter, a tower defense game, and a card game for good measure.

You can tell this software started out mostly as a tool for role-playing games (RPGs). This is not a bad thing, as it has greatly ventured beyond this genre. There are still menus for items, parties, and team alliances (for allied, neutral, and evil actors, respectively). These take nothing away from the engine even if you're not into RPGs much. If you're familiar with the RPG Maker series of game creation software, you'll feel at home in 001GC. Also, the terrain editor is very impressive with a great implementation of lights to boot. You'll be drawing paths on eye-pleasing terrains literally within seconds.

At the heart of the engine is the visual script tool. Although the option for text-based scripting is available, this is rarely needed to create commercially viable titles. In fact, the engine graphical user interface (GUI) warns against text-based input, preferring the user sticks to its mouse-driven approach instead. It's simple enough to drag conditions and events onto the script canvas to get things done.

A word of warning: your mouse's scroll wheel may not play nice with this tool. Scripts are known to vanish off-screen if you use it too much. You have been warned.

Audiovisuals: 4/5

Although the demo games don't give the greatest impression of the engine with sluggish controls and dated graphics, it's obvious 001GC is capable of producing perfectly hip arcade titles. There's an adequate particle system, high-resolution audio, and even some fine (more or less pseudo) 3D graphical abilities available in the engine. 001GC supports several lossless image formats, including BMP, PNG, and TGA. The amount of support for 3D models is more than adequate for an engine with focus on 2D. You can import objects in FBX, OBJ, 3DS, DXF, DAE, and even the good old Microsoft X format. While the 3D capabilities of 001GC aren't AAA quality, they are perfect for casual and/or mobile projects.

The impressive support for different file formats doesn't end there. When it comes to audio, 001GC has your back. You can safely import audio files in WAV, MP3, Ogg Vorbis, AIFF, and even the classic MIDI format (MP3 and MIDI are not supported for HTML5 or Android deployment because of licensing issues). Your speakers and headphones get to churn out audio in stereo or surround in either 5.1 or 7.1.

Support: 4/5

001 Game Creator is pretty much maintained by one person. Having said that, the software clearly is a labor of love for Mike Weir. The engine had a bit of a nosedive in popularity in recent years but seems to have regained momentum. The community around the product has been reinvigorated, and even some downloadable content (DLC) is on its way. The product wiki is extensive and useful (www.engine001.com/wiki/start). There's a ton of additional free resources for the engine on the official web site (www.engine001.com/resources.htm).

This engine is simply pretty much universally well-liked, as is evident from the official forum. The forum has nearly 400,000 posts by mostly enthusiastic users. See for yourself: www.engine001.com/forum/.

Speaking of DLC, you can now purchase an MMORPG kit for the engine. This takes care of the many tedious tasks when creating an online environment for a large number of players. With it installed, a developer is free to invest time on the core product, instead of worrying about user registrations, logins, and networking protocols. At $15 this is very much a mandatory purchase for those looking to make the next *League of Legends*.

Also on its way is first-person shooter (FPS)-based DLC. This obviously can't upgrade the engine into a AAA platform for 3D graphics, but it will open some doors for mobile developers looking to make less resource-intensive FPS titles with lower-poly models. Also, these projects will be stuck in 720p resolution. Another DLC perhaps more suited for the engine is dedicated to the point-and-click genre of 2D adventure games (think LucasArts and Sierra titles from the 1990s). This is more familiar territory for 001GC, and it's doubtful there will be any major technological hurdles to overcome with the expansion.

Overall: 4/5

Perhaps best known for its RPG output, 001 Game Creator is a versatile game engine for several genres. Pretty much only a cutting-edge FPS is out of the picture with the system. Despite its somewhat antiquated GUI, it's a powerful engine for developers of most skill levels.

Here are the 001 Game Creator minimum system requirements:

- Windows XP, Vista, 7, 8, or 10

- 2GHz or faster CPU

- 512MB RAM

- Video card supporting OpenGL 2.1 or newer

- 300MB free hard drive space

Starting Point

After purchasing the engine or installing a demo, watch the video tutorial at `https://www.youtube.com/watch?v=ca1CXm2Y_AY` made by the creators of the software. Explore YouTube for similar videos.

GameGuru by The Game Creators

`https://www.game-guru.com/`

Price (Q1 2017): **$19.99**
GameGuru is for creating 3D (FPS) games.
It deploys on Windows.
GameGuru is a beginner's 3D game toolkit. Although flawed, this software package is frequently updated. It does have some fancy visual effects, such as some great depth of field and motion blur, as well as a rudimentary built-in character creator. Surprisingly, GameGuru offers a fine building editor as well.

Commercial Potential: 3/5

There are no notable games created with the system. The system is barely able to produce commercial output at this stage because of limitations in map size and overall performance.

Usability: 4/5

Described by some as a glorified map editor, GameGuru does offer a lot more. You populate the scenes with objects, attaching Lua scripts to them, where appropriate, for special purposes (e.g., making a car object drive around instead of just staying still).

The software supports DirectX files (.x) for 3D entities. You may have difficulty exporting to this format from your 3D editing program.

When you're done with your game, simply select Save as Standalone from the File menu and you're all set. You now have an independently running 3D game you can distribute.

Many of the visual settings of your map are controlled in real time from within the preview system. You get to see the changes immediately. There are settings for skyboxes, terrain, and vegetation. Surface color, brightness, and other controls are available as well for immediate tweaking.

There are two types of objects in the GameGuru workflow: entities and markers. Entities refer to any 3D objects in the developer's library, such as robots, ducks, or cars (see Figure 4-6). Markers are basically scripts, and this is where Lua comes in. Entities can be set to be either physics or nonphysics objects, the difference being nonphysics objects can't be collided with, but they need less processing power.

Figure 4-6. *A helicopter in the GameGuru editor*

The Easy Building Editor

Released in early 2017, version 1.14 of GameGuru received its most impressive single feature yet: the Easy Building Editor (EBE). This easily adds a point in this category, such is the usefulness of the tool.

You simply add a *site* into your terrain and start adding the walls, floors, and roof elements on top of that building site. Elegantly mouse-driven, the tool is something most people can master in minutes. EBE allows for multilevel buildings, with the Page Up and Page Down keys on your keyboard taking your efforts one level higher or lower, respectively. By tapping the Tab key, you temporarily remove walls to work with the inner confines of your dream house. The buildings created with the EBE are fully explorable by the player, as long as you provide means to an entry to them.

All of the EBE elements naturally come with textures. There are several types of these textures for you to choose from, and nothing is stopping you from either purchasing new ones or making your own, should you feel like it.

What all this means is a) you no longer have to purchase custom structures for your maps and b) you can craft complicated dungeons and spaceship interiors with minimum effort. Well done, The Game Creators.

Audiovisuals: 3/5

You get a resolution scaled to your desktop's; apparently selecting a resolution in-game is a no-no. This can be annoying if you enjoy keeping your OS resolution well over Full HD specs as rendering anything at such high resolution is slow in general, including in GameGuru. There's depth of field and some high-resolution skyboxes to make sure your projects do look presentable.

Despite being primarily made for FPS projects, GameGuru allows for the creation of third-person view games, with ample camera control for the developer to toy with.

The physics in GameGuru are powered by no less than Bullet Physics, a physics engine used in *GTA IV* and *GTA V* to name just two, but here the system seems quite underused. While the advertisements claim full ragdoll functionality, most of the enemies seem to just fall down and stay there after you slay them, not sliding more than an inch down the sides of slopes.

Also, the player cannot easily ride on top of moving physics objects. What's up with that? This means there's no raft or elevator rides in GameGuru just yet. You walk around, maybe teleporting every so often, and that's it. You can only script movement for nonphysics objects it seems (unless you factor enemy soldiers in), and your protagonist just falls through these.

GameGuru was initially criticized for slow visual performance. In late 2015 the Game Creators overhauled the underlying engine with good results. The average project on an average PC now runs between 40 fps to 45 fps, which is relatively smooth sailing.

There are dedicated height-map generating software out there, such as Raiseland and Geovox, which greatly speed up the terrain generation process in game development. Unfortunately, there is no height map support available in GameGuru. This is a mainstay in higher-end engines, but with the GameGuru market segment and price, we can't complain.

The water in GameGuru maps stays on one level at all times (so you can forget about waterfalls), and the maps aren't very big. Also, creating and venturing on high terrain causes unpredictable behavior, such as flickering landscapes.

In 2016 GameGuru got another facelift, in the form of a trio of visual techniques: scalable ambient obscurance (SAO), fast approximate antialiasing (FXAA), and lens flare. FXAA basically softens the whole screen estate, so you see less of jagged edges in objects and terrain. SAO, on the other hand, is a technique to add realistic corner shadows and other soft shadows into and around 3D models—a hit-and-miss effect. While the FXAA especially makes a positive difference on the visuals, the new effects do take a toll on the frame rate with about 5 to 8 fps. The lens flare is simply an age-old halo effect of what happens when one glances straight into the digital sun, but it's a nice little addition nonetheless.

Support: 4/5

GameGuru-related forums are pleasantly busy. The system has a Steam-powered store available, offering thousands of extra 3D entities and other resources for a few bucks each. This in itself offers a lucrative business-to-business opportunity for 3D artists, skybox makers, and Lua script writers, as long as you don't have issues with PayPal.

Game-guru.com has a decent news section with details on each product update. There's also a community-based voting system on future GG features on the web site. Some items on the long list include player-operated boats and planes, a day and night cycle, and antialiasing. Clearly The Game Creators is serious about future-proofing this software suite.

Overall: 3/5

GameGuru has a lot of promise. Its main appeal is in its map editor, which is easy to use and intuitive. The visual side is quite adequate for creating an atmosphere of your choosing (think games circa 2010). However, the waypoints system is extremely poor. Populating your maps with enemies is easy, but making these guys follow paths is a pain. The poor waypoint system aside, GameGuru offers limited terrain creation possibilities. Also, the loading times for the stand-alones are very old-school, meaning you do get a lot of time for meditation and/or watching paint-covered surfaces dehydrate.

Despite its shortcomings, GameGuru is a great choice as one's first 3D game–making tool. It's just such fun. Just keep in mind that using static stock objects in a project isn't a great way to create a commercial product. You probably need a crew of at least three passionate people in order to come up with original 3D objects and other resources for GameGuru. This is not a viable single-person tool for commercial development, unless you have considerable experience in 3D modeling.

Here are the GameGuru minimum system requirements:

- Windows XP, Vista, 7, or 8

- Intel Dual-Core 2GHz or AMD Dual-Core 2GHz

- 2GB RAM

- NVIDIA GeForce 400 series or AMD Radeon HD 6000 series, 1GB video card (minimum Shader Model 2.0)

- Version 9.0c

- 4GB available space

Starting Point

Start working on the tutorials on the official GameGuru site, from the Quick Start and onward (`https://www.game-guru.com/tutorials`).

Also, get acquainted with the official forums for the product (`https://forum.game-guru.com`).

Case Study: Halflight by Soiree Games

For a trailer of this project, see `https://vimeo.com/157925079` (see Figure 4-7).

Figure 4-7. *A scene from Halflight, a GameGuru-project. Notice the use of depth of field.*

GameGuru promises a lot of paper: low price, a decent map editor, fine visuals, and an active developer team. The Games Creators is indeed known to provide frequent updates to many of its products, including GameGuru. Soiree Games, my outfit, looked in-depth into developing its first 3D title with the engine, just to see whether it could be done.

Now, without dwelling too heavily on the storyline, *Halflight* (a working title) will feature a wide variety of vistas. There's a forest, an ocean, beaches on tropical islands, an icy landscape, and even a big metropolis with skyscrapers. At one point you're riding on the back of a big cargo plane. The game will feature very few guns and violence but ideally a lot of dreamy and nightmarish scenes to inspire one's imagination (see Figures 4-7 and 4-8). Using Game Guru in its current form is a challenge. Scripting a decent adventure game in what is primarily a simple first-person shooter engine is relatively taxing.

Figure 4-8. *A second scene from Halflight, a GameGuru project*

The visual engine in Game Guru is decent, and with careful use of color and bloom, any atmosphere can be created quite effectively, from a night downtown to a bright desert noon. The choice of skybox affects a map's ambience greatly. Also, spot lights can be made to shine in any color and brightness level. There are scripts for them to flicker, too. At the moment all lights are immobile, however. The performance is also quite lackluster at this stage. The frame rate is not outstanding even on higher-end hardware, staying in the 30 to 35 fps range most times with more object-heavy scenes.

Terrain creation is still in its infancy in Game Guru. You can start with a flat terrain, which requires plenty of tweaking to make it into anything interesting, or you may pick a randomized, dune-like map, which is also far from interesting from the get-go. There's about 20 very well put together tutorial maps in the map folder (see /mapbank/tutorialmaps). However, turning these into something to call your own is time-consuming. Generally it's bad practice to reuse stock maps in your creations. If you choose to do so, prepare for negative product reviews.

Map sizes are relatively large in Game Guru, although you can forget about a *Fallout 3*-type of seamless flow of outdoor scenery. GameGuru is definitely an old-school map-based tool. You do get to switch these maps at will, and there doesn't seem to be an upper limit on the total number of locations in a project.

And now for the biggest issues: there are constant problems with the waypoint system. On some of the maps, the waypoints just don't show up, no matter how frequently the icon is clicked. It seems the waypoints appear along the edges of the map—sometimes. This is not intuitive, people. We tried everything from validating the Game Guru application cache on Steam to reinstalling the program numerous times. Enemy combatants also displayed some glitchy behavior when assigned a path to follow. Nothing fixed these issues.

Lee Bamber, the lead programmer behind the project, is no doubt a talented coder. Still, Soiree Games will wait until GameGuru matures a little bit before releasing a 3D game made with the engine. Games made with the engine at its current state may not have much commercial appeal, but GameGuru itself holds a ton of potential (see Figure 4-8).

GameGuru Hints

This is where your scripts usually reside: C:\Program Files (x86)\Steam\SteamApps\ common\Game Guru\Files\scriptbank. Just edit these files with WordPad or some other word processor. To make a new script, copy an old one and rename it. You can't edit scripts from within the GameGuru software.

The file name of a script needs to be in the script itself—twice. Say you have made a Lua-script called cheese.lua. You need to incorporate the file name within this script file, in the init and main spots. So, it should have both function cheese_init(e) and function cheese_main(e) inside the script, instead of, say, function program_init(e) and function program_main(e).

Use the Win zone -marker to load a new map. Simply add the name of the map you want to load through the zone in the *ifUsed*-portion of the parameters. This functionality cannot be tested within the preview, only from the finished, stand-alone program. You will get a notification, however, in the preview as well, to signal the marker works.

To require the player to press E in a Win zone, overwrite the contents of the winzone.lua script with the following:

```
function winzone_init(e)
end
function winzone_main(e)
        if g_Entity[e]['plrinzone']==1 then
            Prompt("Press 'E' to fix the radar (or whatever) and move to the
            next level")
            if GetInKey() == "e" then
            JumpToLevelIfUsed(e)
            end
            end
end
```

Make sure you keep your media file names short. For one, your audio files may not play if you use a long file name such as happybigexplosion32423-32433.wav. Instead, try happyexplosion.wav.

Using more than four dynamic lights per scene goes to waste. GameGuru supports up to four dynamic lights in one view simultaneously, so stick to that amount and no more. Two lights can totally make a scene anyway.

Always utilize some DOF. The depth of field in GameGuru is beautifully implemented to add smooth softening to faraway objects. The result is very nice layer of polish. There's really no need to keep this effect switched off.

Shoot-'Em-Up Kit by Tall Studios

`www.tallstudios.com`

Price (Q1 2017): $39
Shoot-'Em-Up Kit is for creating 2D and pseudo-3D shoot-'em-up games.
It deploys on Windows.
Shoot-'Em-Up Kit (SEUK) allows anyone to create visually ambitious retro-ish
shoot-'em-up games. The pseudo-3D visuals are certainly very impressive as is the overall
ease of use. Like the software's title suggests, this is for a very specific genre of games, but
you do get exactly what you pay for.

Commercial Potential: 4/5

There are no notable games created with the system so far. The potential for them does exist.

Usability: 5/5

SEUK uses its 100 percent mouse-driven drag-and-drop approach to video game creation
beautifully. You do not need to type one line of code to create a commercially competent
title. Everything is logically grouped and graphically represented, including your enemies'
attack patterns, in-game lighting, and the physics properties of your game universe.

You do get quite far just by checking boxes and adjusting sliders (in the case of SEUK,
that is). Most aspects of a game's universe are easily manipulated within the software.
Like with many things in life, you will not master SEUK in a few days. Fully grasping what
the system is capable of will still take months. You do have a ton of features including
enemy AI, bullet patterns, camera angles, and particles to work with after all.

Audiovisuals: 5/5

Simply stated, SEUK offers some stunning, commercial-quality audiovisuals (see Figure 4-9).
It also features many graphical approaches from 1980s retro to modern-day arcade blasters
with impressive lighting, amazing explosions, and plenty of detail. Like many current
game-making tools, SEUK comes with a hip physics system. In this case, it's no other than
PhysX from Nvidia, familiar from dozens of smash hits over the past decade or so, appearing
in titles such as *Borderlands 2*, *Fallout 4*, and *Mafia 2* (to name just three). For one, you could
use gravity to make rocks fall on the player's ship when flying inside a cavern in a pretty
convincing manner. Picture the player having to blast through them on their way out with
realistic debris flying around. When it comes to physics, SEUK has you covered.

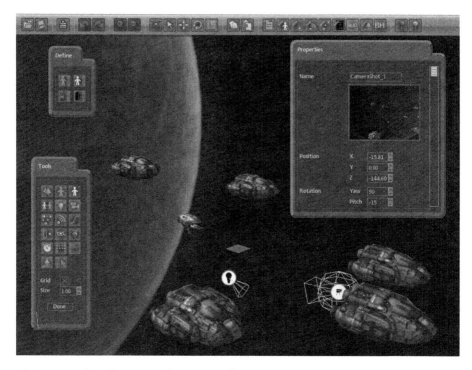

Figure 4-9. *Shoot-'Em-Up Kit has some truly impressive visuals*

Particle effects are also put to good use in the system, offering the developer full customization over their lasers, explosions, and other graphical touches. Shaders are supported with a considerable amount of customization at your disposal for all your post-processing needs. As for in-game 3D objects, SEUK accepts either .x or .obj models.

One of the finest features in SEUK is the camera. The flexibility provided by the camera system is simply outstanding, allowing the developers to create tasty cut scenes and experimental visual approaches with ease. Combine this with the amazing lighting system, shaders, and particles, and you have all the tools you need for some jaw-dropping visuals, if that is your thing. Again, you are not forced to use any of these features if you want to reach that blocky 1970s aesthetic. That would be a "thing" with indie developers after all.

Support: 4/5

Tall Studios in general has an active approach to its customers' worries. Tall Studios clearly cares about the product and has a reputation of responding promptly to whatever concerns developers have. The forums may not be the busiest out there, but that is only because of the relative lack of awareness of the product.

Overall: 4/5

A winner in every regard, the software delivers exactly what it promises. If shoot-'em-ups are your genre of choice as a developer, you couldn't do much better than the Tall Studios offering. Do prepare for a considerable amount of work on custom graphics and audio. Remember, it is a bad idea to use stock resources only, even if they're plentiful, as is the case with Shoot-'Em-Up Kit.

Having said all that, don't rely on this software as your only development tool, just in case you feel like experimenting on other, perhaps vastly different video game genres. That's why I deducted a point in this category. But for your very first commercially viable rooting-and-tooting title, it just might do the trick.

Here are the Shoot-'Em-Up Kit minimum system requirements:

- Windows XP, Vista, 7, or 8

- Intel dual-core 2GHz or AMD dual-core 2GHz

- 4GB of RAM

- 1GB of hard drive space

Starting Point

Start watching the tutorial videos on the Shoot-'Em-Up Kit site, from top to bottom (www.tallstudios.com/tutorials).

Leadwerks Game Engine 4.3 by Leadwerks Software

www.leadwerks.com

> Price (Q1 2017): $98
> Leadwerks Game Engine 4.3 is for creating 3D games.
> It deploys on Windows.
> Leadwerks is a grown-up's 3D system. Visually ambitious, it suffers from some usability issues. Despite the ease of achieving a basic 3D game with it, Leadwerks is for a more advanced user, mostly because of a heavy reliance on scripting. You may want to try it after you're done with GameGuru, for example.

Commercial Potential: 4/5

Here are some notable games created with the system:

- *A Demon's Game*: *Episode One* by RP Studios (2016)

- *Rogue System* by Digits Crossed Interactive (2016)

Usability: 4/5

Leadwerks is definitely not for absolute beginners although it's marketed as an easy game engine. This is a system for moderate to advanced programmers. It supports (and very much requires) either Lua or C++ scripting depending on the edition you choose. The indie version works with Lua scripts only, while the more expensive professional version covers both languages. C++ output in general is faster.

Leadwerks features a built-in script editor unlike, say, GameGuru. Whether you're working in Lua or C++, you will quickly learn to appreciate this workflow. Using the scripts themselves is straightforward: simply add one to an object for the functionality you need. Unfortunately, objects can all take just a single script file each. Leadwerks also includes a nifty graphical tool, or *flowchart editor*, for managing simple game functionality. With it one can easily create most common actions in the game world, such as opening doors when the player flips a switch.

Another great feature is the NavMesh generation, which is pretty much a single-button-click affair. A NavMesh stands for *navigation mesh* and simply defines areas on a map where enemy units can move without hindrance. In the past, on most game engines, keeping enemies from becoming stuck on the scenery may have been a slow and tedious process.

But let's face it, Leadwerks is buggy. All kinds of error messages and crashes are common. The trick is to try many of the available beta versions. One of them just might work on your hardware. The most current version of the software deemed stable may actually be less so than the beta versions on your configuration. Also, the system is very finicky with your video cards. Some cards simply do not work at all with Leadwerks. This may be perhaps because of the software using OpenGL instead of DirectX, which is the preferred API of most video card manufacturers.

Audiovisuals: 4/5

The OpenGL-powered visuals in Leadwerks are of very high quality. The experience of a well-made Leadwerks terrain is simply a feast for one's eyes (see Figure 4-10). The terrain creation system itself is intuitive and powerful. Everything including arid prairies, snow-capped mountain vistas, and dense forests are a joy to create. You have the usual tools to flatten and raise land among others, but you can also import height maps i.e., bring in terrains created externally using specialized software such as Raiseland.

Figure 4-10. *Leadwerks terrain*

The Leadwerks vegetation system is a breeze to use. You simply "paint" an area in the terrain you want your luscious vegetation growing in. Then, with a few adjustments, you can fine-tune your vegetation's attributes to your liking when it comes to things such as plant height, density, and whether the foliage casts shadows or not. However, the water shader isn't all that.

When importing 3D objects, Leadwerks supports the industry-standard Autodesk (.fbx) models. The engine also supports an approach called *constructive solid geometry* (CSG), which is basically the method of creating 3D primitives out of thin air and manipulating them into useful objects in the game world. For example, by hollowing out a rectangular CSG object, you can create a basic but functional tunnel for your game, adding detail with automatic texture maps. You have your box, wedge, cylinder, sphere, arch, tube, and torus shapes to experiment with. Sometimes this can be a time-saving approach, just in case you need something large and simple in your map and don't have anything as an Autodesk 3D model available.

The audio format support in Leadwerks is known to be limited. For a long time, the system only supported traditional WAV files. While this is a high-fidelity format, it takes a lot of hard drive space and is only ever useful for sound effects. Since version 4.3, Leadwerks has supported the popular Ogg Vorbis audio format, which is known for both great quality and small file size. This finally enables music and voice acting tracks for your Leadwerks projects. Also, the engine supports full 3D sound spatialization.

Support: 4/5

The documentation and available tutorials are plentiful and easy to understand. YouTube, too, has a wealth of video tutorials for the software. In particular, Jorn Theunissen has created a formidable number of video tutorials for the engine.

The learning curve remains quite steep. Also, there doesn't seem to be a clear vision for the future (i.e., a road map) for Leadwerks. Updates to the engine are still frequent and show commitment from the development team. Version 4.1 of the software debuted in June 2016 and version 4.2 in December of the same year.

The Leadwerks Workshop (a *workshop* refers to a Steam-based add-on store) is quite well-equipped. There you'll find numerous user-generated 3D models, scripts, and sound effects for your buying pleasure. The quality of the items is above average in all categories.

Overall: 3/5

Leadwerks offers some very professional features, but it's not one for the complete beginner despite what the marketing materials claim. Think of it as a next step on your journey as an indie developer. Also, without the bugs and icky video card support, the software would rate at least one point higher in this category. Having said that, Leadwerks is clearly alive and well and continues to improve every update.

Here are the Leadwerks minimum system requirements:

- Windows Vista, 7, 8, 8.1, or 10

- 2.0GHz dual core

- 2GB RAM

- OpenGL 4.0 or DirectX 11 graphics

- 2GB hard drive space

Starting Point

Start working on the basic tutorials on the Leadwerks site, from top to bottom (www.leadwerks.com/werkspace/page/tutorials).

CopperCube 5/CopperCube 5 Pro by Ambiera

www.ambiera.com/coppercube

Price (Q1 2017): $38/$300 for Pro
CopperCube is for creating 3D games.
It deploys on the following:

- Windows

- macOS

- WebGL (HTML)

- Android

- Flash

A product for lower-end systems, CopperCube 5 is an easy-to-use system for most types of 3D products with a beautiful terrain editor.

Commercial Potential: 4/5

Here are some notable games created with the system:

- *Post Collapse* by Ambiera (2016)
- *Painted Legend* by Vitaly Shikhovtsev (2016)

Usability: 4/5

CopperCube 5 comes in two flavors. The more expensive Pro version differs from the regular one in many regards: you get (in-scene) video playback, an unlimited number of scenes, scene metrics, and a command-line interface. The regular version is perfectly competent for creating any kind of 3D game or app.

The editor interface in CopperCube is as good and intuitive as they come (see Figure 4-11). It's easy to add new objects to a scene, swap textures, or create gorgeous colorful liquid surfaces. The terrain editor is a pleasure to use as well, with the software also able to accept externally created height maps. Unlike some engines (such as GameGuru), you have a large number of textures available to paint your terrains with. You even get to populate your terrains with randomized trees, a feature called a *procedural tree generator.*

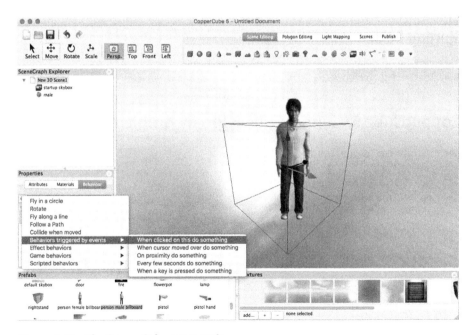

Figure 4-11. *The CopperCube user interface*

CopperCube works in a comfortably codeless, mouse-driven environment. No coding is required to create commercially viable projects. However, the system does have full JavaScript support in case you need to dig deeper.

To create new JavaScript functionality, just put a script file into the extension directory (Documents\CopperCube\extensions on Windows or ~/Documents/CopperCube/extensions on macOS) and call it ScriptName.js (e.g., action_MovePosition.js). Each valid script file will appear within the CopperCube engine upon restarting as an extra action or behavior.

The in-game camera in CopperCube is straightforward to add and manipulate. You simply click the Create a Camera icon and pick from a selection of presets to get the functionality you need. There are six highly useful presets to choose from, including both a first-person camera (with typical mouse and keyboard controls) and a third-person camera that follows the path of an object of your choosing.

Audiovisuals: 4/5

CopperCube features competitive enough graphical capabilities, but there are other engines out there with more modern visual effects available. What CopperCube does well is optimization. You'll no doubt be able to create reasonably attractive games for lower-end systems, such as mobile devices. CopperCube supports Blender (.blend), DirectX (.x), Blitz3D (.b3d), Milkshape (.ms3d), and many other formats for its models. The system may rarely crash trying to import higher-poly objects.

CopperCube has custom shader support. You access this functionality through JavaScript because at the moment there is no extensive shader support in the main GUI. This is not an easy-to-use solution for rookie developers, but it's there.

The audio support in the system is very impressive. All current formats can be imported and used as convincing 3D audio, such as .wav, .mp3, and .ogg-audio files. However, you may also add some classic audio formats from the 1990s, including .mod and Scream Tracker 3 music files. Very nerdy, very chic.

Support: 4/5

The Ambiera forums are busy. There are some free 3D models for you to download as well as a quite few (also free) JavaScripts to add functionality to the system. CopperCube seems to be going places as a viable games development platform.

Overall: 4/5

As a newcomer, you could do a lot worse than CopperCube 5. Basically the only major hurdle to overcome with the program is the same with any 3D engine: you need to have your custom 3D models handy to create a commercial-quality product. With CopperCube you get a great terrain editor and a simple enough interface for most beginners to learn the ropes with. It's perfectly capable of amazing games for mobile systems as well.

Here are the CopperCube minimum system requirements:

- Windows XP, Vista, 7, 8, 8.1, or 10
- Intel Celeron, AMD Sempron or faster CPU
- 1GB RAM
- DirectX 9.0c graphics
- 60MB hard drive space

Starting Point

Study the tutorials provided by Ambiera on the official web site (`www.ambiera.com/coppercube/doc/index.html`).

RPG Maker VX/RPG Maker VX Ace by Kadokawa Games/Enterbrain

`www.rpgmakerweb.com/`

Price (Q1 2017): $37 (VX) / $65 (VX Ace)
RPG Maker VX is for creating 2D role-playing games.
It deploys on Windows.
If you like games like *Zelda*, you'll love the RPG Maker series of software. It provides you with quick means for creating maps, enemies, weapons, and special events. The VX Ace edition is a somewhat more expensive and refined version of the VX system.

Commercial Potential: 3/5

Here is a notable game created with the system:

- *To The Moon* by Freebird Games (2011)

Usability: 5/5

Think of RPG Maker as a database of role-playing assets. It shouldn't take more than a few minutes to get you going and start building your worlds. This database is split into such categories as friends, enemies, items, and events. You enter several attributes for the different categories, associating audiovisual assets with the objects where necessary. As with most role-playing games, the emphasis is on party management. As the "general manager," you must pick the best group of warriors you can find. You must tend to your troop's health as well as to their battle actions on an individual level during combat, equipping them with weapons and gear best suited to their skills.

The software package features an intuitive map editor for all your world creation needs. It is effortless to create good-looking maps in RPG Maker and to make the player navigate between them.

Modern versions of RPG Maker utilize a powerful scripting language, Ruby Game Scripting System (RGSS), which is based on the Ruby language. While not an easy language to master, it is very versatile and, in conjunction with RPG Maker, allows for a lot of control over the proceedings. Anything from graphical effects to overall game mechanics can be adjusted with RGSS.

RPG Maker VX comes with RGSS2. The pricier RPG Maker VX Ace uses a more advanced version of the scripting language called RGSS3. You can create more complicated scripts with this version as it executes code much faster than the previous generation of the language, eliminating most slowdowns experienced with RGSS2.

Audiovisuals: 2/5

The first version of RPG Maker came out in 1992, and it has retained its retro charm admirably. Think Super Nintendo–era output. However, this means the game resolution is very, very low at 640×400 pixels. I could only increase it to 640×480. Hence, I gave it a low rating in this category. If you're into high-resolution graphics, this tool may not be what you're looking for.

The default visual style in RPG Maker is not a great way to go as far as commercial products are concerned. There are a lot of amateur titles that all use the same gaudy look. Luckily, there are a lot of extra scripts for RPG Maker, some of which combined give the software a graphical overhaul. You can, and should, go for that complete overhaul of the menus, map graphics, and character portraits in your RPG Maker games.

The slightly more expensive VX Ace version adds a character generator (see Figure 4-12) into the proceedings, allowing for some customization possibilities right out of the box. With this feature you can (and indeed should) assemble new characters for use with your game. Still, an even better approach would be to draw everything from scratch, if you have the time and the team for it. The Ace version of the software also adds video file support for those cut scenes. Also, an easy shadow system has been implemented in this version of RPG Maker.

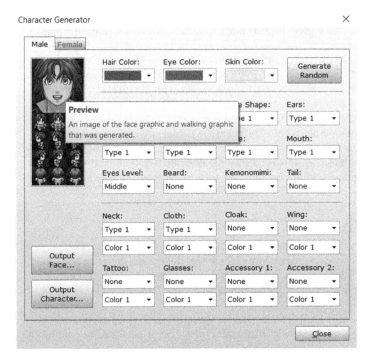

Figure 4-12. *The character generator from RPG Maker VX Ace*

Since all RPG Makers are heavily intertwined with the Ruby Game Scripting System, there is some room to enhance the audiovisuals to your liking. There are dozens of free scripts online for these matters.

Support: 5/5

RPG Maker forums are very busy with hundreds of thousands of posts. This is, after all, a legendary line of software dating all the way back to 1992. You also have several DLCs available on Steam. There are plenty of additional graphics and tunes already. More are probably on their way.

Overall: 3/5

Like its name states, RPG Maker offers quite a narrow experience in game making. It's hardly meant for any other genre than the *Zelda*-ish role players. Luckily, this is a very popular genre of video games, and not just in Japan. However, the online world is flooded with more or less substandard games made with RPG Maker, which has reflected rather poorly on the product, which is the reason for the low rating of 2 in the Commercial Potential category. But what it does it does well. The learning curve for making simple games is lenient enough, and most of the challenge comes from creating fresh audiovisual content, unless you are happy with ready-made assets. Again, you shouldn't work with those as RPG Maker games using stock graphics are considered extremely amateurish in most cases and way, way too common.

The scripting element is really what makes or breaks an RPG Maker game. It unfortunately doesn't share the gentle approach of the rest of the suite. Beginners will have a hard time coding anything useful from scratch. Thankfully, the Internet is absolutely loaded with custom-made RPG Maker scripts. Beginners are advised to download a bunch of scripts and modify the heck out of them to get ahead.

Here are the RPG Maker VX Ace minimum system requirements:

- Windows XP, Vista, 7

- Intel Pentium 4 2.0GHz or faster

- 512MB RAM

- 1024×768 or better video resolution

Starting Point

Start working on the basic tutorials on the RPG Maker site, from top to bottom (`www.rpgmakerweb.com/support/products/tutorials`). Find the tutorials specific to the VX Ace brand of the series.

RPG Maker MV by Kadokawa Games/Enterbrain

`www.rpgmakerweb.com/`

Price (Q1 2017): $75
RPG Maker MV is for creating 2D role-playing games.
There is an editor available for both Windows and macOS.
It deploys on the following systems:

- Windows

- macOS

- Android

- iOS-devices

- HTML5 (browser)

The MV version is the high-end RPG Maker. In addition to export support for multiple platforms, it features improved graphical capabilities and many other updates. At a slightly higher price you get simply a much better development system for your RPG-related projects.

Commercial Potential: 3/5

Here are some notable games created with the system:

- *Corpse Party* by GrisGris (2016)
- *Angels of Death* by Makoto Sanada (2016)
- *The Deed: Dynasty* by Pilgrim Adventures (2016)

Usability: 5/5

Running also on macOS, RPG Maker MV uses the same friendly mechanics as its cheaper counterparts. However, there are some major improvements. For one, it adds an expanded item database. You now get to have 2,000 items, twice the number available in previous versions.

The scripting system also gets a major overhaul. You now get to utilize the very popular JavaScript language for your scripting needs. This provides a high level of compatibility for several new platforms, such as HTML5.

The VX versions did suffer from clunky script management. Now, the MV includes a new feature called the *plug-in manager*, which makes integrating and configuring those JavaScript files a breeze.

They added mouse support for desktops, and with the new support for mobile devices, you also have full touchscreen functionality built in.

Audiovisuals: 4/5

Not only did they upgrade the usability features in the MV version, they also enhanced the graphical capabilities of the software. The screen area is now set to approximately 800×600 pixels, which provides a more modern amount of screen estate in comparison to the VX's 640×400 resolution. In fact, all the visuals were multiplied by 1.5 times, including the sprites. You now have a sharper, less pixelated look available for the first time in an RPG Maker, right out of the box. Installing additional scripts allows for even larger resolutions.

The previous RPG Makers featured only one type of visual battle system, *the front view*, although you could add others using custom scripts. But the MV version has not only the original battle view but a gorgeous *side view* for you to choose from. It's a nice little touch indeed.

And like the RPG Maker VX Ace, there's a built-in character generator, now in higher resolution as per with the overall visual improvement.

Support: 5/5

RPG Maker forums are, again, very busy with hundreds of thousands of posts. The community welcomed the MV version with open arms. It, too, has dozens of free scripts for additional visual effects and functionality. Product updates have ironed out some export-related glitches in the original MV release. Note that because the MV and VX RPG Makers use different languages, their scripts are not interchangeable.

Overall: 4/5

If you enjoy making games in the RPG genre, many would agree this is the superior version of the software with its higher-resolution graphics and additional export options. The previous versions have few benefits over this one, unless you count some older scripts incompatible with MV. However, as the community behind this product is very vibrant, that scenario is becoming less likely.

Here are the RPG Maker MV minimum system requirements:

- Windows 7, 8, 8.1, 10 or Mac OS X 10.10 or newer

- Intel Core 2 Duo

- 2GB RAM

- 1280×768 or better video resolution

Starting Point

Start working on the basic tutorials on the RPG Maker site, from top to bottom (`www.rpgmakerweb.com/support/products/tutorials`). Find the tutorials specific to the MV brand of the series.

Clickteam Fusion 2.5 by Clickteam

`www.clickteam.com/`

Price (Q1 2017): $80
Clickteam Fusion is for creating 2D and rudimentary 3D games.
It deploys on the following:

- Windows

- macOS (paid module)

- iOS (paid module)

- Android (paid module)

- XNA (paid module)

- Flash

- HTML5 (limited free, full support paid module)

Fusion feels like a more hip cousin of the classic GameMaker versions. Such are the similarities in the user interface—and the end results. This is not a criticism. Plenty of successful games have used this tool. It has a solid reputation among platformer-fanatics, but any other genre is an option, too.

Commercial Potential: 5/5

Here are some notable games created with the system:

- *Spryke* by Volnaiskra (2017)

- *Concrete Jungle* by ColePowered Games (2015)

- *Angry Video Game Nerd Adventures* by FreakZone Games (2013)

Usability: 5/5

The user interface in Fusion is quite sleek and accessible, if ever so old-school. And there's no coding to be done—it's all drag and drop with the mouse. The software comes bundled with a massive library of drag-and-drop modules, and a lot of additional ones are out there just waiting to be installed. The free edition of Fusion is perfect for getting started with the system, but as soon as you begin to feel confident with it, you should upgrade to a paid version (see Table 4-3). Creating anything commercially viable with the free edition of Fusion is an unlikely prospect. The limitations in it are simply too overbearing.

Table 4-3. *Fusion License Options*

Product	Notes	Cost (Q1 2017)
Fusion 2.5 Free Edition	Limited HTML5 export only; projects may contain three frames (i.e., rooms) only	Free
Fusion 2.5	Exports only to Windows out of the box	$80
Fusion 2.5 Developer	Contains additional objects and interface enhancements; removes Clickteam logo from your projects	$220
Android support	Exports an .apk package	$70
HTML5 support	Enables full HTML5 exporting for Fusion	$60
Flash support	Supports Flash video (.flv format)	$60
iOS support	Exports an Xcode project	$100
UWP support	Enables exporting to Xbox One, Surface, and other Windows platforms	$180
Firefly 3D	Additional 3D functionality for Fusion 2.5 and Developer	$80

Now, you have an action module in Fusion for all the usual game mechanics: play sound, move object, display image, and, indeed, tons of others. These are then associated with the corresponding objects within your game in the so-called event editor (see Figure 4-13). It's quick, logical, and very friendly to beginners.

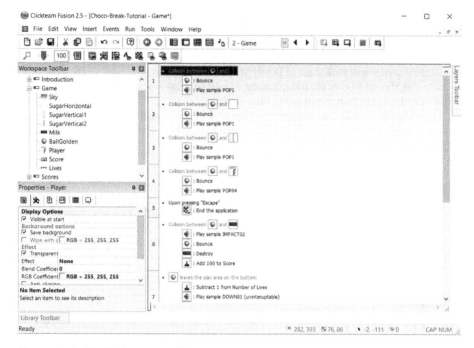

Figure 4-13. The Fusion event editor

Audiovisuals: 4/5

Fusion produces smoothly updating 2D graphics, perhaps even faster than the GameMaker versions do. In addition, it has easy-to-use shader support built in. This comes at the expense of fine-tuned manual control, which is a prominent feature of the shader support in the GameMaker versions. But for beginners, Fusion does win hands-down in the shader department. The building time for projects is also light-years ahead of GameMaker Studio. There's no need to wait for three to five minutes to run a more visually complicated project.

For software that has changed externally so little over the years, Fusion 2.5 is lenient when it comes to choosing resolutions for your games. Unlike the previous generation of GameMaker versions, choosing wide-screen resolutions isn't difficult. There's minimal 3D support, too, for those able to do something with it, but Fusion is clearly a tool for those with a hankering for classic arcade action.

Firefly 3D

Price (Q1 2017): $80

Clickteam released Firefly, a 3D extension for Fusion in late 2016. While a far cry from the 3D quality of, say, Unity, Firefly expands Fusion's capabilities considerably. It's fascinating to see the venerable ChocoBreak tutorial of Fusion get its 3D update.

However, there seems to be quite a few technical issues with Firefly's visuals; ragged object edges and strange shadows pop up from time to time. The lack of AAA shaders give Firefly an aura of visual antiquity. Think 3D from 2007 at the most. Having said that, the visuals on offer are far from unusable. While not suited for cutting-edge FPS projects, more casual genres will look great in Firefly 3D. Also, it's easy to implement FPS-style controls with this add-on or even implement a flight simulator–style control method. Doing that in plain Fusion might cause a few strokes.

Knowing Clickteam's commitment to its products, Firefly will surely be getting the updates it needs and thus have a better future ahead of it. It's a fine product but not quite worth $80 yet. Caveat emptor.

Support: 4/5

A lot of budding developers have found this tool, making the forums a lively experience. Clickteam products have been around since 1993 after all.

A rather impressive asset store, dubbed Clickstore, is online, providing developers with massive amounts of extra graphics, audio, and other resources.

Overall: 4/5

Fusion has a lot going for it. It's neck to neck with GameMaker Studio in features. It even uses the same robust physics system of Box 2D. However, Fusion is severely limited by not having any scripting language support. You are more or less stuck with the drag-and-drop interface. Some developers are fine with that, but others crave the flexibility of, say, GML. Despite this shortcoming, Fusion is an amazing product for beginners, especially those who enjoy making games in the platformer genre.

Here are the Clickteam Fusion 2.5 minimum system requirements:

- Windows XP, Vista, 7, 8

- Intel Pentium 4 2.0 GHz or faster

- 512MB RAM

- 1024×768 or better video resolution

Starting Point

Open Fusion and click Display Tutorial. Select and complete the legendary ChocoBreak tutorial. Work down the list of tutorials at your leisure.

Table 4-3 lists *the* license options.

Game Salad 1.25 (Mac)/Game Salad 1.00 (Windows) by GameSalad Inc.

www.gamesalad.com

This is an editor available for macOS and Windows.
Price (Q1 2017): Starting at $19 per month
Game Salad is for creating any type of games.
It deploys on the following:

- Windows 8

- macOS

- iOS

- Android

- Tizen

Game Salad is 100 percent a programming-free, mouse-driven game engine perfect for 2D games of most kinds. It features a lightning-fast preview mode of your projects and a logical layout for the editor. Game Salad is simply a great piece of software for beginners.

Commercial Potential: 4/5

Here are some notable games created with the system:

- *Stickman Highbar* by Boxed Up Studios (2015)

- *Spooky Hoofs* by Gamesmold (2014)

- *Tiny Goalie* by Fat Fish Games (2014)

Usability: 5/5

Game Salad is a joy to use. You can create simple game mechanics comfortably even without any tutorials. The main program logic is divided into scenes, actors, behaviors, and rules. Scenes are simply the views in a project, whether they represent an intro screen or a particular level/map in a game.

Dragging a sprite onto a scene turns it into an *actor*, which can then accept *behaviors*. These behaviors in Game Salad consist of the usual kinds, such as "move actor around the scene" or "change scene." There are a couple of dozen useful game-related behaviors built in.

Rules in Game Salad context refer to conditional checks, as in "if mouse button is pressed then (activate behavior)." An attractive combination of rules and behaviors make a game (see Figure 4-14). It's all pretty standard and intuitive logic. One is hard-pressed to find faults in the Game Salad interface.

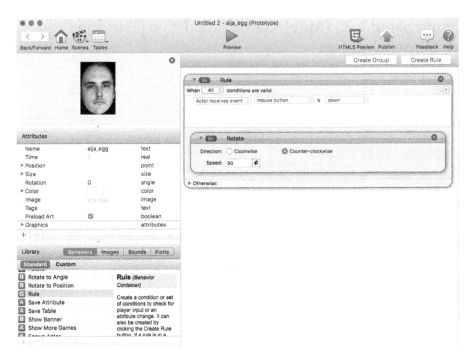

Figure 4-14. *The rule-editing view in Game Salad*

Remember to copy and paste rules when you need several similar events, such as when implementing WASD controls, to speed up the development time.

Audiovisuals: 4/5

Marketed primarily as a mobile phone engine, it's understandable that Game Salad doesn't support any type of 3D game development. You are given the tools to make perfectly commercially viable 2D output with decent particle and physics support built in. Most, if not all, popular image file formats are supported in Game Salad. The engine supports MP3, WAV, M4A, and OGG audio formats, too, of which the Ogg Vorbis seems to be a staple among mobile developers thanks to its excellent size-to-quality ratio.

Game Salad has an acceptable proprietary physics system, which gives the typical attributes of friction, bounciness, and center of mass to its actors. A global gravity setting called Scene Gravity affects all actors. The only flaw with Game Salad physics is the lack of built-in collision shapes because you get only two: rectangle and circle. You can assign custom collision shapes in Game Salad, but this is somewhat tricky for beginners. An external program (such as the Physics Body Editor by Aurelion Ribon) is needed to generate a collision shape data file in JavaScript Object Notation (JSON), which is then imported into Game Salad.

Support: 5/5

Game Salad has been well-received by budding developers. The forums are densely populated. Not only that, the makers of the software have made sure the engine is as beginner-friendly as possible. There are a commendable number of resources online for getting one's bearings with Game Salad and/or getting acquainted with some advanced topics. The tutorials are useful and plentiful. There's even an online "cookbook" chock full of useful tips available for both Mac and Windows versions of the software, in particular when it comes to exporting your projects to the various available platforms.

GS Helper (`http://gshelper.com`) is the official Game Salad marketplace with tons of resources for your purchasing pleasure. The store features audiovisual assets and many game templates to get you started in most genres. There aren't that many free resources in GS Helper, but the item quality in general is very high.

The store also sells custom coding services starting at $40 an hour, apparently provided by the Game Salad team. They claim their clients include not only clueless indies but multinational corporate clients as well.

Overall: 5/5

One of Game Salad's strongest pros is the device emulator; there's no need to hook up your iPhone or other devices to your computer to develop games for Game Salad. This is great news for developers who prefer to test their projects after even the smallest of changes.

The whole Game Salad ecosystem is geared to facilitate quick and painless mobile game development. Not surprisingly, the engine is marketed for educational purposes. The clientele ranges from high schools to higher institutions of learning (`http://edu.gamesalad.com`).

To sum it up, Game Salad is perhaps the best beginner-friendly game engine for iOS and Android. It's both simple and powerful. Let's hope it doesn't go away anytime soon.

Here are some Game Salad minimum system requirements:

- Windows 7, 8, 8.1 or Mac OS X 10.7 (Lion)
- Core 2 Duo CPU
- 2GB RAM

Starting Point

Complete the free tutorial labeled My First Game on the Game Salad Academy (`http://learn.gamesalad.com/`) for Mac or Windows, depending on your system. They are presented in video form and come with all of the audiovisual assets necessary to complete them.

S2 Engine HD 1.4.6 by Profenix Studio SRLS

www.s2powered.com

Price (Q1 2017): $20
S2 Engine HD is for creating 3D games.
It deploys on Windows.
In short, this is one visually stunning system. This is clearly a labor of love for Fabio Di Paola, who is a very able and motivated programmer. Older versions of this software are available to download for free, but we'll take a look at the latest commercial version of the S2 Engine HD.

Commercial Potential: 3/5

Here are some notable games created with the system:

- *Blacksoul* by Xeniosvision (2014)

- *I'm Not Alone* by PixRev (2010)

Current bugs reduce the points in this category.

Usability: 3/5

The main editor program groups your project's resources in a logical fashion as 3D models, audio, fonts, animations, and so on. Terrain creation is quick and painless in S2. You have the usual tools of raising and lowering land, as well as the option to autogenerate a terrain or import one created externally. Since the technical aspects of the software are so advanced, it's possible to create some breathtaking scenery within minutes. The time of day of your virtual world can be adjusted to the minute, affecting the artificial sun in a very believable way.

The testing of your levels from the player's perspective is a simple affair of clicking Start in the Game menu. You then get the usual WASD controls to run around in the scenery with.

Presentation is obviously high on the list of priorities with the S2 system. Like the Leadwerks engine, S2 utilizes a visual flowchart system for game logic, called GameEngine, which is interwoven with a handy GUI editor. This makes creating game menus a breeze. However, beginners may be confused with the flowcharts in S2 as they present themselves in a relatively complex array of boxes and connections.

Every aspect of the impressive visuals in S2 is controlled mostly with the graphical user interface, enabling quick adjustments. Shaders can be switched on and off from a simple menu. Also included is a cut-scene editor that feels like a video editing suite à la Premiere Pro: a definite bonus. S2 even allows for some modification of your project's 3D models geometry, so if you feel like fine-adjusting a model, there's no need to fire up an external 3D editor program.

Scripting in S2, when needed, is based on the C programming language. This is not an easy language to master, and beginners are better off using the visual GameEngine tool to coordinate events in their games (such as "if player pulls lever, open door").

Audiovisuals: 5/5

S2 Engine HD features some of the best visual capabilities of any engine in this book. The engine is absolutely packed with some of the most modern visual technologies available. According to the creator, the software deploys on Windows only in order to reach the very best potential of a single system, instead of compromising the visual output, which is the case for many multiplatform engines. When it comes to visual finesse, this approach pays off. The attention to visual detail is remarkable. Shadows are cast beautifully by every object without much (if any) flickering or strange behavior. Also, you can scale your 3D models to massive sizes and they still manage to look presentable in the engine. You can import objects in many common 3D model formats.

The physics in S2 are provided by none other than Nvidia's venerable PhysX system, providing robust, realistic portrayal of the way real-world laws of physics simulate. The engine has extensive physics options for all of your models—that's another impressive and easily adjustable set of features in the S2.

Also, the water shader is perhaps the most convincing one out there. You may think this is a somewhat trivial matter, but any open world game suffers greatly if some of the largest masses in it look mediocre. That is not the case with S2. One could gaze for hours at the formidable foam and wonderful waves of water in this engine. Remember, if utilized in the slightest, water is just as important as terrain.

Impressive as the vast oceans in S2 are, the fun with digital liquid doesn't stop there. Unlike some lesser engines, you have multileveled, dynamic water. This means realistic waterfalls, rivers, and ponds are an option in S2; even the foaming is calculated to look as realistic as possible under all scenarios.

The vegetation in S2 reacts beautifully to the wind settings in the program with the grass and trees flailing in a faux storm quite convincingly. Thunder and rain, too, have numerous settings both making for a fine, atmospheric experience when need be. The raindrops even bounce off surfaces and mix with larger bodies of water in a convincing manner. Sadly, there's no snow.

Now, on to the problems of the S2 engine. There have been numerous reports of the software crashing periodically on even some newer video cards. Also, the frame rate may stoop as low as less than 30 fps on some hardware, even on a decent CPU. Your mileage will vary. The engine runs currently on an OpenGL platform, but there are plans to provide a DirectX implementation, which will probably reduce the number of these issues. Your best bet is to go with a video card with decent OpenGL support. It's a close shave, but in general Nvidia delivers better on this front. Also, while their CPUs are great, do stay away from Intel's graphics chips. Even the developer-stated minimum requirements on Steam for the software warn against those.

Oddly, S2 supports only `.wav` audio files, which is not great for music or voice acting in games distributed online as the file sizes are just too big for comfortable downloading.

Support: 4/5

There's plenty of documentation and support available online for this engine. The S2 forums are active, and replies to questions in the separate Q&A section are provided promptly. The engine has a small but loyal customer base.

There are a few DLCs available for the engine since early 2017, such as the Medieval Town Pack and an Easy Game Pack. While the first one is self-explanatory, the Easy Game Pack contains numerous resources in many categories. These include additional items such as a couple of new weapons (the iconic M4 rifle), implementing a third-person perspective, and the ability to drive vehicles. If you invest in the S2 engine, you should get the Easy Game Pack as well, as it really enhances the experience. There's talk of even more DLCs for the S2, so the fun won't stop here.

Overall: 4/5

The S2 engine has a moderately steep learning curve for the beginner. It's easy to create beautiful outdoor maps with it, but it's harder to come up with a commercially viable title as you then have to dig much deeper into the underlying mechanics, such as the flowchart editor. Do persist with the tutorials as the end results are worth it. Once you master the GameEngine flowchart technique, you can practically create any kind of 3D game with the system.

Also, the system still has some bugs to be ironed out, as well as some frame rate issues. The hardware support in the program is not quite there yet; the performance and stability of this engine may or may not be adequate on your PC (granted, some of these issues have to do with video card manufacturers and their driver support). However, if Di Paola continues his impressive work into the future, it's quite likely his product will be among the gold standard of game development suites, standing proudly with the likes of Unity within a couple of years. Features such as outstanding visuals, a built-in cut-scene editor, and a mostly mouse-driven workflow make the S2 an appealing software package. Therefore, this engine is highly recommended with only some minor reservations.

Here are the S2 Engine HD minimum system requirements:

- Windows 7, 8, 10

- 4GB of RAM

- Dual-core CPU

- Nvidia Geforce 640 GTX, Radeon HD 5850, or IntelHD 4000 video card/chipset

- 2GB of hard disk space

Starting Point

Start watching and working on the introductory S2 Engine tutorials on the official web site (www.s2powered.com/copiasito/?page_id=2487).

Tyranobuilder Visual Novel Studio by STRIKEWORKS

www.tyranobuilder.com

Price (Q1 2017): $15
Tyranobuilder Visual Novel Studio is for creating visual novels.
It deploys on the following:

- Windows

- macOS

- Linux

- Android

- HTML5 (browser)

The visual novel is a genre of video games no longer popular only in Japan. Thanks to the proliferation of anime culture on a global scale, the visual novel is here to stay—and the tools are more and more numerous. Tyranobuilder is one of the more accessible ones with very few flaws.

Commercial Potential: 4/5

Here are some notable games created with the system:

- *Panzermadels: Tank Dating Simulator* by DEVGRU-B (2016)

- *True Lover's Knot* by Sapphire Dragon Productions (2015)

Usability: 4/5

Tyranobuilder prides itself on being a fully codeless game engine. Game events are entered using the mouse-driven interface. If you want to dwell deeper into visual novel mechanics, you can access the underlying scripting language, Tyranoscript, directly. This is a JavaScript-based universal programming language, which explains the multiplatform nature of the product.

Audiovisuals: 4/5

The visuals in Tyranobuilder are probably the best in any game engine of the visual novel genre. For one, the system supports video backgrounds in .ogv or .webm format. These can greatly enhance the immersion level of these types of games, especially if shot on a (semi)pro camera rig—or rendered in a professional 3D animation suite.

Tyranobuilder also supports Live2D, which is a very impressive technology for creating pseudo-3D animated characters. You do not need 3D models to create rather convincing 3D characters using Live2D. Instead, these objects are constructed from layers of flat 2D images (of body, eyes, attire, etc.). When combined, they create an animated character full of depth and emotion.

If you're not happy with the Live2D material shipped with Tyranobuilder, a separately sold software suite, Cubism Editor, is needed to create new Live2D characters.

The only visual issue with the engine is the lack of full-screen support. To some, that in itself is a deal-breaker. A smaller issue may be the lack of support for custom fonts. Developers are stuck with four clean and classic fonts for their games.

Because of licensing issues, Tyranobuilder doesn't support `.mp3` audio or `.mp4` video files. Ogg Vorbis, however, is fully supported. Actually, the Ogg file format is all you need. It's perfectly usable in a game-making context thanks to its high fidelity and small file size. Interestingly, the old `.mpa` format is also supported.

Support: 4/5

Some 1,200 threads can be found in the Tyranobuilder Steam Discussions, the product's official support community. A comprehensive FAQ section adorns the official web site, too.

Overall: 4/5

Tyranobuilder is very much a beginner's game engine in the best sense of the term. If visual novels are what interest you, you shouldn't hesitate to get this product off of Steam. The learning curve is gentle, but underneath the hood there's plenty of potential to unleash. Also, the fact that Tyranobuilder exports to such a vast array of devices is one of its major selling points. For a single-genre game engine, you can't do much better.

Here are the Tyranobuilder minimum system requirements:

- Windows XP, Vista, 7, 8
- 1GB of RAM
- Video card with 512MB of memory
- 500MB of hard disk space

Starting Point

Start working on the basic tutorials on the Tyranobuilder site, from The Basics and onward (`http://tyranobuilder.com/1-getting-started/`).

RTS Creator by Infotread, LLC

`www.rtscreator.net`

Price (Q1 2017): $10
RTS Creator is for creating 3D and 2D real-time strategy (RTS) games.
It deploys on Windows.

The real-time strategy genre is a big one. You can trace its roots back to *Dune 2* by Westwood Studios in 1992. Then, in late 1990s, a franchise called *StarCraft* happened, ending up selling more than 15 million copies. Clearly the genre is here to stay. RTS Creator is an ambitious and user-friendly take on building your very own *StarCraft* killers. It features high-quality graphics, but sadly the development seems to have stopped.

Commercial Potential: 1/5

While RTS Creator is still on sale on Steam, the last time the software received an update was in late 2015. That pretty much means the product is a nonviable option. You may, however, learn a few things by experimenting with it, in particular if you are a big friend of the RTS genre. Luckily, there's a free demo version available for download.

Usability: 3/5

Every aspect of your RTS project—from particles to textures to audio—is easily editable with mouse-driven tools in RTS Creator. Scripting is not required. The interface is user-friendly to a great degree and serves users of all skill levels. The default key controls are, however, oddly mapped and largely counterintuitive. You can use this engine without typing a line of code. For those who do want more functionality, there's the option of using Lua for event scripting. Lua, of course, is a solid choice because of its popularity and stability.

RTS Creator is quite prone to crash. If you want to experiment with it, save frequently.

Audiovisuals: 3/5

RTS Creator features fairly modern visual output all around (see Figure 4-15), from supporting high-screen resolutions to providing decent particle effects. One could create a competitive offering with this tool if only it wasn't so broken. The graphics do tend to lag even on decent systems as the armies grow bigger, however, which is why it gets a 3 in this category. There are settings to make the visuals less demanding on lower-spec hardware. You can switch off antialiasing, ambient occlusion, bloom, and shadows at your will.

Figure 4-15. *Despite its shortcomings, the visual rendering is impressive in RTS Creator*

The engine accepts 3D models in several popular formats, mainly Blender (.b3d), Autodesk (.fbx), and 3D Max (.gmf). Despite the numerous bugs in RTS Creator, importing 3D models in these formats works just fine. Therefore, it is, in theory, possible to create a game with any theme with the software. Generic land war strategy games aside, you could set your epics in space (à la Sierra's *Homeworld* series), in medieval times, or in some wacky, cartoony setting.

Support: 1/5

The forums were densely populated, and replies to questions were provided promptly. Notice the past tense. The user documentation for the product is also lacking in many areas. Some informative tutorial videos would be nice, as they are pretty much a requirement for these types of software.

Overall: 1/5

It does what it promises—barely. Last updated in late 2015, RTS Creator has some serious technical limitations in the form of bugs, slow screen update, and poor keyboard controls. Despite this, it's a fine prototype for a specialized game-making tool with a future ahead of it, if the team behind it suddenly pulls together and takes criticism seriously. However, it's becoming less and less likely.

The RTS Engine is a classic case of great unrealized potential. With continued development, the engine would make an easy 4 in this category. As it stands, it cannot be recommended. Even the basic event of exporting a ready-to-play file out of the RTS Creator editor sometimes results in a crash.

Here are the RTS Creator minimum system requirements:

- Windows XP, Vista, 7, 8

- 1GB of RAM

- Video card with 512MB of memory

- 500MB of hard disk space

Starting Point

Watch this two-video tutorial series on YouTube: `https://www.youtube.com/watch?v=Qu9CWetoCi0`. There's hardly any other documentation available.

CHAPTER 5

■ ■ ■

Freeware Game Engines

The quality of free game creation software is surprisingly high. Many engines in this chapter actually represent a hybrid business model, offering a free, fully functional version of the system and also a paid version with additional functionality.

The answer to the following question determines whether a game engine is fit for this chapter:

- Can a developer make commercially viable games with the free version of the software?

If that answer is yes, you could do much worse than downloading said development kit for free and starting work on your first games. Like in the previous chapter, the software is not presented in any particular order, and the following categories are rated on a scale of 1 to 5.

Commercial Potential

- Are there any notable games created with the system?

- Does the system allow export to more than one current platform?

Usability

- Is the engine intuitive to use?

- Is the user interface uncluttered and logical?

Audiovisuals

- Does the engine provide adequate technologies to create modern visual output?

- Do the engine's audio features allow a good degree of flexibility in formats?

Support

- Does the engine have busy forums?

- Do the engine developers respond swiftly to technical and other queries?

© Robert Ciesla 2017
R. Ciesla, *Mostly Codeless Game Development*, DOI 10.1007/978-1-4842-2970-5_5

Overall

- This is the bottom-line grade based on the four previous factors as well as various intangibles.

Unity 5.5 by Unity Technologies

`https://unity3d.com`

This is an editor available for macOS and Windows.
It's for creating any type of games.
It deploys on the following:

- Windows

- macOS

- Linux

- iOS

- Android

- Tizen

- Browser (via the Unity Web Player plug-in or HTML5)

- VR

- PS4 and Ps Vita

- Xbox One

- Nintendo Wii U, 3DS, and Switch

First appearing for Mac OS X in 2005, Unity is perhaps the most popular suite of tools for creating any type of modern game. It comes with a massive track record of successful games. There are four tiers of Unity, one of which is free to download and use. For this reason, this is the first noncommercial engine in this book.

Commercial Potential: 5/5

Here are some notable games created with the system:

- *Super Mario Run* by Nintendo (2016)

- *Kerbal Space Program* by Squad (2015)

- *Slender: The Arrival* by Blue Isle Studios (2013)

Usability: 4/5

The Unity editor has a logical, well-organized user interface split between four main windows. Hierarchy shows all the logical objects (called *GameObjects* in Unity) in the project, Scene is where you assemble and view the project at hand, Inspector allows you to set the properties for any selected objects, and Project is there to display all the files (i.e., scripts, images, audio) in your game. It's pretty standard fare.

When starting a new project, Unity asks whether you'd like to work in 2D or 3D. This choice sets the program settings appropriate for the respective approach.

For 3D projects, terrain and vegetation creation in the engine are relatively simple processes. You have the usual terrain-shaping tools as well as a tree generator in the editor. There are, however, many tools in the well-received Unity Asset Store that facilitate even easier terrain creation. Some worth mentioning are World Creator and Gaia.

Unity scripting works both in C# and in JavaScript. Thanks to the way Unity is built, you may not have to type large amounts of elaborate code to create a game. Depending on the project, a few lines of code here and there may be all that is needed. Also, Unity comes shipped with a fine programming IDE called MonoDevelop.

There are some beginner-friendly aspects to coding in Unity. Memory management, a rather tedious aspect of programming, is automated in the engine. This will only upset expert programmers who crave that extra amount of control over the proceedings.

Compared to competing products such as GameMaker Studio, Unity isn't really a framework for rapid games development for those just starting out. If Unity Technologies figures out a way to pander to the low-attention-span crowd with an even more simplified UI, the engine will score full marks in the usability department. As it stands, the system works.

Audiovisuals: 5/5

Unity is perfectly capable of creating commercially viable visuals. It wouldn't have gained the support it has otherwise. Virtually every modern graphics technology is available in the engine, and the quality and scope of post-processing effects are quite striking. This wasn't always the case, as the first few versions of Unity were considered lacking in visual immersion among developers.

One of the most impressive features of Unity, the *post-processing stack,* is a collection of easily implementable shaders for that trendy film-like look. Available from the Asset Store, the stack is provided free of charge and consists of more than a dozen effects. The stack includes bloom, motion blur, depth of field, and two types of antialiasing, among others. There really aren't many flaws in Unity's post-processing capabilities in terms of quality. The effects are optimized to work together in any configuration, and the graphics rendering doesn't suffer from any particular combination. Using them in your projects is very easy; you simply check boxes to enable these effects in the Unity editor, whether working in 2D or 3D. For those with experience in writing shader code, Unity leverages a shader language known as Cg, which is quite similar to Microsoft's HLSL.

There are two isolated physics systems in Unity, one for 2D and the other for 3D. On offer are Nvidia's PhysX for 3D projects, and Box2D, which is also found in engines such as Gamemaker Studio. Physics support in the engine is available as drag-and-drop components within a scene.

For rendering, Unity uses OpenGL on Mac and Linux, while defaulting to DirectX on Windows. This setting, however, can be changed to either in Windows. The engine also supports a wide range of audio formats, including some rather obscure and geeky ones, such as Scream Tracker 3 and Impulse Tracker for the ultimate in chiptune goodness. Best of all, Unity comes with some wonderful real-time audio-mixing capabilities out of the box. A dedicated sound mixer component is there to allow for in-project audio processing, reducing the need to switch between Unity and an external sound editor. Also, the 3D positional audio is both convincing to the ears and easily implementable.

Support: 5/5

Because of its popularity and proven track record, Unity has an extremely vibrant community behind it. The Unity Asset Store is full of 3D models and other resources. The engine forums are very populated, and the available additional resources grow pretty much on a daily basis. When it comes to game engines, it just doesn't get any better support-wise. There's a clear road map for Unity on the web site, and the future seems bright.

Overall: 5/5

While primarily known as a small-time indie developer's engine of choice, Unity has outgrown its somewhat humble reputation when it comes to visuals. Unity Technologies has kept adding hot new shaders into the engine and will no doubt be doing so in the future. The community behind the product is massive and doesn't show any signs of stagnation. There has been somewhat of a tidal wave of less than fantastic games made with Unity, but that's hardly the game engine's fault. The developers of those titles simply needed to put in more work with the engine.

Unity is a robust, still developing system that deploys for many platforms with ease. There have been dozens of very successful games on several platforms over the last 12 years made with Unity. That says it all really.

Here are the Unity minimum system requirements:

- Windows 7 Service Pack 1, 8, 10/Mac OS X 10.8 or newer
- Video card with DirectX 9 or DirectX 11

A Beginner and His Unity Experience: Developer Interview

So, what is the Unity experience like for the complete beginner? Let's ask Jim Baker, a game maker and host of the increasingly popular JimPlaysGames channel on YouTube. Mr. Baker is behind such quirky and innovative titles as *Conker the Universe* and *The Day Earth Got Mooned*. Check them out at jimmakesgames.com.

Jim: If you're looking to get into coding and game development as more than a hobby, Unity is a good way to go. It has a graphical interface that allows you to get things happening on-screen with only a few lines of code. There are tons of tutorials by the Unity developers and third parties that make it easy to get started too.

The programming languages Unity uses aren't the worst either. C# and JavaScript don't have the complexities and pitfalls of languages that are more powerful but harder to use like C++. However, there might be better ways to get a start in learning game development, like RPG Maker or GameMaker.

Couldn't agree more, Jim. Unity does have a learning curve, doesn't it?

Jim: Resist the temptation to jump in. Take the time to research and design. Look at other games in the same genre and analyze their design, UI, and aesthetics. There's nothing wrong with trying to take an existing game type and building on it. It doesn't have to be the most original thing ever, as long as it's well made and engaging to play.

Make a simplified version of your game's core mechanics and try it out, without any of the fancy stuff that you're planning for later. Make sure the core concept of your game loop is engaging before taking on the development fully. Depending on the game type, you can even make a pen-and-paper version or use miniatures, if you're making a turn-based tactical game, for instance.

Finally, don't worry if you struggle and feel like you're spending a lot of time staring at your code in complete puzzlement as to why it isn't working. That's all part of the process. Take advantage of the community of coders and designers on the Unity forums and Stack Exchange. Oh, and I almost forgot. Don't forget to comment your code. You'll thank yourself for it later.

So, how would you sum up your advice to games makers starting out in Unity?

Jim: My advice to someone who wants to get started with Unity is at first to watch all the tutorials on the Unity site and follow along with them. Look around for other tutorials relevant to your interests too. It'll be tempting to just jump in and start making something, but you'll likely get frustrated if you try to do too much too quickly.

Your first project should be just a learning experience. Make something simple, like *Breakout* or *Space Invaders.* I've had a problem myself with biting off more than I can chew and then getting discouraged because I don't yet have the skills to make it as well as I could have if I'd learned the fundamentals first.

Starting Point

Take a look at the excellent selection of tutorials on the official Unity web site (`https://unity3d.com/learn/tutorials`). There are countless more by third parties on YouTube and other sites.

Unity Tips

Here are some tips for using Unity:

- Use subfolders in your hierarchy view. Group objects by role. For example, make a subfolder for bonus items, another one for enemies, etc. Clutter is a big issue among Unity developers.

- Click an object and press F to center on it in the scene view.

- Unity can automatically build a texture atlas for your sprites to optimize 2D performance. The Sprite Packer utility can be enabled by selecting Edit ➤ Project Settings ➤ Editor.

- In Unity parlance, a *prefab* is simply a class (see Chapter 3 for more about object-oriented programming).

- WASD controls are easily added in 2D projects. Just attach a script to the object you want to control and add this function in it:

```
void FixedUpdate() {
float moveHorizontal = Input.GetAxis ("Horizontal");
float moveVertical = Input.GetAxis ("Vertical");
Vector2 movement = new Vector2 (moveHorizontal, moveVertical); }
```

Unity License Options

Unity offers several types of licenses for developers at different points in their careers (see Table 5-1). Since 2015, Unity also offers a free Personal edition. This is obviously the best way to get acquainted with the engine as there is no financial risk involved. Nothing is stopping you from developing the next big indie hit with this edition, unless you count the splash screen displayed for a few seconds at the beginning of your projects. Also, multiplayer games are limited to a maximum of 20 participants. You may still earn up to a rather generous $100,000 under this license. Unity doesn't charge royalties at any license level.

Table 5-1. *A Rundown on Unity License Options*

Product	Notes	Revenue Capacity	Cost (Q1 2017)
Personal	"Made with Unity" splash screen, 20-user multiplayer	$100,000	Free
Plus	No splash screen, 50-user multiplayer, 20 percent off asset kits	$200,000	$35 per seat per month ($420 per year)
Pro	200-user multiplayer, 40 percent off asset kits	Unlimited	$125 per seat per month ($1,500 per year)
Enterprise	Custom multiplayer, 40 percent off asset kits	Unlimited	Contact Unity Technologies for details

For the more established developers, Unity offers the Plus, Pro, and Enterprise editions. Going up the tiers gradually reduces the limitations on multiplayer and revenue capacity. The costlier licenses use *seats* to calculate the price. A seat is simply a member of a development team that uses the software. So, if your team has five programmers and you want a Unity Plus license, the cost would be $175 per month (5 × 35) or $2,100 per year.

An *asset kit* is a large compilation of resources for specific genres of games when working in Unity. Each kit contains scripts and/or various audiovisual assets for different types of projects. Think of them as booster packs to accelerate your Unity development.

There are asset kits for racing games, first-person shooter (FPS) games, and dungeon crawlers, to name just three. They are priced between roughly $100 to $300 each. Unity Plus, Pro, and Enterprise licenses cover asset kit discounts at either 20 percent or 40 percent.

Construct Classic/Construct 2 by Scirra

www.scirra.com/

Construct is for creating 2D games.
It deploys on the following:

- HTML5 (Construct 2 only)

- iOS and Android (Construct 2 Personal and Business licenses only)

- Windows, macOS, and Linux desktop (using node-webkit)

- Native Windows (Construct Classic only)

Scirra's offerings are beginner-friendly, 100 percent drag-and-drop, game development tools. Construct Classic is a free, unlimited development kit (for Windows export only), while Construct 2 offers three tiers of licenses, one of which is a somewhat compromised free version. In Construct 2, in particular, the feature set is extremely impressive, from the sheer number of templates to the shader support.

Commercial Potential: 4/5

Here are some notable games created with the system:

- *Super Ubie Island Remix* by Notion Games (2016)

- *Cosmochoria* by Nate Schmold (2015)

- *Airscape: The Fall of Gravity* by Cross-Product (2014)

Usability: 4/5

Construct Classic and Construct 2 share most of their usability features. The most obvious initial difference is the lack of built-in game templates and other material in Construct Classic. Also, their project files are not compatible as Construct 2 was rewritten from the ground up. Classic supports manually coded scripting in the Python language, while Construct 2 is a drag-and-drop interface only.

While it's possible to export to desktop platforms with Construct 2, this is only achieved through a node-webkit system. This refers to an HTML5 project wrapped in a Google Chrome browser. The visual output of these types of exports is likely to be slower than native desktop applications. Construct Classic exports straight to Windows in DirectX, giving excellent visual performance.

Since 2012 Construct Classic has not been officially developed by Scirra, but an active team of volunteer developers still work on it and release occasional updates.

Download the latest version of Construct Classic from `https://sourceforge.net/projects/construct/`.

The free version of Construct 2 is not time-limited or lacking any sets of tools. However, it has some very specific limitations in the form of being able to export only smaller projects. You can have a maximum of 100 events, 4 layers per layout, and 2 effects (shaders) per project exported from the free version. Also, there's the barely noticeable three-second waiting period when you close the program. These limitations still allow a developer to come up with some virally friendly and thus simplistic browser games, in the mold of the venerable *Flappy Birds* and the like.

To make full use of the software, you really need to purchase the Personal license from Scirra for about $99. This enables iOS and Android export as well as the creation of multiplayer games among other additional features. If you get comfortable with Construct 2, you should invest in this type of license at some point as it's well worth it.

As an indie starting out, there's very little benefit from the much more expensive Business license at $330. This version of Construct 2 features exactly the same feature package as the Personal license, except the $5,000 revenue limit is removed.

Audiovisuals: 4/5

The visual output of Construct 2 is highly competitive. Virtually any type of modern 2D graphics technique is implementable with the system. Construct 2 includes some 70 shader effects, ranging from classics such as grayscale and sepia tone to more exotic types.

The Classic version of Construct features support for HLSL language scripts, meaning one can import shaders into the program. This is not possible in Construct 2. Advanced programmers may enjoy this feature.

Support: 5/5

The communities for both software versions are vibrant. As stated, even the "obsolete" Construct Classic has a huge fan base with more than 80,000 posts about it on the official Scirra forums. The fact that a team of volunteer developers are still updating the software speaks volumes about its quality.

Of course, the current version of the software, Construct 2, commands even more attention from its users and developers. This is an immensely popular product with more than 600,000 posts in the forum.

The Scirra Store holds approximately 60,000 additional assets for Construct 2, ranging from extra audiovisual resources to complicated software extensions. With this store, you can both expand your Construct 2 experience and cut down on the development time.

Overall: 4/5

You literally can't write code with Construct 2. It takes that much pride in its drag-and-drop approach. This is, naturally, great news for the junior developers out there. The incredible number of extensions available for the software further facilitates quick and painless game-making.

The output from Construct 2 is only hampered by the HTML5 approach. Although great for browsers and platforms like Facebook, this is not a flawless format of delivery. Since most forms of export require wrapping your project in a browser, including desktops, you will fail to reach optimal the frame rates the hardware is capable of. If Scirra fixed the performance approach with true native deployment, the software would reach a perfect 5 in this category. This doesn't mean your projects can't be visually ambitious, but you need to optimize them carefully. Most importantly, keep the number of on-screen objects as low as possible in Construct 2.

It is a worthwhile idea to start your Scirra journey with Construct Classic as it is unrestricted in every way. For Windows desktop development, it is actually a much more robust system than the newest iteration of the software. The few remaining bugs are being neutralized by the team of volunteers one by one, meaning Construct Classic will stick around for many years to come. Having said that, Construct 2 contains such a huge amount of game templates, even the free version is quite likely to jump-start your indie development career.

Starting Point

Complete the official *Beginners Guide to Construct 2* (`https://www.scirra.com/tutorials/37/beginners-guide-to-construct-2`). This will result in a simple shoot-'em-up game and teach you most of the essential elements of Construct 2 development.

Here are the Construct Classic/Construct 2 minimum system requirements:

- Windows XP SP 3

- 1GHz or faster CPU

- 512MB RAM

- 500MB of free hard drive space

Ren'Py 6.99.12.3 by Tom Rothamel and His Team

`www.renpy.org/`

This is an editor available for macOS, Windows, and Linux.
It is for creating visual novel games.
It deploys on the following:

- Windows

- macOS

- Linux

- Android

- iOS

One for the more code-savvy or wanting to learn the ropes, Ren'Py is a popular choice for visual novel enthusiasts. In development since 2004, Ren'Py has inspired game makers to create more than 1,000 games. Some of these titles are even sold on major digital distribution platforms like Steam.

Commercial Potential: 4/5

Here are some notable games created with the system:

- *Max's Big Bust: A Captain Nekorai Tale* by Lached Up Games (2017)

- *Sound of Drop: Fall into Poison* by Sekai Project (2015)

- *Heileen 3: New Horizons* by Winter Wolves (2012)

Usability: 4/5

Ren'Py is all about programming. There's no dragging and dropping here. However, don't let that trouble you. There are only a handful of commands needed to create basic visual novel core mechanics. The engine is outwardly rustic but very powerful underneath the lack of UI gloss.

The first thing you see running Ren'Py is the launcher. The engine works in tandem with any text editor capable of creating plain text. You are provided with the option of downloading Editra, a rather fine text editor on its own merit, in the launcher program.

Deployment to all of the available desktop platforms is painless. Simply clicking Build Distributions on the launcher menu gives you the options needed to build for Windows, Mac, and Linux in both 32-bit and 64-bit versions. Exporting to iOS requires the installation of the Renios software, a free download available from in the launcher and on the main Ren'Py web site. For Android, you need the RAPT software, which is also free and readily available.

The Ren'Py launcher also provides an error-checking function for your script and the option to extract dialogue from your game into an external text file. Very handy!

Audiovisuals: 4/5

One of the benefits of working in the visual novel genre is the low hardware requirements for both developing and playing the games. Ren'Py is no exception. To a degree, this guarantees some extra global market penetration.

The engine supports a wide variety of formats for images, video files, audio, and fonts. Virtually any high-resolution 2D image files will work with the engine. Videos can be looped in your games to create impressive animated backgrounds. Supported video formats include Ogg Theora, several MPEG types, and Google's new VP8 and VP9 formats. Google's formats are lossless and work great for even higher resolutions than Full HD, too. While the support for these video formats is impressive on paper, getting a video to actually play in Ren'Py in the past has been a hard task. Apparently, the software is still somewhat picky when it comes to video files. Your mileage may vary. Read the Ren'Py documentation carefully and encode your files accordingly.

The engine also supports quite a few audio formats, including Ogg Vorbis, WAV, MP3, and even MP2, which is best known from almost all European DVD releases of popular movies. You shouldn't use the MP formats in your commercial games, as they are patented technology. However, Ogg Vorbis is probably all you need for both sound effects and soundtracks.

Support: 4/5

Updates for Ren'Py are frequent and useful, and the engine is not going to disappear anytime soon. The Ren'Py community is absolutely crowded with enthusiastic users of the engine as is evident on the Lemma Soft forums (`http://lemmasoft.renai.us/forums/`). Since 2003 they have catered for the visual novel genre in general, but a sizable part of the forums is dedicated to Ren'Py. Some 100,000 messages have been posted about the software. Much of the genre knowledge is not engine dependent anyway.

Overall: 4/5

The coding aspect is actually one of Ren'Py strengths. After you conquer the gentle learning curve, you will have grasped some universal aspects of programming in general.

Ren'Py has proven to be a commercially viable choice for visual novels. It gives developers lots of control over their projects and has virtually no limitations when it comes to working in the genre. It is obviously not an all-purpose tool, but as a single-genre engine it's probably the best one out there. You cannot beat this price-to-performance ratio.

Here are the Ren'Py minimum system requirements:

- Windows XP SP 3

- Mac OS X 10.6 (Snow Leopard)

- Linux (32- or 64-bit)

Starting Point

Create a new project in the Ren'Py launcher (see Figure 5-1). Open the main script file with Edit File ➤ Script.rpy. Using the mechanics presented in this section, create a set of characters, dialogue, and working menus that point to labels by following the tutorial. Use the Open Directory command in the launcher to open the images folder. Download or create some graphical content and place it in that folder.

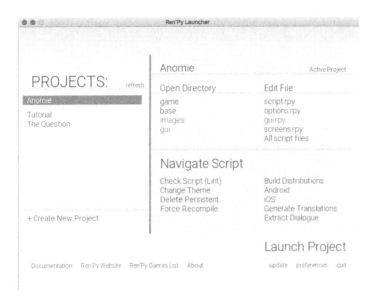

Figure 5-1. *The mighty Ren'Py launcher*

A typical Ren'Py project consists simply of working on a single main script file (called `script.rpy`) and its related preference files and audiovisual resources. The nongraphical interface might scare a few people off, but it actually provides the maximum amount of control for your projects as soon as you grasp the basics. I'll now go through these basics.

Click Projects ➤ Create a New Project. You are then given the option to choose between New GUI Interface and Legacy Theme Interface. The latter is only ever useful for specific aesthetic reasons when deploying to desktop platforms. In general, it's better to pick New GUI Interface as it works best for mobile systems. Next, give your project a name and select the game interface color theme. You now have a new Ren'Py project with all the right folders and files.

The next section is intended for your reading pleasure only. You don't have to integrate any of the following code to your project. It's there only to decipher some of Ren'Py's inner workings. See the "Starting Point" section for actual tutorials you should be working on with the engine.

Now, the graphics files are generally stored in a subfolder of your main project folder, usually named `images`. Just open this folder via the launcher by clicking Open Directory ➤ Images. In our example, you would create a file called `dungeon.jpg` in your favorite visual editor (or download and rename some image file) and drag it into the `images` folder.

A word of warning is in order to all Ren'Py developers. The language is indentation-sensitive, meaning you can't have any arbitrary number of spaces before each line of code. Notice in the example the first line (`init:`) is on a different level of indentation compared to the following three lines. It has to be this way; otherwise, the project will refuse to run. These levels of indentation are known as *blocks* in Ren'Py and Python language parlance. So, work that Tab key in an orderly fashion with these fine, if slightly finicky, programming languages.

The following are the contents of a simple Ren'Py script, called `script.rpy`, which isn't much of a game, but it'll demonstrate the engine basics well enough. Let's take a look at a basic Ren'Py project file and then go into more detail, shall we?

```
init:
        image backdrop dungeon1 = "dungeon.jpg"
        image backdrop dungeon2 = "darkerdungeon.jpg"
        define man = Character("Man", color="#0000ff")
        define potatoperson = Character("Potato", color="#00ff00")
```

This is the initialization portion of a Ren'Py script. Here you define things such as which audiovisual files are used, what the different game characters are called, and what color their dialogue text is.

Now, let's dissect the second line. You shouldn't address image files directly. Instead, you use intermediary handles (i.e., variables) to do this. So, the second line in the script assigns an image file called `dungeon.jpg` to an image variable I decided to call `backdrop dungeon1`. The first part of the variable, `backdrop`, is a base name for the image. The second part, `dungeon1`, is an additional tag for the image. Images sharing the base name (in this case `backdrop`) can be easily swapped with one another, as replacing one will position the new image in the same place and capacity as the old one. More on this later.

Next, the following lines create two characters for the project, called Man and Potato, the latter whom is some kind of sentient perennial plant. Again, you are assigning specific handles for these characters so that you don't need to specify the attributes over and over. You do this with the `define` command. The displayed name and the color of text for both characters are stored in the variables `man` and `potatoperson` in the syntax provided by this example.

As with web sites and many other applications, colors for the character dialogue in Ren'Py are designated using the RGB method. This refers to *red, green,* and *blue* presented in hexadecimal (base 16) notation. The first two digits after the hashtag define the amount of red in the color. The following controls the amount of green, and—you guessed it—the last two digits indicate how much blue is in the color. Mixing these three primary colors is what makes all the colors of the rainbow possible in the digital realm. In this example, the character `man` is represented by an electric blue color, while `potatoperson` will receive a rather lovely toxic green as their color of choice.

There are very few limits as to how many characters and audiovisual assets you can use per project in Ren'Py, but don't overdo anything to avoid player confusion. Now, let's move on to an actual scene. You'll notice some lines beginning with a hashtag in the next segment.

```
# This is a code comment. Yes, hashtags turn lines into comments in Ren'Py.
# These are not expected to do anything, except store reminders for the
coder!
# You can insert these in your script file at your leisure.

label start:

        # First, we show a background.

        scene background dungeon1
```

```
# These three lines display lines of dialogue.

"Once upon a time.."
man "Dear Potatoperson. What is your favorite movie?"
potatoperson "That would be Zardoz starring Sean Connery"
```

The label command represents just what you might think: it's a label meant for navigating the storyline and script. Here I have named the label start. By labeling segments of the script, you allow the player to reach that precise point at a later time by making specific choices.

Now let's take a look at another core Ren'Py concept: the menu. A menu is where a player interacts with the game universe. All menus are designated by the command "menu:", as is the case with this example. An integral part of the menu mechanic is the command called jump. It is simply used to take the player to a different, labeled part of the script. In the case of the example menu, the player may choose to jump to the agree or disagree labels with their corresponding text prompts.

```
menu:
        "Agree with Potatoperson.":
                jump agree
        "Strongly disagree with Potatoperson.":
                jump disagree

label agree:
        "It is a wonderful piece of cinema!"
        return

# If we disagree with Potatoperson, we get to witness a new
# background graphic fade in

label disagree:
        scene background dungeon2
        with fade

        "I find Zardoz un-watchable."

        return
```

Remember the image tags? In the previous lines, one is being put to good use. The image designated as background gets replaced with the image with the same base designation, but a different image tag. So, the image file pointed to in the dungeon2 variable (i.e., darkerdungeon.jpg) will now become the background graphic in this example. Not only that, it's done via a fancy fade to black, thanks to the with fade command. For a film-like dissolve between two graphics, you would replace that line with with dissolve.

Finally, you have the `return` statement. This simply returns the player to the main menu, where they may either play the magnum opus again or quit the program. And with this you reach the end of the little demonstration of the Ren'Py basic mechanics.

Make sure to visit the Ren'Py cookbook and start experimenting with the various techniques presented there (`www.renpy.org/wiki/renpy/doc/cookbook/Cookbook`).

Gamelooper by Oyun Döngüsü Ltd

`www.gamelooper.com`

This is an editor available for macOS and Windows.
It is for creating simple mobile 2D games.
It deploys on the following:

- iOS

- Android

Definitely an engine suitable for absolute beginners, Gamelooper has its limitations but also some serious strengths. One of these is the 100 percent drag-and-drop approach, which works very well.

Commercial Potential: 3/5

There are no notable games created with the system. The potential for making hits with this engine is modest, but it's there.

Usability: 3/5

The main editor view in Gamelooper is logical enough, with different categories for screens and objects, audiovisual resources, and variables. The engine offers a choice between Basic and Pro interfaces (see Figure 5-2), with the professional mode adding extensive controls for analytics and in-app purchases, among other things. Splitting the interface this way is a good approach to keep beginners less confused.

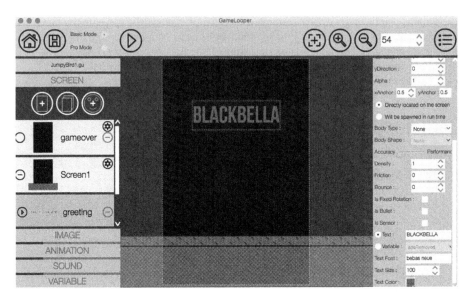

Figure 5-2. *Gamelooper in Basic Mode*

Because the deployment will be for mobile devices only, the supported player controls are based on touchscreens only. You won't be integrating any key presses or mouse action into your Gamelooper projects, ruling out accurate desktop-based testing of your games. There is a rather clumsy and incomplete simulator method available for the engine, but it doesn't really do the trick. Make sure you've invested in an iOS or Android device before downloading a copy of Gamelooper.

When it comes to keeping your workflow simple, this engine is among the best out there. Parts of the user interface, however, are unintuitive. Why are there two red icons side by side in confirmation dialogs? Get it right, developer people. Go with the traffic light logic.

Some of the best features of Gamelooper are the publishing options. You can either publish with the development team's help or do it by yourself. Now, should you go with team-assisted route, you get a lot of the technicalities of the publishing process taken care of for you. First you need to upload your project to the Showcase section of `Gamelooper.com`. Should the team deem your game commercially viable enough, they will help you get it distributed on the Apple App Store and the Google Play Store. This publishing method won't cost anything. The revenue from games published via this method will be then split between the Gamelooper team and the developer.

The self-publishing route with Gamelooper projects costs $199 per game and requires a whole lot of working with digital certificates and the like. However, you do get to keep all of the revenue. This may be a better publishing method if you're sitting on a sure hit (if one can ever be sure of these things). Luckily, there is an extensive guide on the main site for all of the technical specifications needed for self-publishing.

You do need a cloud storage account from Dropbox for both testing and publishing your projects on Gamelooper. However, these are free and facilitate on-the-go development of your games. Running your projects on your mobile device is pleasantly trivial with Gamelooper. There's no need for those pesky digital testing certificates at that stage.

Audiovisuals: 3/5

Simplicity (or elegance, depending on how you want to look at it) seems to be a crucial tenet in Gamelooper. The engine only supports PNG image files and MP3 audio files. There's no shader support for post-processing or anything of the like. Animations are made from sprite sheets by specifying the number of rows and columns in the file as well as the playing speed in milliseconds. It's all very basic, but it works.

Support: 3/5

There are some fine tutorials built right into the software. Apparently the engine has more than 50,000 users as of early 2016. There is a smallish forum for the product on Facebook (`https://www.facebook.com/groups/gamelooperforum/`), and the developers seem to respond to queries in a timely manner. The followers of Gamelooper on social media are not very numerous. Clearly, it's still a relatively small-scale operation.

Overall: 3/5

A most delightful little piece of software, Gamelooper allows pretty much anyone to create visually modest mobile games within an hour. For one, the engine is perfectly capable for the rather popular infinite runner genre, and it can handle simple shoot-'em-ups just fine. Complexity does not necessarily make a good game. Extra kudos to the team in Turkey for the unique publishing options in Gamelooper. Based on these factors, the system is definitely worthy of downloading as a "my first game engine" for mobile development.

Here are the Gamelooper minimum system requirements:

- Windows 7
- Mac OS X 10.7 (Lion)

Starting Point

Download Gamelooper for your Max OS X or Windows computer from Steam or `http://gamelooper.com/download/`. Run the program and select Go To Tutorials. Start working on the *Bananas* tutorial. To learn the ropes even more thoroughly, complete *Jumpy Bird*, *Bug Shooter*, and *Spin Stick Soccer* at your leisure.

To test these projects on your iOS or Android mobile device, you need the mobile versions of the Gamelooper software, as well as a free Dropbox account.

Stencyl 3.4 by Stencyl, LLC

`www.stencyl.com`

This is an editor available for macOS, Windows, and Linux.
It is for creating 2D games.
The freeware version deploys on Flash.

The paid version deploys on the following:

- Windows

- macOS

- Linux

- iOS

- Android

- HTML5 (browser)

Branded as a beginner-friendly toolkit for making hit mobile games, Stencyl is a fully codeless environment. The engine is free only for Flash development, which is what I'll focus on in this review. Getting access to other available platforms requires the purchase of additional modules. However, the Stencyl development process is the same for all exports.

Commercial Potential: 4/5

Here are some notable games created with the system:

- *Battle Slimes* by DoDreams Fairytale Company (2015)

- *Foxtrot!* by Bull and Gate Ltd (2014)

- *Impossible Pixel* by 99 Up Games (2013)

Usability: 4/5

The Stencyl motto "Design Once, Play Anywhere" says it all. Great care has been taken with this approach, making multiplatform releases the main appeal of this engine.

The projects in Stencyl are divided as Resources and Logic in the editor. Resources contain audiovisual assets, tilesets, and game objects (called *actors*), while Logic stores object and scene behavior and scripts.

The Stencyl editor includes built-in access to StencylForge, which is a modest collection of free, downloadable assets of all types. It's worth using these assets when you're experimenting with the software, but using these resources in your finished games isn't a wonderful idea. Always keep your content as original as you can.

The language of choice here is Haxe, which shares most of its syntax with the Flash scripting language ActionScript. Although the Stencyl GUI runs on top of a Haxe-based framework, you are not required to type a single line of code to complete your projects. If you do end up coding manually in Haxe, rest assured the code will be compatible with all the available export platforms in the engine. The whole programming language was built on the premise of delivering compatible code for all modern platforms, making it ideal for this engine.

Some say Flash is dying. Apple cofounder Steve Jobs hated it, and hence it won't be supported on iOS devices. Granted, Flash has some security and stability issues. However, the format is still very much alive on some rather massive online gaming sites, such as Kongregate among others. The dying process for Flash sure seems to be a drawn-out one.

Audiovisuals: 4/5

The engine is capable of modern 2D visual output with basic shader support available for Windows, macOS, and Linux exports. It's simple enough to implement, say, a grayscale effect, some film grain, or a combination of the two. Desktop platforms also get advanced shaders in the form of GLSL scripting for those willing to work with that language.

Stencyl has fine physics support in the form of Box2D. Each object in the system has a set of controls for mass (in kilograms, no less), friction, and other physics attributes. There's a reason Box2D is popular. However, if your project doesn't need realistic physics (think board games) or you want to keep things running fast as possible, you can opt for simple physics instead.

Audio support in Stencyl is limited to Ogg Vorbis (`.ogg`) on all platforms, apart from Flash, which uses MP3 files exclusively. The engine has handy, live controls for fade-ins and fade-outs for your soundtracks.

Support: 4/5

Stencyl has a reasonably packed Extensions Market with free and low-cost extensions for the engine. These range from additional ad service functionality to extra visual effects.

The software was clearly well-received and has a thriving online forum community. The Stencylpedia is a comprehensive collection of tutorials and sample projects available on the main engine web site (`www.stencyl.com/help`).

Overall: 4/5

If you are looking to develop 2D mobile games in a rush, Stencyl is a fine engine for this purpose. Impressive as the list of export platforms is, the issue with the engine is the simplicity of the output from the drag-and-drop interface. Basic tile-based games (think *Pacman* or *Gauntlet*) are quickly crafted with the system, but you will have to go knee-deep in scripting in Haxe to come up with anything more advanced. However, as a beginner's tool, Stencyl is among the best out there.

Here are the Stencyl minimum system requirements:

- Windows 7

- Mac OS X 10.9 (Mavericks)

- Ubuntu Linux 10.04

- Java version 8 for all systems (free download from `www.java.com`)

Starting Point

Start working on the Stencyl *Crash Courses* from top to bottom (`www.stencyl.com/help/start/`). The downloadable assets needed by the lessons are provided on the site.

In addition, you may benefit from downloading actual completed mini-games and examining how they work (`www.stencyl.com/developers/samples/`).

Godot 2.1 by Juan Linietsky and Ariel Manzur

www.godotengine.org

This is an editor available for macOS, Windows, and Linux.
It is for creating 2D and 3D games.
It deploys on the following:

- Windows
- macOS
- Linux
- iOS
- Android
- Blackberry OS
- HTML5 (browser)

Godot is a lesser known engine with a lot of power and potential. The editor is available for all major desktops and exports to as many as seven platforms. While it relies quite heavily on scripting, it's worth looking into perhaps as your second-ever game engine. It may be the only engine you'll need.

Commercial Potential: 4/5

Here are some notable games created with the system:

- *The Interactive Adventures of Dog Mendonca & Pizzaboy* by Ravenscourt (2016)
- *Steno Arcade* by For All To Play (2016)
- *Egg Returns Home* by PigelPix (2015)

Usability: 4/5

The GUI layout in Godot is intuitive and has very little to fault (see Figure 5-3). I'll next go through the necessary basics of Godot to ease you into the engine. There are four central concepts in the system: scenes, nodes, signals, and singletons.

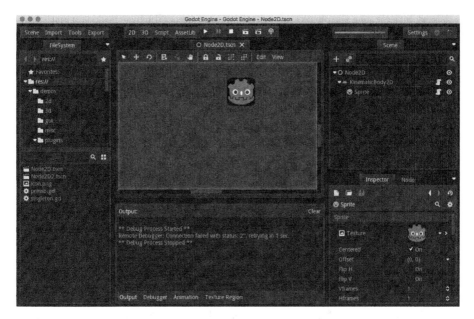

Figure 5-3. *The Godot GUI with the seminal icon put to great use*

Scenes

A scene is basically a level or a room in a game. You need to define a *main scene* before trying your project, which refers to the first scene to be displayed. You do this by activating the scene you want, selecting Scenes ➤ Project Settings ➤ Application, and selecting the main scene check box. Lastly, you need to click the folder icon on the right and navigate to the actual scene file in your project folder.

Now, on to how to change scenes. Let's assume you have two scenes, scene1.tscn and scene2.tscn. Simply add the following line of code to a script in some node in scene1 to change to the other scene:

```
get_tree().change_scene("res://scene2.tscn")
```

Nodes

Nodes are the building blocks of a project, which include clickable buttons, enemy units, jukebox objects, and so on. Think of nodes simply as *objects of all kinds*. Let's now create a couple of useful Godot nodes, shall we?

First, you need to click the plus sign in the Nodes window to create your first node. A window will open. Click Node2D. The description window will state "Base node for 2D system." Now click Create. All scenes need a base node, and this is what you just created. These don't do a whole lot, but they are required for functional scenes in Godot. Try renaming the base node to **Main** or **World**.

117

Next, let's create a simple player-controlled node. Select the base node you just created. Click the plus sign. Type **body** in the search box. Three search results should come up: StaticBody2D, KinematicBody2D, and RigidBody2D. These are the main node types for 2D objects in Godot.

- A StaticBody2D is used for static objects that don't need to be affected by physics properties.

- A KinematicBody2D will collide with physics objects but is not affected be the physics simulation. It's great for player-controlled objects.

- A RigidBody2D is a general-purpose node/object.

Create a KinematicBody2D node. You'll notice it is now underneath the previously created base node. Rename the new node to something like **Player**. You'll also notice the new player node has no visual representation yet. That's easily fixed: select the player node from the node view and create a new node of the type Sprite. The player node now has a subnode of the type Sprite with the default name of Sprite. Next you assign an actual sprite (i.e., image file) to this sprite node. Select the Sprite node and focus your attention on the Inspector module in the GUI. On the top there's a field labeled Texture. This stores visual data for the node. Click the part where it says <null> and select Load. Find an image file on your hard drive and select it. That's it. The sprite node now has an image associated with it. Because the sprite node is a child node of the player node, it will inherit this visual representation.

And that's how you attach sprites to your nodes/objects in Godot. The sprites can be easily manipulated inside the inspector in Godot when it comes to attributes such as scale and rotation.

Signals

Now, *signals* are the actions in the Godot engine. A robot node on a scene may receive a signal of, say, having the A key pressed on the keyboard, which then results in movement of said node.

Let's get some WASD action going. To begin adding user interaction in your Godot projects, you should first get acquainted with the input map. Go to Scene ➤ Project Settings ➤ Input Maps. Here you can map your keys to specific signals (i.e., actions). Type a name for the actions in the top bar. Let's start with W.

The way to implement player control into Godot is based on scripting. You simply need to attach a script to the player character node, which contains the interactive elements you need for your game.

The following script, when attached to a node, enables WASD controls in Godot. It may look complicated, but it actually isn't.

```
var location

func _ready():
        # Called every time the node is added to the scene.
        set_fixed_process(true)
        pass
```

```
func _fixed_process(delta):
      if(Input.is_action_pressed("W")):
            location=get_pos()
            set_pos(location+Vector2(0,-100)*delta)

      if(Input.is_action_pressed("S")):
            location=get_pos()
            set_pos(location+Vector2(0,100)*delta)

      if(Input.is_action_pressed("A")):
            location=get_pos()
            set_pos(location+Vector2(-100,0)*delta)

      if(Input.is_action_pressed("D")):
            location=get_pos()
            set_pos(location+Vector2(100,0)*delta)
```

Let's break down the input code block in GDScript.

- `Input.is_action_pressed` is a GDScript command for observing when an input event registers.

  - That command checks out each of the key mappings you stored in the input maps (W, A, etc.) and, when triggered, stores the current coordinates of the node into the location variable using a command for that purpose, called `get_pos()`.

- The variable called `location` is used to track and change the location of the node. Look back and you'll see you defined this variable in very first line of the script.

- You then tell Godot to set the position of the node with a dedicated command, `set_pos`.

- That command takes the current location and a two-dimensional vector as its attributes.

- The `Vector2` command sets a direction for the node its working with, on the classic Cartesian coordinates (i.e., x and y). The first variable in the command sets the *x* or *horizontal direction*. The next one works with the *vertical direction*.

  - Negative numbers input into the vector simply move the node in the reverse direction on the respective plane!

Singletons

Singletons are data storages for global variables. These are needed when the player navigates from scene to scene and specific variables need to persist throughout the scene changes (e.g., a score variable would benefit from being stored in a singleton). Simple games may not need this functionality, but you should get acquainted with it as it is a core concept in Godot.

To begin working with singletons, you start off by creating a new script. Click Script ➤ File ➤ New. Type **singleton1.gd** in the path box. You can type any name for this script, of course, but for the sake of simplicity I chose the most obvious one. Now, you need to work with a feature called Autoload. Go to Scene ➤ Project Settings ➤ Autoload. Navigate the path to the file you just created. Click Add and make sure the check box called Singleton is enabled. The very spartan `singleton1` script creates a variable called `score`, which is globally available for all scenes and their nodes in the project.

```
extends World
var score = 0
```

That's your script. Now, how to access this singleton data from within some other node? Just use the syntax of `<name of singleton>.<singleton variable you want to access>`, i.e., `singleton1.score`.

GDScript

Godot supports a C++ API but relies primarily on a proprietary language called GDScript for scripting. This is based on the Python language. The developers claim GDScript is easy to learn and gels best with the engine. The C++ API is recommended only for performance-critical parts of a project and requires quite a bit of prior experience in that language. All projects made with Godot require varying degrees of scripting. The software does have a learning curve, but it's worth investing the time.

Overall, the engine is comfortable to use. Godot has a well-integrated and beautifully color-coded built-in script editor. The IDE has both autocompletion and auto-indentation. The latter feature is quite useful, as GDScript is a whitespace-sensitive programming language, much like Ren'Py.

In addition to all this, Godot is very much a lightweight program coming at you at hardly 30MB in size. With broadband, it's yours within ten seconds.

Audiovisuals: 4/5

Godot has a custom physics engine, which does the job well. In addition to the three types of 2D physics bodies, the engine naturally caters for 3D nodes/objects as well. Note that there's a strict division between 2D and 3D node types. For one, the base class for projects in 3D is called `Spatial`.

Godot supports full-scene importing in 3D. Individual models in the Wavefront format (`.obj`) can naturally also be imported.

The particle system in Godot is extensive and fits the bill just fine. However, it would be nice to be able to use animated sprites for your particles. You only get nonanimated sprites for your explosions and other effects. Still, there are four phases of color available in addition to comprehensive particle attributes, including gravity direction, orbit velocity, and spread. You do get to craft some pretty convincing fire and magic effects with the system as it is.

The engine also has a visual animation tool for both 2D and 3D projects. This is a very user-friendly, timeline-based feature, reminiscent of many popular video-editing software applications.

Imported audio can only be in the venerable .wav format. You can, however, normalize the samples (i.e., pump up their volume level) and/or convert them to mono upon import, which may come in handy. Godot also allows you to resample your audio files at a sampling frequency of your choosing and/or convert them into 8 bits, if disk space is a priority in your project.

Support: 4/5

The Godot team has a clear vision for the future of the engine, and there's a very detailed road map available online. Updates to the engine are frequent. Social media is pleasantly getting more and more saturated with all things Godot. In addition to the (as of yet small) official forum and a busy Reddit thread, there's some real-time support available in the form of Discord and IRC chats. In short, people seem to love this engine because the developers take it seriously.

However, the official Godot documentation, while ample in scope, can be patchy in places.

Overall: 5/5

Godot is a great new engine on all fronts even for beginner developers. It got its first stable release in August 2016, but it's already gaining major ground among indies. Once you internalize the core concepts, you can come up with some rather ambitious titles for several popular platforms. The audiovisuals are strong. Although not AAA quality, the output from this engine is technically impressive and lends itself well to both professional 2D and casual 3D development. Best of all, this software is 100 percent open source.

In my opinion, Godot is the best game engine presented in this book. It deserves a much larger user base among indies and established developers alike.

Here are the Godot minimum system requirements:

- Windows 7

- Mac OS X 10.7 (Lion)

- Any Linux distribution

- OpenGL 2.1 or newer capabilities

Starting Point

Start working on the "Step by step" section in the online tutorials (http://docs.godotengine.org/en/stable/tutorials/step_by_step/_step_by_step.html).

■ ■ ■

## CHAPTER 6

Audiovisual Assets

Most of the time video games are audiovisually engaging. Good old-fashioned text adventures, while they are still played by many, speak to only a handful of potential customers. This means a developer must know his or her way around at least some basic audiovisual terms, which are presented next. First, I'll take on some core audio concepts followed by a look at current audio-editing software. Then, I'll do the same for graphics.

The Basics of Digital Audio

Compact disc–quality audio is still the gold standard you want to aim for in video games. This method of capturing audio in a digital environment is known as *pulse-code modulation* (PCM). It means using a 44.100 sample rate in 16 bits for all recording and playback. Going higher with these numbers (such as doing the 24-bit thing) in a video game context is overkill, no matter what some audio card manufacturers claim. The bigger the bit depth and sampling rate, the more disk space the audio eats. This may not matter at the delivery stage, but on a sound designer's workstation it does.

Now, the term *sample rate* refers to the number of times a sound source is sampled per second by the hardware/sound card. This information is donated with the hertz (i.e., Hz). The bigger this number is, the higher the frequencies you can record. Material sampled at a low frequency of, say, 8000Hz, sounds muffled or muted to our ears. That's why you want to keep your audio at that magical CD sampling rate of 44.100Hz. Most audio played back at this rate sounds natural enough to the majority of listeners.

Let's take a moment to learn about the *Nyquist theorem*. As physicist Harry Nyquist demonstrated, the actual highest frequency we can hear after sampling audio is *half* the rate the audio passage was recorded in. In other words, a sampling rate of 44.100Hz results in audio with its highest frequency being 22.050Hz instead of 44.100Hz. But don't worry—22KHz is enough for our precious ears.

There's also a great anatomical reason we stick to the CD standard. Human ears detect only up to 22.000 Hz at age 18 or so. After that, our ears begin to lose sensitivity and we hear only up to about 16.000 hertz at 25. At age 75 you're lucky to have 10.000 Hz available. This age-induced type of hearing loss is known as *presbycusis*. It happens to everyone.

Now, let's tackle the other important number in digital audio, the *bit depth*. To put it simply, the bit depth in digital audio simply means how many volume levels are available for the signal; 16 bits provides adequate dynamics with its 65,536 possible levels of volume. The bigger the bit depth, the more "volume ladders" there are—and the less background hiss there generally is. Sixteen bits is plenty to reproduce any kind of audio,

© Robert Ciesla 2017
R. Ciesla, *Mostly Codeless Game Development*, DOI 10.1007/978-1-4842-2970-5_6

including classical music with quiet passages, heavy metal, beeps, explosions, and even poorly voice-acted dialogue.

One may argue for 24 bits in a recording studio context (with its impressive on-paper 16.7 million volume steps) if you intend to record very quiet audio passages, but in the video game industry we're happy with 16 bits.

Say, do you want to go retro? Convert (i.e., downsample) your audio material to 8 bits. It's an instant 1990s sound. There are also some chic effects available to downgrade the hell out of your audio material, taking your players right back to the 1970s and Pong.

MIDI

Musical Instrument Digital Interface (MIDI) is just that: a way to interface specific instruments, usually keyboards, with digital workstations, such as computers. MIDI data differs from pure digital audio in several important ways. Think of it as messages instead of audio. MIDI devices transmit streams of notes (i.e., songs), their pitches, and velocities. You can't listen to a MIDI stream without a computer or some other device, which provides the sounds for all this note data to trigger.

There are many benefits to MIDI-based music making. For one, you can easily change entire instruments without touching the rest of the song's arrangement in any way. Also, MIDI song data takes very little room, often way, way less than 1MB. MIDI music used to sound cheesy, but these days there are some very convincing sound libraries available for any instruments you can think of, including the human voice. These libraries do take a lot of space, often being distributed on several DVDs. Needless to say, downloading them might take a few days in a row.

MIDI was made public in 1983 as a U.S./Japan partnership. It completely revolutionized music creation, enabling countless hobbyists to make pro-grade arrangements. MIDI is still a very large part of the global music industry, also in video games.

Lossy Audio Formats (i.e., Delivery Formats)

As is the case with graphics, there are two major groups of audio formats: lossy and nonlossy. Lossy includes MP3, Ogg Vorbis, Windows Media Audio, etc.

Think of lossy formats as old audio cassettes or VHS tapes—remember those? If you took a copy of one such recording onto a similar format, the new copy would be inferior in quality. In other words, lossy formats degrade after each copy, or after each "save as" in computer software.

The most well-known lossy audio format is our good friend MP3 from 1995. Other popular ones include Ogg Vorbis and Windows Media Audio (WMA). What is the purpose of all of these lossy formats? Well, because of their small file size, they make for fine delivery formats in a finished product. So, when there's no need to work on an audio file anymore, you save it as a, say, MP3. Remember, you do want to try to provide the customer the shortest possible downloading time in these times of digital distribution.

MP3 files, still the most popular lossy format, can be saved at different quality settings, known as *bit rates* (or *kbps*). The higher the bit rate, the closer the file is to a noncompressed file in overall fidelity. These rates range from 32 kbps to 320 kbps. Needless to say, you want to stay away from the low bit rates at all times. This is not 1996 anymore. There's plenty of Internet bandwidth for all.

Nonlossy Audio Formats (i.e., Source Formats)

Nonlossy audio formats, such as WAV, AIFF, and FLAC, are what you need when you're still working on some sound effects or music. You can safely save and copy in a nonlossy audio format without any degradation in audio quality. Large nonlossy audio files can take hundreds of megabytes in size. Therefore, you usually want to end the audio workflow with that "save as lossy" step.

The bosses of uncompressed audio formats are WAV in the Windows environment and AIFF on Macs. They're not system-specific, so you can work on both formats on either type of system. Both are archive ready and just love working with you and your musicians.

Now, here's some no-nonsense advice:

- *Deliver high-quality lossy files only*: Everything you release with your game should reflect well on you, including the audio quality in your files. Keep your MP3 output at 160kbps minimum to retain decent high-frequency fidelity—think hi-hats, cymbals, the "edge" in a vocal. Nobody wants to listen to that hip soundtrack shipping with your product at 32kbps. The same goes for sound effects. At lower bitrates they lose all "punch."

- *Make sure you keep your master audio material backed up and handy*: In case you decide to alter the audio in your project, you need the uncompressed master audio tracks at your disposal. Never go back and "enhance" a lossy piece of audio. Load up the master, work on it, and then save it as lossy, overwriting the old lossy file. There's nothing worse than an MP3 that's been compressed twice or more.

- *Keep the "holy numbers" with compressed audio as well*: Remember, 44.100 is the ideal sampling frequency for MP3 and other lossy formats, too—not 32.000Hz and certainly not 22.000Hz, unless you really need to keep your file sizes small.

- *Test your audio on several sets of speakers and headphones before release*: I'm assuming that as an indie developer you aren't going to invest in expensive and ultra-accurate monitoring speakers.

  - So, what might sound great on your personal setup may sound muddy or harsh on some other system. Try to minimize the amount of variation of quality between setups.

Plug-in

A plug-in is any type of extension to an audio editor's effect library. Some manufacturers of note include Waves, Slate Digital, and IK Multimedia. Plug-ins are a big business and are widely responsible for the sounds you hear on records, the radio, and in-video games. You can do any kind of effect with the right collection of plug-ins, from creating natural-sounding reverberations to enhancing specific frequencies in the audio.

There are roughly two types of plug-ins: effects and instruments. Plug-in effects consist of various mixing tools and special effects applicable on any type of audio with a graphical user interface usually modeled after studio hardware. Plug-in instruments refer to MIDI-based software synthesizers as well as MIDI-triggered instruments sampled from actual recorded strings, pianos, and other instrumentation.

Different operating systems support different types of plug-ins to a varying degree (see Table 6-1). Apple systems are 100 percent compatible only with Audio Units, which is no surprise since Apple implemented the specification itself. You may or may not have success running VST-based plug-ins in macOS, as is the case with Linux. Windows supports all plug-in types, apart from the aforementioned Audio Units.

Table 6-1. *A Rundown on the Typical Plug-in Formats for Current Systems*

Plug-in Format	System	Developer	Type
Virtual Studio Technology (VST)	Windows, Linux, and macOS with partial support	Steinberg	Effects, instruments
Audio Units (AU)	macOS	Apple	Effects, instruments
LADSPA	Linux, Windows, macOS	Various	Effects
LV2	Linux, Windows, macOS	Various	Effects, instruments
Nyquist plug-ins	Linux, Windows, macOS	Audacity	Effects, instruments

The Fundamental Concepts of Audio Processing

When working with any kind of audio, some concepts are universal. Even if you never work in this exact field, it is useful to be aware of their meanings. These effects are to be found pretty much in every single decent audio-editing tool.

Decibels (dB)

A decibel is a sound-pressure unit used to measure relative audio loudness. Human ears experience pain with sounds clocked at around 130 dB. These may include gunshots or someone performing low-quality slam poetry at you through a megaphone. Decibels are commonly used in audio workstations to exhibit volume levels and the intensity of any applied effects, such as EQ.

EQ

EQ is short for *equalization*. This is the most crucial component in audio post-processing. EQ is used to manipulate—and in many cases fix—audio material, using mostly digital, software-based filters. These filters boost bass or cut treble or work on any frequencies in the middle. Remember, your average digital audio track contains frequency data from the hardly ever audible 20Hz all the way up to 22.000Hz. Only in rare cases should you leave a freshly recorded audio track as it is. Let's take a look at some of the most common points of frequency intervention.

- *Below 50Hz is the very low end and is felt more than heard*: This is the domain of the rumble and the chest pain. Material rich in these frequencies might sound great on a pair of headphones, but it might cause earthquakes on the average subwoofers. Don't overdo this and monitor closely.

- *200Hz, the mud*: Try cutting this for extra clarity on any type of material.

- *3KHz to 4KHz, the upper mids, which is the area the human ear is most sensitive to*: Too much of these and your listeners will get ear fatigue. Too little and the material sounds unfocused; this will work for background ambience but not for gunshots or dramatic interludes.

It's always better to cut than boost, unless your material is incredibly lacking on wanted frequencies. Boosting a frequency may introduce unwanted artifacts into your audio material, changing its character to something more artificial or unpleasant.

Not all EQs are built the same, however. Most of the built-in equalizers in audio-editing software are intended to deliver a precise, sterile effect. There's nothing wrong with that, but a whole industry has emerged around digital emulations of actual studio hardware. Big-name studio EQs, such as Neve, SSL, and Trident, have been emulated to a great extent in plug-in form. The reason for this? A thing called *character*. None of these boutique EQs sounds the same even when working on the same frequencies. A great equalizer can change a miserable audio file into a decent one—and beyond. This naturally goes for any type of material, including video game sound.

Common Types of EQ Filters

EQs and individual filters come in many types. You'll now take a look at the most common varieties.

- *High-pass filter*: These types of filters cut frequency content beneath a set point in the frequency spectrum. A common use for high-pass filters is to tame the rumble at the very low end (< 50Hz).

- *Low-pass filter*: Basically the opposite of a high-pass filter, these filters cut content above a set point in the frequency domain. They are used mostly to tone down harshness in the upper frequencies (> 10KHz).

- *Graphic EQ*: Like the name suggests, these types of EQs provide a visual representation of their workings in the form of a sliders set at specific points in the frequency spectrum.

- *Parametric EQ*: These devices/plug-ins usually feature between two to six adjustable frequency bands with separate cut and boost knobs for each. With a parametric EQ, you essentially get to carefully define which are the most relevant frequencies in the material you're currently working on.

  - Parametrics also usually feature a control labeled Q, which refers to the reach (i.e., amplitude) of each frequency center. A wide Q affects more frequencies next to the one being worked on than a narrow Q does.

How to EQ Your Material

The best way to get acquainted with the critical skill of equalizing audio is simply to open an audio file in a digital audio workstation and start adjusting the parameters. There's always room for taste in these matters, but don't even think about releasing a game with lackluster audio. Again, your game's audio should sound decent in as many speakers and headphones as possible. To achieve this, you should adhere to the following tips:

- *Chisel off the sonic marble*: This refers to simply removing frequencies that are not crucial to an audio track. A tambourine doesn't need anything below 300Hz, most of the time, so high-pass that track. A bass line or an explosion doesn't benefit much from content upwards of 12KHz. Take out the unnecessary bands from your material, but don't overdo it. Go for a neutral or natural sound overall.

- *Deal with frequency competition*: Many different audio sources have similar frequency components. A busy audio collage with lasers and human voices might need you to adjust the fundamental frequencies of one element at, say, between 1KHz and 2KHz. Overlapping these elements without EQ might create a subtle cacophony and, at worst, an undecipherable mess in which every other syllable is inaudible. Sometimes a mere volume adjustment doesn't work, creating instead a glued-on sound.

- *Cut, don't boost*: To boost frequencies, it's often better to do some cutting. Paradoxical as it sounds, this technique, known as *subtractive equalization,* is a must. This is how it works: let's assume your explosion is missing some bass rumble. Instead of boosting below 160Hz, try cutting between 800Hz and 2KHz. The technique works the other way around as well. Not enough mid? Try cutting the low and/or high frequencies.

Dynamics (Compression and Limiting)

Compression is an effect that reduces the dynamic range of audio. In essence this means decreasing the volume of the loud parts and increasing the volume of the softer parts to create a nice, audible, and commercially acceptable track or sound effect. You don't want the user to fiddle with the volume controls mid-song, do you?

Limiting, on the other hand, is an extreme form of compression. A limiter evens out a track in a less subtle way, pumping out solid and usually loud material. Both effects may be used to eliminate digital distortion (i.e., clipping), which is the least desirable end result in digital audio and a sure sign of an amateur at work. Think of a limiter as an aural safety net to keep overly loud passages in check.

Here are examples of dynamics processing in daily life:

- FM radio uses heavy limiting to guarantee audible broadcasts even in busy urban environments.

- Any sporting event PA system has a limiter to guarantee overload-free sound amplification.

- Almost all tracks on a pop music album that make up each song are compressed to varying degrees.

Clipping

Clipping occurs when the overall signal level overloads its boundaries. This results in a very unpleasant popping sound in most cases. In addition to your ears, this type of signal overload can also damage speakers and headphones. You do not want clipped audio in your projects.

Here are some examples of when audio usually gets recorded with major clipping without compression:

- Gunshots at close range

- Gigs and concerts (in-field)

- Low-flying jet airplanes

- Your roomie's parties in the other room

Down in the land of bits, if your 16-bit audio with its 32,767 possible volume values is boosted too hard over the maximum value of 32,767, you enter clipping territory. In practice, this means keeping an eye on the volume levels in your digital audio workstation (DAW). Stay away from the red zone. If you clip a signal badly enough and are unfortunate to save and overwrite the original file, restoring the original audio fidelity may be impossible.

Normalization

There are two main types of normalization: peak and root mean square (RMS). I will now briefly discuss the former. This is a rather crude but common method of bringing the average volume level of audio up to a target level. While it obviously does make your material louder, which can be a necessity in many cases, peak normalization also boosts the noise level. It doesn't discriminate; everything in your material gets a lift.

Instead of normalizing your material, you should stick to limiting and/or compression to control its overall volume. This goes especially for soundtracks. Only normalize when the source material is completely unusable because of being of extremely low volume and when you have no chance of replacing it with material of a higher caliber.

Reverb

Short for "reverberation," *reverb* is a digital simulation of acoustic spaces, sometimes emulating a realistic environment, such as a cathedral...or your average toilet. This should be the last effect you apply. Pros approach the audio material with their open ears first, then EQ, then dynamics, and only then, maybe, reverb.

In a video game context you may be better off using real-time reverberation systems, keeping your sound effects effects-free. This way you can alter the acoustics within the game engine as the project unfolds. Of course, audio processing on the go is quite hard on the CPU, so if you're absolutely sure you don't mind not having real-time effects, go with the traditional approach by all means. Many smaller, casual projects don't need the exact, live approximation of the Taj Mahal.

Free Audio Resources

Here are some free audio resources:

- `http://dig.ccmixter.org`: Dig ccMixter, despite its clumsy name, provides hundreds of looped sounds and other types of audio for your game projects, 100 percent free of charge. Just visit the site, preview, and download. You must give credit to the composer, however.

- `www.freesound.org`: The Freesound Library contains thousands of samples of varying quality, most of which are good. It's great for your background ambience needs.

- `www.soundbible.com`: Sound Bible is another, smaller library with hundreds of usable sound effects.

- `www.incompetech.com`: Incompetech is a project by the venerable composer Kevin Macleod. You are free to use his multigenre work in your games provided you give full credit. While somewhat overused these days, the Incompetech library provides at least some fine placeholder music for your projects.

Some Tools of the Audio Trade

Presented next are some of the best tools for working with game audio in my opinion. Pick an audio editor you feel comfortable with and stick to it. You will need one; stock sound effects get you only so far. Some audio manipulation is necessary.

Modern freeware audio editors are very close in features to the available commercial software. The major differences are in the availability and quality of MIDI and plug-in-support and stability.

Most audio software packages these days support all major compressed and uncompressed formats. As a games entrepreneur, this is what counts most. You have plenty of choice when it comes to this type of software too.

Audition CC by Adobe

`www.adobe.com`

Price (Q1 2017): $19.99 per month
This is available for Windows and macOS.
Audition is a fine piece of software with excellent, time-saving features. In particular, the multitrack section of the program is quite flawless, if you can live without MIDI support.

Starting its life as Cool Edit Pro in the late 1990s, Audition has evolved into a popular professional audio-editing suite. While the support for plug-ins is robust, Audition has virtually every sound-editing capability built in, including great compressors. However, the multitracking section still does not support MIDI instrumentation. This makes Audition a great choice for a sound effect person, but not one for the composers, unless you are planning to record actual sound sources/instruments only.

The latest versions of Audition are very stable and not likely to crash. For comprehensive sound effects and ambience work, you could do a lot worse.

Audacity 2.1.2 by The Audacity Team

`http://audacityteam.org/`

This is available for Windows, macOS, Linux, and Unix. Slightly older versions of Audacity are also available for PowerPC Macs on the official site.

A classic among freeware audio editors, Audacity is the clumsier sibling of Audition. It does provide fine basic features for the game maker, however, such as wide format support. There's no MIDI support, but this is a great free program for small-time game developers looking to work with their audio.

First released in 2000, Audacity has reached close to 100 million happy users as of early 2017. The software has an old-time charm about it. The interface remains somewhat unintuitive, relying quite a bit on your operating system to set up the audio routing. You have several windows to navigate to get to some basic adjustments in Audacity.

However, underneath the clumsy exterior there are lots of great processing capabilities. For one, the noise reduction effect included in the software is among the best. When it comes to plug-ins, Audacity supports VST, Audio Units, LADSPA, LV2, and the emerging Nyquist format, for the respective platforms.

Ardour 5.8 by Paul Davis

`http://ardour.org`

This is available on Windows, macOS (Intel and PowerPC), and Linux.

Continuing the theme of audio-editing software starting with the first letter of the alphabet, Ardour is one of the finest programs out there.

Ardour is capable of some serious work with great plug-in support. You are asked to donate a minimum of $1 to keep the "nag screens" at bay, which is a fair price to pay for such a high-quality product. Mixing tracks works wonderfully in the program's multitrack view. Crashes are few and far between. Ardour seems extremely stable.

There's very little to fault with Ardour. At some early point in its development it featured an experimental collaborative system called Ardour Session Exchange, which was unfortunately dropped. It's wholeheartedly recommended you download this software and make the aforementioned donation to keep the development cycle going.

Ohm Studio by OhmForce

http://ohmforce.com/

This is available for Windows and macOS.

Ohm Studio is a collaborative audio workstation. This means you get to work on your material online with team members and strangers alike.

The software opens with a chat screen and a view of both your personal, local projects and all the public projects available for participation. The projects are associated with keywords when it comes to the genre and overall vibe of the song (e.g., *happy, epic, tense*, and so on).

Ohm Studio lacks the versatility of many other audio workstations. It's clearly built around its collaborative capabilities, which is not a bad thing. However, this comes at some price in regard to the processing prowess and stability. Ohm Studio is not the fastest when it comes to mixing your projects. There are continuing issues with both plug-in and hardware support. You may or may not be able to even launch the program with your particular setup.

Ohm Studio comes in four editions, as presented in Table 6-2. While you are limited to exporting in the Ogg lossy format in the free edition, you at least get the full-quality setting of 500kbps. This is not source-quality audio, but it's pretty close.

Table 6-2. *A Rundown on Available Ohm Studio Editions*

Product	Features	Maximum Projects	Cost (Q1 2017)
Ohm Studio	16-bit recording and compressed audio format export only	10	Free
Ohm Studio Pro	24-bit recording; export also in uncompressed WAV format; two extra plug-ins by OhmForce	10	$39
Ohm Studio Pro XL	All Pro features and seven additional plug-ins by Ohm Force	10	$89
Ohm Studio Cloud		200	$9 per month

Overall, Ohm Studio is an impressive concept and sadly one of the few collaborative audio tools available. The software isn't updated frequently, which is a shame, as this type of solution is sorely needed.

sfxr/cfxr

```
www.drpetter.se/project_sfxr.html
http://thirdcog.eu/apps/cfxr
```

sfxr is available for Windows, and cfxr is available for macOS.

This duo of sound-generating software makes it simple and fun to populate your projects with old-school sound effects. It doesn't get much easier to create 8-bit audio on your modern desktop.

There are some presets for various types of common sound effects on the left of the interface. Clicking one of these buttons creates a new sound in the chosen category, which include "laser," "explosion," and "powerup." Alternatively, select the main type of audio from a variety of waveform types, adjust some parameters, and click Play to preview. If that feels like too much work, you can always click "random" to generate just that—arbitrary sounds that may or may not work in your projects.

When it comes to usability, these two are second to none. However, the audio output itself is rarely usable out of the box. The samples are quite hard on the ears with vast amounts of upper-mid frequencies (2KHz to 4KHz). These can be tamed with EQ in any audio-editing program, of course, making this software a must-have for indies.

Wavosaur 1.3 by The Wavosaur Team

```
http://wavosaur.com
```

This is available for Windows.

A most lightweight piece of software, Wavosaur offers competent audio processing for Windows with great file format support.

You can run Wavosaur from a USB stick; there's no installation is needed. This is one highly portable piece of software. That's the reason there's a limited number of effects coming with Wavosaur out of the box. You get your basic audio cut-and-paste editing, normalization, frequency analysis, and other expected features. Instead of a ton of built-in effects like most audio editors, you are advised to add them using VST plug-ins at your leisure.

Wavosaur has extensive file format support, covering everything you need from current audio staples to more exotic formats, such as Akai S1000 samples and even some Amiga file types. For an audio file format converter and basic editor, Wavosaur is an impressive piece of software. Just add a few EQ and compressor plug-ins, and it'll do everything you need for your sound effects.

Digital Audio Questions

Finishing this section, you should be able to answer the following questions:

- What are the gold standard settings for audio in a video game context and why?

- What are the differences and uses for lossy and nonlossy audio formats?

Software for Game Visuals

By now you are probably familiar with pixels, resolutions, and some of the basics of digital graphics. These and many other related concepts were covered in Chapter 1 and will be discussed more in-depth in Chapter 10.

In this section I'll mostly focus on the tools that allow you to actually create visuals for your games. There are a plethora of fine software applications for this purpose, both commercial and free. This section of the book will be divided between software geared toward 2D and 3D visuals. By the latter, I mean products that output models and height maps (i.e., actual 3D resources).

Before beginning the software review, let's take a look at a few more crucial concepts for the subject matter you may not be familiar with.

Lossy Image Formats (i.e., Delivery Formats)

As is the case with audio, there are two major groups of image formats: lossy and nonlossy. When you're ready to publish a game, downgrade its image files into a lossy format of your choice such as JPEG or GIF whenever possible. In this context, *compression* refers to the reduction in file size and quality of lossy images. Heavily compressed images take less space but are also less faithful to the original, uncompressed files. Go with the smallest file sizes you can attain without compromising the color and detail too much. It's a balancing act, especially on size-critical platforms such as mobile games. Remember, you can't convert a lossy image file back into a nonlossy one and expect great results.

Graphics delivery in lossy formats usually works best for presentation (e.g., title screens and related contexts). Lossy formats aren't great with transparency.

Nonlossy Image Formats (i.e., Source Formats)

Nonlossy image files are large but immune to image-quality degradation when saving. Not always fantastic for delivery, they are a must when still in the editing phase. Make sure you keep the latest version of your work in a nonlossy image format such as PNG, TIFF, BMP, and TGA. Portable Network Graphics (PNG) is perhaps the darling of the day among image formats. To know it is to love it.

There are usually several varieties to nonlossy image formats. Images in PNG come in 8-bit type, too, meaning a maximum of 256 colors per such files. This often gives the effect of an image originating from 1995 or so, at least in the case of more complicated scenes. Stick to the highest bit depths when editing your image files. In the case of PNG, that would be a color depth of 32 bits, offering millions of colors per file.

Now, there's also a format called Fireworks PNG. This format is used by Adobe's now sadly discontinued Fireworks graphics-editing suite (which is still much loved by me, for one). This format allows for layered image files with high fidelity and offers a great source format for video game graphics.

Transparency

This term simply refers to the "invisible" parts in an image file. Most, if not all, nonlossy image formats support transparency. Sprites (i.e., moving objects) are in many cases deliverable in the PNG format as it offers sharp image quality and excellent transparency. Although GIFs have basic transparency support, they are limited to a maximum of 256 colors per image. In the context of hip retro games this is rarely an issue; however, as the whole, an aesthetic thrives on limited color palettes.

There are two types of transparency: *alpha transparency* and *index transparency*. The former has multiple levels of transparency, which allows for those smooth drop shadows and a higher fidelity of the effect in general. You can also adjust the level of alpha transparency, from complete to partial, making these types of images jell with others with sometimes interesting results.

Index transparency, found in some GIF files, is simply a specific color in the image file's palette, which will be interpreted as transparent. It offers a rudimentary type of the effect that mostly works with images with more simple, jagged edges and no need for partial transparency. Again, this approach is fine for retro titles in most cases.

Tools for 2D

Now you'll explore some options a developer has for 2D tools, after which you'll take a peek at 3D software. Of course, these approaches are not mutually exclusive. Most 3D projects feature quite a bit of flat 2D artwork in the form of presentation. Also, even some of the most retro-like 2D titles may include elements of 3D in their presentation. Before getting into the software, let's take a look at some terms of this particular trade.

PD Howler 11/PD Artist by Dan Ritchie

www.thebest3d.com/dogwaffle/

Price (Q1 2017): $49 for PD Howler/$27 for PD Artist
This is available for Windows.
The Project Dogwaffle line of software, like the name may suggest, is an eccentric one. There's a lot underneath the hood; it's very powerful and rich in features but suffers from some usability issues. If you persist, however, some truly impressive art can be yours.

PD Howler has a long list of possible applications: digital painting program, realistic terrain generator, Photoshop replacement, and animation suite, just to name a few. Note that PD Artist differs from PD Howler mostly in that it doesn't feature the aforementioned animation tools.

The learning curve for the PD line of software is relatively steep. You can do the average color correction and resizing of images in no time, but the more advanced features can take a while to master. The design philosophy behind this software gives artists some great tools for rapid expression.

Creating any type of near-photorealistic terrain is a simple process in PD Howler. It shouldn't take more than a few minutes, and the end result is very impressive. Start by selecting Render ➤ Plasma Noise to create a topographic representation of the terrain. Adjust parameters according to your taste. Next, go to Transform ➤ 3D Designer. You now get a rotatable 3D view of the terrain with some powerful options for further refinement. Additional controls are enabled by clicking More on the top-left corner of the window. You can now adjust properties like erosion and sediment, both of which are implemented very well in the software. By clicking Create Texture, you get a customizable texture for your terrain simulating snow, grass, and rock, applied on three respective levels on your vista. You have full control over the intensity and distribution of these elements, as well as the option of infusing the scene with some artificial sediment of any color, which is great for wintery scenes.

One of the most iconic Howler features is the *swap image*, which can be accessed most easily by pressing J on your keyboard. Think of the swap just as a secondary, spare image layer. Use it to sketch your ideas or combine it with the primary layer. This is a useful feature and a callback to 1990s painter programs, such as Deluxe Paint by Dan Silva.

Pixen 4 by The Open Sword Group

`http://pixenapp.com`

This is available for macOS.

One for friends of old-school graphics, Pixen is a tried and trusted companion of many a 2D artist. The feature set is more than adequate for most tasks in the hallowed halls of pixel art. Since going commercial, Pixen has become even more enjoyable to use.

Once an open source piece of software, Pixen has been turned into a commercial project in recent times. The biggest reason probably was the fact that the Apple App Store got flooded with clones of this program. This naturally didn't please the developers. Going commercial ensured a proper development path. The price is still very low for such a fine 2D image editor.

Apart from a new look, Pixen 4 feels like the Pixen you may have grown up with. The classic approach is still there: you get to assign a separate drawing tool for each mouse button (e.g., you may choose to have a plot pixel function for the left mouse button and an erase pixel function for the right one). But since version 4, Pixen has added quite a few features. These include filters (i.e., post-processing effects), video card–accelerated processing, and optimized CPU utilization of drawing operations. The new Pixen will run great on even the most modest of Mac minis. Animation is still one of Pixen's strong suits. Using a filmstrip approach, developers can effortlessly craft sprite sheets for their game engines of choice or plain old animated GIFs.

You may be able to download an older, free version of Pixen for quite some time at some software repository. However, Pixen's commercial edition is the recommended one for those working in the chic realm of 2D pixel art. It's the tool of choice for many mobile game artists and indies in general, for a reason. The feature set, simplicity, and continuing support are what makes Pixen 4 a winner.

Spriter by Brash Monkey

`www.brashmonkey.com`

Price (Q1 2017): $60
This is available for Windows, macOS, and Linux.

Spriter emphasizes rapid 2D art creation, without compromises. It makes that approaching deadline much less daunting for those in a hurry to deliver.

Spriter has a modular approach to sprite making. This means you compose your characters, limb by limb or part by part, from different resources at your will, instead of plotting each pixel as you do with programs like Pixen. This speeds things up considerably for the 2D artist. But that's not the only thing Spriter does to accelerate your creative impulses. The animation system in the program utilizes an approach where you define a second set of invisible elements (called *bones*) over your character image elements. This virtual skeleton then controls the angles and motion of the underlying parts, making for some smooth animations. This speeds up the animating process quite a bit.

There's a limited version of Spriter available for download in addition to the full commercial Pro version. Spriter's free edition disables animations-within-animations and image set swapping among other features. The Pro version also ships with a whopping 260 animations to make your characters walk, jump, and punch like there's no tomorrow.

Spriter is not a mere stand-alone tool. It can be integrated into several game engines, making the workflow even more convenient. An API of the software is available for GameMaker Studio, Unity, and Construct 2, to name a few. This extension adds some programming commands to your respective engine for operating directly with the Spriter system. It may be too cumbersome and/or unnecessary for beginners to implement, but more advanced developers (especially those working in larger teams) will benefit from this approach.

Brash Monkey sells quite a few art packs for Spriter. These include characters and other graphical resources tailored for platform games, role-playing games (RPGs), and sci-fi shoot-'em-ups. The prices range from $12 to $24. You can start your Spriter journey with a free Essentials art pack available from Brashmonkey.com and see if you and the program are a fit.

Spine by Esoteric Software

http://esotericsoftware.com

Price (Q1 2017): $70 for Essentials Edition, $300 for Professional Edition
This is available for Windows, macOS, and Linux.

Stemming from the same school of ideology as Spriter, Spine is a modular sprite maker. The biggest difference seems to be in the price, with Spriter being the wallet-friendly option.

The cheaper Essentials Edition might work for smaller game project, but the Professional Edition is where it's really at. Spine allows you to export your image files in PNG, GIF, and JPEG. Your actual character data can be saved in either binary or JSON formats. The game engine API support in Spine isn't as impressive as that in Spriter. Some major technologies are supported out of the box, and these include Unity, HTML5, and Flash. Although lacking official support, a Spine API has been developed for such systems as GameMaker and Construct 2.

But what do you get for the steeper price in Spine that you don't get with Spriter? Well, the biggest feature would be *freeform deformation* (FFD). This refers to the approach of having a transformable mesh cover your objects, which can then be used to alter their overall shape at will. You can add bounciness with this method, as well as making hair and cloth on a sprite more realistic. Spriter includes a somewhat similar (if ever so experimental) feature called *skin mode*, which is simply not as versatile.

Spine is a popular and rather powerful tool for speeding up your sprite making. The interface is professional, and the documentation is adequate. Tons of smaller-scale commercial games have used Spine during development to save the developers some time. You should do so, too.

Creature by Kestrel Moon Studios

http://creature.kestrelmoon.com/

Price (Q1 2017): $99 for Basic version, $199 for Pro
This is available for Windows and macOS.

Creature is a highly advanced sprite creator. It offers both rapid development of visuals and a ton of features, some of which can enhance your original artwork.

The software comes in three flavors: the free trial, Standard, and Pro. Saving is disabled in the trial version, but otherwise you get to experiment with Creature without many limitations with it.

Creature is an amazing piece of software from a technical standpoint. The main buzz with it is in its capability to create perfectly usable animation from a single image file. This actually works and is done with a clever use of freeform deformation. You can also import an image file containing several body parts, and the software will automatically create separate elements for you to animate (based on the space between the different body parts). Very handy.

Next, you rig your character, i.e., create the virtual skeleton. This is a simple, intuitive process in Creature as there are several preset rigs available for your starting points. You then assign weight to your "bones." The Auto Weighting option in the software usually does a good job at this.

Creature offers a decent number of formats when exporting. These include individual PNG frames or sprite sheets, Autodesk FBX, and Alembic. When exporting in an image or video format, there's the option of doing so using a technique called High Quality Super Sampling. This is a video card–accelerated approach that reduces jagged edges and makes the end result look more polished. There's also some convincing GPU-accelerated post-processing available, including a pixel-art filter with variable block size (this is great for that 8-bit or 16-bit look, if you start with high-resolution material). Most of these features in Creature work in a wide variety of both Nvidia and AMD video cards. Your mileage may vary.

Making impressive sprites has perhaps never been as fast or fun. Not only does Creature speed up your sprite making, it actually can actually add artistic value to it with lighting and other effects. The software is well worth the money, even at $200 for the Pro version.

TerraRay 6.5 by Synium Software

www.syniumsoftware.com/terraray

Price (Q1 2017): $10
This is available for macOS.

Not capable of animated scenes or exporting height maps for 3D game engines, TerraRay is still a valuable addition to your 2D graphics arsenal. If your projects need high-quality, still 2D sceneries, this program will do the trick.

In addition to the intuitive interface, TerraRay is powered by an impressive array of visual technologies. You get some pretty realistic lighting rendering, volumetric (i.e., god ray) clouds and fog, high-quality water, and even some decent vegetation to plot on your terrains with. The most impressive feature in the software is, again, the user interface. The tools are grouped in a very understandable fashion. Most of the time you simply paint your terrains with the various elements (e.g., vegetation, water, and others). TerraRay is very much a beginner-friendly piece of software.

The camera tool in TerraRay is versatile, offering five types of perspectives in addition to complete freedom to pan and zoom as much as you like. A handy, resizable preview window helps you keep an eye on the proceedings. You can speed up the previewing by going to Preferences > Preview and switching the antialiasing settings to 1.

If you don't feel like sculpting a terrain from the ground up, you can speed things up by allowing TerraRay to generate one for you. You do this by selecting the Terrain Elevation tab. Then, simply select Filters and Add Noise. By adjusting a few sliders and clicking Apply, you get great starting points for your work. The best approach usually is to combine a noise map with some manual adjustment where necessary.

There are a few built-in 3D objects included in TerraRay for you to insert into your vistas. You can import 3DS models into the program, too. While external models usually import just fine, the associated textures may not. However, for simple objects, at least you can easily assign a flat color surface or a stock texture within TerraRay, in case the original texture doesn't quite import successfully.

For such a low price you might think TerraRay is not quite up there with the visual quality. That is not the case; the output from the program is on par with most commercial solutions. Just make sure you set the detail level to Very High Quality in the render settings by the time you're satisfied with the view.

VUE Infinite 2015 PLE by E-on Software

www.e-onsoftware.com/products/vue

This is available for Windows and macOS.

VUE is a terrain generator with a strong track record. It's been used to create backdrops in such movies as *Avatar* and the latest *Indiana Jones*. While obviously powerful, VUE is also surprisingly comfortable to use. It won't take hours to come up with some impressive vistas, including animated ones.

VUE is available as a free *personal learning edition* (PLE) with some limitations. These include limiting animation exports to the base HD resolution (1280×720) and watermarked output after 30 days of use. Also, you are not allowed to use any output commercially. However, the PLE never expires. This is still a great way to learn the basics of this rather splendid software.

Another option for the dilettante users is VUE Pioneer. It's pretty much the same product as the PLE, although it watermarks your output from day 1. Also a free piece of software, this edition differs from PLE mostly in that you get Full HD (1920×1080) export and you can upgrade it to a nonwatermarking product with a paid module.

The user interface in VUE is intuitive. You simply use the left mouse button to select elements in the terrain, hold down right mouse button to pan, and use the scroll wheel to zoom in and out. To get started, simply go to Object ➤ Create and select the type of element you want to incorporate in your scene. The available selection includes procedural terrain, celestial bodies, rocks, and everything an artificial landscape can use.

Before rendering a scene to a file, you are treated with the option of a few common post-processing filters, including contrast, brightness, and color filtering. While not exciting on paper, these filters work exceptionally well with VUE's visuals and can really change the ambience in a terrain. You then get to save your image in some gorgeous, high-resolution formats such as Targa, TIFF, and PNG. Good times!

The animations in VUE are effortlessly made. An Animation Wizard inside the program takes care of this in a very enjoyable manner. First, you select an object on your terrain or the camera, in case you want a first-person perspective animation. Then it's time for the wizard to work some magic. By selecting Animation ➤ Animation Wizard, you get to pick your type of object or camera movement in your animation. There are motion presets for both airborne objects (such as an airplane or a missile) and ground vehicles, all with differences when it comes to banking behavior and other attributes. Next, you define the behavior of the object at the end of the animation. You get to either have it play just once, set it on repeat, or have the object reverse its movement upon completion. Next there's a visual waypoint system for you to plot the object's course with on the terrain. Finally, you get to set the duration of the sequence in seconds. That's all it takes to animate objects in VUE.

There's also a comprehensive collection of plug-ins available for the VUE family of products. These include exporting functionality for 3D programs and various extra visual capabilities, such as plug-ins for populating your terrains with highly realistic vegetation.

VUE is great for creating some jaw-dropping presentations within your projects. The output is of a very high technical standard and, if used carefully, can really add to the atmosphere of a video game. Not surprisingly, AAA video game houses like Activision and EA have used VUE in their products. Thanks to the ease of use of the software, so can you. Just make sure your video card has solid OpenGL support before you give VUE a spin. In fact, your entire hardware setup should be ample in resources before trying this one. Not even your average quad-core CPU combined with an above-average video card can make the most of software as demanding as VUE.

Tools for 3D

Now it's time to look at some common solutions for creating 3D visuals. This is a more challenging realm of content creation. However, each featured product does have a robust community behind it. Naturally, plenty of online tutorials are also available to get you started.

Blender 2.78 by Blender Foundation

www.blender.org

This is available for Windows, macOS, and Linux.

A free piece of software since 2003, Blender has amassed a massive user base over the years. Primarily a 3D modeling program, Blender is the most versatile suite of 3D tools out there.

With power comes a steep learning curve, and Blender is no exception. Absolutely packed with features, the software suite takes a while to master. As is the case with all complex software, the secret to working comfortably in Blender is to memorize all of the most useful keyboard shortcuts. Do this and your experience with the software will be greatly improved.

It can be daunting to create an interesting 3D model from scratch for a beginner. If you are one, you're better off importing a ready-made object and modifying it to get to grips with the Blender tools and interface. There are plenty of free 3D models out there in the Blender community.

Blender includes a built-in game prototyping system. While not very beginner-friendly, the game engine can produce impressive results with more experienced developers. It has been used to make commercial titles such as *Tomato Jones* and *KRUM: Edge of Darkness*. Clearly Blender has the potential to be a game engine in its own right. Unfortunately, the developers behind the project are having some issues with this feature, so it might get dropped at some point. The Blender game engine uses the Python language for scripting but can be also controlled to a degree by a visual logic engine.

Blender supports a wide variety of the most common export formats. While hardware accelerated on both Nvidia and AMD video cards, the former is supported to a much greater degree. Many elements of rendering, such as smoke and fire, remain unaccelerated on AMD hardware.

Not only a fan favorite, Blender has friends in high places. Its users include Marvel Enterprises (for the movie *Spiderman 2*) and good old NASA, no less. One of Blender's main appeals is its use of a world-class physics system that lends itself well to both cinema and scientific applications. Bullet Physics has also been used in several AAA titles.

In technical terms, Blender output is just as impressive as that from any of the expensive software applications. The GUI is consistent over different platforms, so if your Window PC melts down, you can continue your work on your nerdy friend's Linux version of Blender without any usability issues. There's also a lightweight video editor in there with some basic built-in effects. You shouldn't forsake your Premiere and Final Cut just yet, however.

If you're just starting out on the long and uphill journey in 3D modeling, Blender is a great choice for a multitude of reasons, the biggest one being the supportive community behind it. Not only is the built-in feature set impressive, but Blender is constantly getting new extensions and features for you to experiment with. And if you persist, some rather dazzling visuals can be achieved with it for pretty much any type of project.

Daz Studio Pro 4.9 by Daz3D

https://www.daz3d.com

This is available for Windows and macOS.

While very much a beginner's toolset, Daz Studio offers plenty of uses if you dig deeper. The final output from the software, especially when it comes to realistic 3D humans, is among the best.

Daz Studio Pro is not the most feature-rich piece of software. It can't be used to create new 3D models *per se*. Think of it as an accessible character poser, a simplified animator, and a file format converter. It does support wonderfully realistic human characters available at the Daz3D store and elsewhere. There's only so much you can do with the spartan objects that ship with Daz Studio Pro, but they are great for learning the workflow. The interface is intuitive with a collection of sliders controlling the various attributes.

Animating your models is a joy. There's a keyframe-based editing system for you to play with. Posing your characters is easy and fun with the Daz universal tool. Some preset poses are also available built in and in the store. Also, Daz Studio projects are supposed to link up with Adobe Photoshop via a plug-in called 3D Bridge, but this seems to be an experimental feature.

Daz Studio Pro has robust OpenGL support for rendering in both basic and intermediate varieties, the latter which allows you to experiment with the "passes per light" parameter. Interestingly, Daz Studio Pro also supports Nvidia's Iray, which is a technology that can add a whole new level of photorealism to your renders. Iray is based on a technique called *physically based rendering* (PBR), which simulates the interaction between light and material in the 3D world as realistically as possible. For a free product, this is no small feat. Naturally, for hardware-accelerated Iray work, you do need an Nvidia video card.

Daz Studio Pro allows you to export 3D models in a variety of formats, including Wavefront (.obj), Collada, and Autodesk FBX. You also get to import models in more than a dozen formats. Of course, nothing is stopping you from exporting a still image with the highest-quality settings from Daz Studio for 2D presentational purposes. For working with realistic 3D human characters, Daz Studio Pro is a beginner's best friend.

Fuse 1.3 by Mixamo

https://www.mixamo.com/fuse

This is available for Windows and macOS.

Fuse is a modular 3D character creation tool. You combine various body parts to your liking, animate the character, and export to your game engine of choice. Fuse is a fine addition to your rapid development arsenal.

Fuse is an ambitious but somewhat troubled piece of software. The main desktop program used to create your characters is a free download. Now, to animate them, you need a free Adobe account on the Mixamo web site and upload your files there. You used to be limited to making two character animations per week on this free setup. You could break this limit by paying $50 for the service, but thankfully this business model is no more; animating is free for all since mid-2015.

Adobe has deemed Mixamo a worthwhile partner, and the quality of the product is indeed quite high. When it comes to the user interface, Fuse shines. It couldn't be much simpler: you are given dozens for choices for your character's head, torso, limbs, and clothes. Countless combinations are therefore available.

You can also tweak and fine-tune your character elements' shape to your heart's content. You do this by clicking and dragging on the several points of modification provided for each part of the character. Alternatively, you can adjust a rather large number of sliders—so large, in fact, that it might get slightly confusing at times operating them. There are buttons in the GUI, too, for randomizing the shape and size of both the individual elements of the character (e.g., legs or torso) and the entire character. You also have a choice of texture sizes ranging between a meager 64×64 to a more presentable 1024×1024. Some of the elements are provided with the option of high-resolution 2048×2048 textures. Fuse exports in the Wavefront format (.obj), which is supported by many popular game engines.

Although criticized for dropping support for a few additional output formats, Fuse offers exactly what it promises: fast and easy 3D character creation. In technical terms the models created with the software are quite impressive as well as being compatible with a wide range of game creator software.

Raiseland by David Manzanares Miguel

`http://raiselandsoft.com`

This is available for Windows and Linux.

Most serious 3D game creation tools have some type of terrain creation capabilities built in. However, developers are usually delighted if the game engine they use supports the importing of external terrains, as these can be designed more easily inside dedicated terrain creation software. Raiseland is one of these specialized programs, and it does offer much.

Basically, Raiseland operates with a very streamlined user interface. A collection of sliders control the height, type, and other properties of a terrain. The most important properties implemented are *amplitude* (terrain height scale), *frequency* (terrain width and depth scale), and *exponent* (terrain sharpness and uniformity). Simply adjusting these attributes is how you create some rather impressive terrains in Raiseland.

The program features some decent enough textures for you to work with, but you are encouraged to import your own in the PNG format in a square (i.e., 1:1) aspect ratio. Raiseland supports exporting height maps in the `.raw` format. The exported terrains can be used in Unity and Leadwerks, to name but two engines.

Raiseland is a so-called hybrid terrain creator. While it's powered by a procedural approach, it also allows some manual fine-tuning in real time where necessary. The design paradigm behind the software exhibits a nice sense of simplicity, allowing for a rapid workflow. You will become best of friends with the scroll wheel in your mouse. There is no typing to be done. The game-like WASD controls are also a pleasure to navigate the terrains with.

There are no apparent limitations when it comes to the size of the terrains in Raiseland. These are only set by the hardware you run the software in. But as you go, for bigger terrain sizes the program does turn down the detail level somewhat. Experiment and avoid overkill.

For previewing purposes only, Raiseland allows you to experiment with different lighting setups. In addition, fog and water are available inside the program too. Please note that how these elements of the terrain will ultimately look depend on the game engine you will be importing into; Raiseland will merely simulate them for you.

The software offers some impressive crater effects. This is achieved with a feature known as the *probability density function* (PDF). A set of sliders control the number of meteor-like impact craters on the surface of your land masses. These look great in any lunar/sci-fi terrains you might come up with.

In closing, Raiseland is a fine piece of software for its elegance and real-time nature. It does crash a few times, but it will work just fine 99 percent of the time. For an apparently one-person project, this is to be expected. If you are in need of highly detailed and vast landscapes for your games, you can no wrong by investing in Raiseland. Do remember to keep your terrain sizes under certain commonsense limits. While your system may be able to run them comfortably, your eventual audience could be using much more modest hardware.

CHAPTER 7

■ ■ ■

Selling Your Game

First, there's the thirst to create. Then, there's the process of making the game. Finally, the third (and perhaps the most unintuitive) act is selling that game. Let's take a look at what you need to know about the business by the time you're ready to go pro in games development.

To succeed in any business, you need an understanding of the fundamentals of marketing. Mentioned in countless business textbooks, the *four Ps* is an essential concept for you, too, as an indie developer. Here they are in no particular order: product, price, place, and promotion. All successful business owners need to understand how to properly approach these concepts to make it. I'll now go through all four of these magical Ps in detail.

Product

In the case of video games, there's less of the tangible to worry about than before when digital distribution wasn't a thing. Product packaging is mostly a concern for big-name AAA titles and special editions from smaller development teams. All this means more focus on the core product, which works to your advantage, saving time and other resources.

What you also need to focus on is the product life cycle. The four stages in a product's life are introduction, growth, maturity, and decline. Care must be taken to ensure your customers get updates to your projects. Digital distribution guarantees easy update delivery to your games. While focusing most resources on the introduction phase is a good idea, what follows is equally important for your brand reputation. The most overlooked stages in a game's life cycle are the two in the middle.

Price

Although there are many long-term strategies when it comes to pricing, in general there's only one motivation behind selling video games: making a modest to decent profit. You probably won't be doing a lot of social engineering with your product pricing, as might be the case with overpriced cigarettes and other hazardous products. Having said that, there are many creative short-term tactics to approach the pricing of your precious products with.

© Robert Ciesla 2017
R. Ciesla, *Mostly Codeless Game Development*, DOI 10.1007/978-1-4842-2970-5_7

Psychological Pricing

Prices ending in specific digits are more appealing to the masses. This is the case with the number nine, in particular. Simply put, a game that costs $0.99 is perceived as more tempting than one that costs $1, even though it's only 1 cent less. This is a universal technique, and there's no reason to not use it in your business, too. In part, it gives the impression of a bargain.

Penetration Pricing

A new business enters the market with lower-priced products than most (or all) of its direct competitors. This might secure a lot of brand awareness. Eventually, the business compensates for this initial cheapskate phase, possibly with a range of premium products. Quirky retro titles benefit from this pricing model when it comes to video games.

Honeymoon Pricing

This tactic is a variation on penetration pricing and is used in established businesses. A new game is introduced to the market with a low price point only to get more expensive after a while, perhaps after additional features are introduced into the product to justify the extra dollars.

Premium Pricing

Maintaining high prices enforces the idea of a business that sells superior products. It rarely works for humdrum products and should be used when the concept is so unique it isn't offered by many, if any, competitors. In the realm of video games, never-before-seen visual technology often warrants this price tag. Think *Call of Duty* or the *GTA* series of games.

Economy Pricing

When a business focuses on delivering low-end products on the cheap with minimal marketing costs, it is working from the economy pricing model. This is perhaps the best approach for low-end products with very few innovations in them. Think run-of-the-mill genre games or your average first-person shooter (FPS) or shoot-'em-up.

Product Bundling

Bundling games has always been a common approach in the world of games, and more so in the era of digital distribution. There's no harm in applying this concept to your marketing efforts. The idea of discounts is always appetizing to potential customers. Flexibility with product options only sweetens the deal from the customer's perspective. By offering several tiers of games or related assets (e.g., soundtracks), the buyer feels more comfortable making a payment. You don't even have to set rigid prices. Giving customers a degree of freedom by merely setting a minimum payment amount for your products usually works to your advantage. The very successful Humble Bundle online brand of game compilations isn't (and doesn't have to be) the only example of these approaches.

Free-to-Play (Also Pay-to-Win and Freemium)

An increasingly common approach for newcomers and established developers alike is to use a business model known as *free-to-play* and sometimes, mockingly, *pay-to-win*. This refers to releasing the core product as a free download, with the game having some more or less serious limitations. This usually includes providing players with rather lousy virtual equipment to fight their battles and saving the big guns for those willing to engage in microtransactions with actual dollars.

This business model has been criticized both for limiting the gameplay artificially unless payments are made and for shoving in-game add-ons down the players' throats. The free-to-play approach has also garnered criticism from angry parents whose offspring sometimes manages to spend thousands of dollars on virtual items.

Microtransactions

The purchase of virtual goods is generally referred to as *microtransactions*. They range from cosmetic aspects (i.e., new costumes for characters) to items that enhance functional gameplay aspects. Microtransactions are usually delivered through an in-app interface. Apple and Google provide their own frameworks for embedding these transactions into games. They both let developers keep 70 percent of any microtransactions they manage to sell.

Gamers hooked on a particular free-to-play game give game companies enormous amounts of money each year for virtual equipment. The total amount of virtual goods in the games industry was a colossal $15 billion in 2012, most of which came in from the Asia-Pacific markets.

Place (Distribution)

Let's now take a look at some viable alternatives for the distribution of your video games. All portals reviewed in this section offer nonexclusive contracts, meaning you can sell your product (or products) on competing platforms without issues.

Steam (steampowered.com)

For Windows, macOS, and Linux games.

Although briefly discussed in Chapter 1 of this book, it's time to remind you of probably the most lucrative method of video game distribution. Launched in 2003, Steam is a client-based software and media distribution system available for all major desktop platforms. As of mid-2017, Steam has some 12,000 titles on sale. Although Valve is tight-lipped about statistics, it's been estimated the store holds 70 percent of the digital distribution market share. The reach is, in a word, monumental.

Getting your titles on Steam isn't cheap, unfortunately. Steam Greenlight, implemented in 2012, asked for a one-time payment of $100 per developer to get their titles listed on the community voting system. Since June 2017, Greenlight was no more, replaced by Steam Direct. Under the new system, developers are required to pay $100 per title. Instead of a community vote, Valve does the judging, which might take up to 30 days. This does at least remove some of the bureaucracy from the proceedings. In addition to your precious funds, you'll be required to share your tax forms and other digital paperwork upon submitting your games.

Amazon Appstore (amazon.com/appstore)

For Android and BlackBerry games.

Online since 2011, the Amazon Appstore is among the most popular mobile app stores. Some 600,000 Android titles are available as of early 2017. The submission process is easy and best of all completely free. All you need to submit your games to the store is an Amazon developer account, which doesn't cost a thing. Developers receive 70 percent of revenue from their sold apps. In-app purchases are also supported by the portal. All games must simply adhere to the Amazon Appstore content policy requirements. These are pretty standard fare as far as content-related limitations are concerned; excessive violence and pornographic material are not well tolerated.

Amazon caters to Apple developers, too. Although the Amazon Appstore doesn't distribute software for iOS devices *per se*, iOS developers can still enjoy the benefits of various tried-and-tested Amazon solutions. You get to integrate services such as Amazon Drive and Amazon Mobile Ads into your iOS projects courtesy of Amazon, to name just two.

Amazon Digital Game Store (amazon.com/gamedownloads)

For Windows, macOS, and various console games.

Amazon has offered a way to sell downloadable games since 2009 for desktop computers. The store is still doing some good business. Amazon Digital Game Store provides distribution also for popular console platforms, including for the PlayStation and Xbox families of devices. The store uses the same application procedures and requirements as the Amazon Appstore.

Google Play (play.google.com)

For Android, ChromeOS, and online games.

In February 2017, Google Play had 2.7 million apps on sale, with the total number of downloads rapidly approaching 100 billion units. Like many of its competitors, Google Play offers developers 70 percent of revenue from their app sales. As of early 2017, developers may have also opted to sell their products at a discount for limited periods of time. The store supports both traditional installable apps and the more lightweight Android Instant Apps. There are some discovery tools on the store, such as automated personalized collections of software for fans of specific genres.

True to Google, the statistics on Play are quite detailed and rather formidable in their scope. The platform naturally supports Google's AdMob in-app advertisement service for extra income (and user annoyance) you may want to integrate into your games.

For a one-time fee of $25, a Google developer account and thus Google Play distribution are yours. All Android developers are advised to look into this service.

Apple App Store (apple.com)

For iOS games.

The Apple App Store has turned out to be a resounding success. Since its launch in the summer of 2008, the store has garnered well over 2 million titles. With a total of 140 billion downloaded apps as of late 2016, the platform definitely has a large reach. The most popular category in the store is games, so developers of mobile entertainment should make distribution on the Apple App Store a high priority.

The submission process to the App Store is a relatively painstaking one. It isn't quite as simple as uploading a file for Apple's approval. There are many steps to be taken before that, including both technical and content-related considerations. Thankfully, the turnaround is usually only a week or so for the average app.

A developer should look carefully into Apple's Human Interface Guidelines (HIG) way before the submission stage of their games. This is a set of guidelines for the look and feel of what Apple finds acceptable in its App Store content. Also, Apple takes software security very seriously. All distributed apps are expected to use sandboxing, which is a technique to provide a set of tightly controlled resources from the operating system instead of granting full access. Whatever apps Apple deems offensive are also a no-no. Pornographic or overtly political apps will not be well received.

Developers receive 70 percent from any App Store revenue. There are no file hosting fees, and Apple gladly handles all payment processing for you.

To submit an app to the Apple App Store, you first need to enroll in the Apple Developer Program for $99 per year. You also need access to a physical iOS device such as an iPhone and iPad. A digital iOS development certificate and an iOS distribution certificate are also needed to identify you, which you can generate from inside current versions of Xcode, Apple's free programming IDE. For Xcode and the certificates, you need a computer running a modern version of macOS. iTunes, primarily known as Apple's digital music software, can also be used to purchase and manage iOS apps.

Apple Mac App Store

For macOS games.

In addition to the distribution of iOS titles, Apple naturally provides for its sizable macOS clientele. The Mac App Store started its run in 2011 a few months before the release of macOS Lion. The store has been integrated into all versions of macOS from Snow Leopard version 10.6.6 onward.

The Apple Developer Program license ($99 per year) covers both the App Store for iOS and the Mac App Store. As you would expect, all software submitted to the Mac App Store must meet some rather stringent sets of requirements. The Apple Human Interface Guidelines still apply and so does the sandboxing requirement. Also, Mac App Store doesn't accept demo versions of games. The free-to-play approach is naturally acceptable (i.e., titles with in-game purchases are fine).

Both Apple App Stores use an online interface called iTunes Connect to provide content management tools for developers (https://itunesconnect.apple.com/login). User accounts on the system remain live even if the yearly Apple Developer Program license expires. However, the program membership is needed to update or upload apps.

Good Old Games (gog.com)

For Windows, macOS, and Linux games.

Specializing in older games like the name suggests, Good Old Games also offers newcomers some decent distribution possibilities. It introduces a lot of classic games for both the current Macintosh platform and modern Windows PCs. It used to be a hassle to get 1990s games running properly on newer machines, but GOG usually provides a fine experience in retro gaming with their pre-optimized games. A smaller platform with some 2,000 games as of 2017, Good Old Games is nonetheless a viable option for new developers with a dedicated staff behind it.

As for indies getting their first taste of digital distribution, the submission process is painless at GOG. For one, there's no submission fee. You simply fill out a submission form on the site, under Submit Your Game. You're asked to provide a gameplay video and enter some basic information about the game. Click Submit and wait. The GOG folks will respond rather promptly, often with constructive criticism. Soiree Games' first offering, *Office Quest*, didn't quite make the cut, but the team was met with tender words of advice and encouragement. Apparently toilet humor is not a major priority with GOG.

The best way to acquaint yourself with what Good Old Games is looking for is perhaps to visit the indie section on the web site. You'll see some classic independent titles such as *Don't Starve* and *Undertale*, and there's clearly room for creative titles in all genres. The pricing of these titles will also give you a hint on what your products might be worth on GOG.

In addition to a free submission process, GOG grants developers a decent marketing package in the form of social media exposure and banner graphics for a limited time.

Itch.io (www.itch.io)

For Windows, macOS, Linux, Android, and iOS games.

Itch.io is an increasingly popular distribution platform with more pros than cons. For one, there are no submission fees. Also, like Steam, the platform offers a desktop program for its customers to browse and purchase games with. You can even accept bitcoin for your games! The feature set of Itch.io is, in a word, splendid.

The platform uses a business model called *open revenue sharing*. Basically it means you, as the developer, get to decide both the price of your products and what percentage of your sales go to Itch.io. This amount ranges from 0 to 100 percent, with the default setting being 10 percent. Believe it or not, this is a great model for both developers and the service itself as is evident from its popularity. As of 2016, Itch.io was hosting well over 40,000 titles.

Itch.io offers free online web site storage for your projects with decent customization options. It doubles as a relatively hip web site for your efforts, but it doesn't offer much in the way of cool, custom e-mail addresses and the like. In addition to games, you may also sell pretty much any kind of digital products on the site, such as comics, music, and graphical assets. There's also a sizable amount of tools available for general use and for various game engines. The latter includes a keyboard shortcut extension for Unity and a particle editor for GameMaker Studio.

In closing, Itch.io is a pretty smart way to sell your products. With no up-front costs there's very little to lose. Take that, Steam.

Humble Store (humblestore.com)

For Windows, macOS, and Linux games.

Launched in 2013, Humble Store is an online distribution platform based on the Humble Bundles, which entered the fray in 2010. The concept was to promote indie games and donate part of the proceeds to charity. The Humble Bundles utilize a pay-what-you-want model requiring a minimum of just $1 for purchases. The more you pay, the more software you get in your bundle. Since 2010 the concept has made more than $65 million for 50 different charities, with the developers making a total of $100 million across 10 million or so customers.

The Humble Store uses a more traditional business model of a set price for its selection of games. Any indie can approach the store with offerings and potentially get some exposure next to AAA titles in the store. After 5 percent of processing fees, the revenue is split between 75 percent to developers, 10 percent to charity, and 15 percent to Humble Bundle.

Originally for video games only, Humble Store has expanded its business into e-books and comics. Since early 2017, the business has branched also into publishing on several platforms.

IndieGameStand (indiegamestand.com)

For Windows, macOS, and Linux games.

Starting out as the now-defunct crowdfunding platform 8-bit Funding, IndieGameStand offers a wide variety of indie games for the exact price of pay-what-you-want. A portion of the sales go to charity. Instead of bundled software, as is the case with Humble Bundle, the company showcases a new single game every 96 hours on the site.

IndieGameStand is definitely a low-risk option for distribution. There are no submission fees when uploading your games. Developers choose which charity receives a 10 percent donation per sale.

Playism (playism-games.com)

For Windows games.

Playism is an ambitious business that localizes and distributes games to the very big video game markets of Japan. Playism's publishing arm is impressive, spanning several PlayStation stores in Japan and several popular online stores in the English-speaking world. The latter include Steam, Good Old Games, Humble Bundle, Gamersgate, and Desura. If you score a deal with these guys, you are well and truly in business.

All of this comes understandably with a price, however. Playism's services are probably not for indie novices, but if you are seeking to break into the Japanese market later in your career, they are your best bet. Moreover, they don't seek AAA titles *per se*. They've worked with developers behind such runaway hits as *Papers Please* and *Dear Esther*, which is great news for the quirkier indies among us.

Promotion

A great game on its own is never enough. There are some additional materials a developer needs to make it in the business. Luckily, there are not a lot of these, and they can be attained with very little cost.

Web Site

You need an interesting, inviting web site for your games. You should approach your indie ventures as your future profession. Come up with a cool and memorable name for your business. There's something about the aura of a larger organization that reflects well on one's games.

Route A: Custom Domain and Hosting

This approach is most impressive to future employers, casual gamers, and their grandparents. First, you need to register a domain name (e.g., `www.happygames.com`) for your business. Introduce each game on this site as a microsite. This way you not only have a memorable website but also get your own custom e-mail address (e.g., `theresa@happygames.com`) too. Next, you require hosting for your site. In many cases, both domain registration and hosting are provided by the same businesses. These are some popular services:

- HostGator (`hostgator.com`)
- GoDaddy (`godaddy.com`)
- Dreamhost Web Hosting (`dreamhost.com`)

Now, if you are working on a ground-breaking game or you have no shortage of funds, you may want to register a domain on a single game basis (e.g., `www.mygreatgame.com`). This certainly draws more attention to your projects and makes them seem rather special. Make sure your web site is designed and tested to work well on mobile devices. Also, keep those gigantic image files in check. JPEG should be your format of choice.

There's no need to create a web site from scratch. There are plenty of great services offering solid frameworks for mobile-friendly web sites of any kind. Such solutions include the following:

- Bootstrap (`www.getbootstrap.com`)
- Foundation (`http://foundation.zurp.com/sites.html`)
- Wix (`http://wix.com`)

Route B: No Budget

Use free hosting for your business and games. Most edgy gamers don't really care how you host your products. Blogging platforms are therefore a worthwhile option for indie developers. Some of these free platforms include the following:

- Tumblr (`www.tumblr.com`)

- Wix (`www.wix.com`)

- Blogger (`www.blogger.com`)

- Medium (`www.medium.com`)

- Itch.io (`www.itch.io`)

Screenshots

Screenshots are a necessary part of your promotional campaign. Make sure you have at least ten interesting stills per game demonstrating all the core mechanics of your project. Include presentation screens if they are of high quality, but keep the focus on the game itself. Make that Print Screen key on Windows your friend. Cmd+Shift+3 works for Mac (or Cmd+Shift+4 if you want to grab a specific area on the screen). Store your screenshots in a place you can keep them easily organized.

Video Trailer

A video trailer is a must for your game. In this day and age it's virtually impossible to promote a game successfully in any genre without one. Also, gamer channels are very popular on sites such as YouTube and Twitch.tv. For this reason the Web is flooded with screen capture software, both free and commercial. The benefits of expensive video capture software are often exaggerated. Also, not every piece of software works equally well for everyone; much depends on your hardware profile.

Settle for nothing less than smooth 60 fps capture in at least HD resolution (1280×720). Do keep in mind a lot of video capture success also depends on the software settings. Experiment with different formats. Don't try to capture video while other programs are running in the background; shut them down first. If you still get stutter or screen artifacts, it's time to try different software or invest in a more powerful hardware, especially when it comes to your video card or CPU.

The online world is increasingly a world of video. Both major video card brands, Nvidia and AMD, are very much aware of this and are doing their best with their own cost-free offerings. The Nvidia Geforce Experience software suite contains a video capture feature called simply Share. It provides reliable, stutter-free screen capture even on average systems. AMD released its Radeon ReLive screen-sharing software in early 2017 to great acclaim. Depending on your video card, you could do a lot worse than capture with either of these programs. Nvidia's and AMD's software offerings are naturally highly optimized for their respective hardware platform. However, double-check that your video card drivers are up-to-date before clicking Record.

Other popular video capture software includes MSI Afterburner, which doubles as a video card overclocking suite, and Open Broadcaster Software (OBS). Both of these programs work with a wide assortment of video cards.

Social Media

There's no question current social media services have a massive worldwide reach. The literally billions of combined users of Facebook, Twitter, and YouTube get bombarded with content every single minute of the day. A lot of that content, especially from newcomers to those platforms, is understandably ignored. You should still want to put yourself out there in these crowded social media platforms because they are both free and it can lead to a variety of opportunities.

Your comments and tweets are your calling cards on social media. To get your foot in a potential customer's (or collaborator's) door, participate in the debates at hand. Like, comment, and subscribe. Target your original content at those who are most likely to be interested. In your case it's gamers, game developers, and related technology buffs.

On Facebook, there are quite a few major indie-friendly groups you should engage with. These include Indie Game Developers Public Group, Indie Game Promo, and GameDev Beginners, to name but three. YouTube has countless channels dedicated to the subject. Twitter has hashtags related to indie games emerging on a constant basis, such as #IndieGameInitiative and variations on #indiegames. These are all fine tools of promotion available for you, for free.

Many indie games share traits with software in the world of retro gaming. The charm and aesthetics of 1980s and 1990s video games are definitely a thing. Therefore, it pays to network with this branch of the online community if your output can be considered retro-ish to at least some degree.

Invest yourself into the proceedings as a personality. Always network offline as well to whichever degree you're comfortable with. Use social media not only to advertise your games but to share behind-the-scenes stories and shed light on the decisions you make as a developer.

Now, make sure you familiarize yourself with the following tidbits of social media know-how:

- Have all of your social media profiles share a unified visual theme and company logo.

- Join as many groups as you can on every platform made specifically for indie games developers.

- Always respond politely even if approached by asinine individuals on social media.

- When posting, use good grammar and punctuation, but don't be boring.

- Be quirky with your posts; never sound like a head of marketing at work.

- Be more than just a business name; it's about *your* games, *your* face, and *your* personality.

- Cross-link your social media content thoroughly.

- Do not waste time uploading your material to unpopular social media platforms; obscurity rarely helps.

- Here are indie-friendly keywords for all media: *indie, game dev, retro, arcade games, digital distribution.*

In-Game Advertising (IGA)

According to *Forbes* magazine, in-game advertising generated more than $7 billion in revenue in 2016. Many free-to-play games usually feature several types of in-game advertising from splash screens to banner ads. IGA has the benefits of being both engaging and highly targetable, based on properties such as customer age group and location. Actual product placement, while very lucrative in both movie and video games, is usually not a realistic option for indie developers. Some more palatable advertising solutions for indie mobile apps include the free-to-use AdMob by Google and the Singapore-based InMobi.

Festivals

If you have an innovative product to promote, indie game festivals are among the best ways to do it. The competition, however, is stiff and the placement space limited. Still, if you have the money for a couple of submission fees, you might want to hand it over to an indie-friendly games convention. For best results, you should study past winners at each festival and see how your projects measure against them.

Indiecade (indiecade.com)

- 2017 venue: Culver City, California

- Submission fees in 2017: $95 regular, $140 late

Founded in 2005, Indiecade offers promotional opportunities for budding indie developers. It's open to the public, and indies are encouraged to submit their games to the jury. A few dozen titles are featured at the festival each year. The main exhibition takes place in a so-called GameWalk, which consists of a series of improvised galleries in downtown Culver. This is a free event for the public. There are several other events as well under the Indiecade auspices, such as the GameSlam, which offers developers 90 seconds of pitch time in front of a live audience. Past titles featured at Indiecade include *Rollers of the Realm* in 2013, *iO* in 2014, and *1979 Revolution: Black Friday* in 2016.

Independent Game Festival (igf.com)

- 2017 venue: San Francisco, California

- Submission fees in 2017: $75 regular, $25 for students

The Independent Game Festival (IGF) is the largest annual gathering of the indie games industry. Open to developers worldwide and founded in 1998, IGF is offering more than $50,000 in prize money to its participants in 2017. The Seumas McNally Grand Prize is worth $30,000 alone. The prize was named after the programmer behind *Tread Marks* (a winning title of three IGF awards), who sadly passed away in 2000. Past winning entries of the grand prize include *Darwinia* in 2006, *Minecraft* in 2011, and *Papers, Please* in 2014. There are also categories for browser games, technical excellence, and narrative. The IGF audience prize, worth $3,000, has been given to titles such as *FTL: Faster Than Light* in 2013 and *Undertale* in 2016.

Assembly Summer (assembly.org)

- 2016 venue: Helsinki, Finland

- Submission fees in 2017: 80 to 115 euros, depending on the seating

A place of pilgrimage for Nordic nerds, Assembly has been around since 1992 to uphold demoscene technical excellence. The term *demoscene* refers to a computer art subculture. Perhaps Finland's finest ever export, Assembly has been split between Summer and Winter editions since 2007, with the wintery gathering focusing on e-sports. While primarily for noninteractive technical presentations (i.e., demos), Assembly Summer also caters to indie game developers and is worth a shot.

Business and Finance

Game development may start out as a hobby, but eventually you are likely to want to make a living out of what you enjoy doing best. Whenever money and transactions are in the picture, it pays to know what you're talking about somewhat. Let's go through some fundamental concepts of business next.

Return on Investment (ROI)

ROI measures the amount of return on an investment relative to the cost. To calculate ROI, the benefit of an investment is divided by the cost of the investment, and the result is expressed as a percentage. So, the formula for return on investment is as follows:

$$ROI = (Benefit - Cost) / Cost$$

It's time for an example. If you buy 30 shares of Soiree Games for $11 a share, your investment cost is $330. If you sell those shares for $420, then your ROI is ($420 - 330)/$330 for a total of 0.27, or 27 percent.

Economies of Scale/Economies of Scope

Economies of scale refer to the *cost advantages* that a business can exploit by focusing on their production output. The effect of economies of scale is to reduce the average product unit costs. Think of a development house pushing out 99-cent games in large numbers. They have all the basic building blocks of creating an immense number of these games after producing just a handful of these titles. Such a business embodies the philosophy of economies of scale.

Economies of scope, on the other hand, refer to product diversity or benefiting from outsourcing company functions. This approach refers to releasing products in different price ranges or on different platforms. Economies of scope also arise from cooperation between businesses; a development house may gain the means of outsourcing part of their production process such as marketing or conversions to different platforms or to other specialized businesses. Other examples of economies of scope are product bundling and diverse distribution chains.

Securities

A security is any tradable financial asset, such as banknotes (i.e., cash), bonds, or stocks.

Securities and Exchange Commission (SEC)

The SEC is an agency of the U.S. federal government granted with the responsibilities of proposing federal securities laws and enforcing these laws. The SEC came into existence in 1934 in the aftermath of Black Thursday, the stock market crash of 1929. Basically the SEC is there to hold companies accountable on the nature of their business and the risks in investing in them. The SEC becomes relevant to your business, too, when your stocks hit the exchange.

Nonaccredited Investor

This is an investor who does not meet the net worth requirements for an accredited investor as defined by the SEC. A nonaccredited individual investor is one who has a net worth of less than $1 million, including a spouse, and who earned less than $200,000 annually ($300,000 with spouse) in the last two years.

Accredited Investor

To be an accredited investor, a person must have an annual income of $200,000 (or $300,000 for joint income) for the last two years. An individual must have earned income above the thresholds either alone or with a spouse over the last three years.

Crowdfunding

A lot of smaller-scale projects are funded with a bedroom model, i.e., a single individual working on his or her games in their spare time. While a lot of successful titles have been created using this approach since the 1970s, it's not the only option for funding your projects.

Crowdfunding is an increasingly popular method of securing adequate financial resources for your games. Pay attention to your local laws and terms of service for each platform as they may or may not be compatible. Let's take a look at some of the more popular crowdfunding solutions.

Kickstarter (kickstarter.com)

Project creation available to citizens of the following countries only: the United States, the United Kingdom, Canada, Australia, New Zealand, the Netherlands, Denmark, Ireland, Norway, Sweden, Germany, France, Spain, Italy, Austria, Belgium, Switzerland, Luxembourg, Hong Kong, Singapore, and Mexico.

Since its inception in 2009, Kickstarter has garnered a hefty $1.9 billion in project donations from nearly 10 million supporters. As of 2017, roughly a quarter of a million creative projects have been featured on the site. These include movies, music, hardware projects, and video games. Top projects make millions on this platform. Currently, the undisputed king of Kickstarter projects is *Star Citizen*, a video game by Chris Roberts of *Wing Commander* fame. Roberts has made a staggering $140 million for his team's efforts, and the funding is still ongoing.

Kickstarter operates on the principle of all-or-nothing. The developers set a specific financial goal for the project, and if that goal is never reached, nobody pays a thing. This approach is less risky for both developers and their audience. In addition, it provides potentially more word-of-mouth advertising, as the backers usually want to see the funding behind their project of choice reach its goal. Many developers provide additional incentives in the form of special rewards for donations. These include, naturally, the finished product in question (if feasible) as well as related merchandise or customized items.

There are three simple rules to qualify your project for crowdfunding on Kickstarter: creators can fund projects only, all projects must fit within one of the site's 13 creative categories, and creators must abide by the site's prohibited uses. Charity or investment projects are not allowed. Also, heavily regulated or potentially dangerous items (such as weapons or drugs) cannot receive funding in Kickstarter. Projects of the offensive kind are often discarded. Try to be politically correct with these guys. The service takes 5 percent in fees for all successful projects. In addition, free processing removes another 3 to 5 percent.

Of course, while all developers appreciate millions, even more modest amounts of crowdfunding cash can make all the difference in helping newcomers get their games off the ground. Such indie hits as *Faeria*, *Undertale*, and *FTL: Faster Than Light* all received considerable financial gains from Kickstarter. Dozens of indie developers have benefited from leveraging the community on the site. In short, there's very little to lose in trying out this route of financing.

Fig (fig.co)

While Kickstarter offers more or less a general-purpose platform for crowdfunding, Fig is a specialized service working solely in the domain of video games. Established in 2015, Fig offers not only the typical crowdfunding experience for pledgers but an actual cut of the revenue once the game is released. Revenue shares are meant for anyone who invests a minimum of $1,000 in a project. The SEC has approved of Fig's revenue shares in late 2016. Investing is optional for all projects, and Fig is perfectly happy with the established crowdfunding approach of public pledging. Naturally, the amount of general community support a title generates helps potential investors assess the risk involved.

Fig takes a curated, restricted approach to crowdfunding. The focus is on quality and overall viability of projects. This has translated into a much bigger success rate than its competitors. Some completed campaigns on Fig include *Psychonauts 2* by Double Fine Productions, which made an impressive $3.8 million, and *Outer Wilds* by Mobius Digital, which took in more than $126,000.

The company also has a Fig Finishing Fund, which aims to help with the costs of successfully backed projects should they have any late-stage budgeting hurdles to overcome. For this purpose alone Fig has budgeted $500,000 in 2017. Projects qualified for the fund receive up to $20,000 each.

Fig is a brave attempt at tackling the rather overpopulated scene of crowdfunding by careful curation and allocation of resources. The business has made a great track record for such a new company; clearly their approach works. Fig is perhaps best suited for more established game developers with some success already looking to take their projects to the next level.

Indiegogo (indiegogo.com)

Project creation available to citizens of most countries except Iran, Syria, Sudan, North Korea, and Cuba.

As of 2017 Indiegogo has raised more than $1 billion for well over 200,000 projects in various categories. An all-purpose crowdfunding service, Indiegogo has been around since 2008, launching also many successful indie game projects during its continuing run. The site receives roughly 15 million visitors each month. These include *StarForge* by CodeHatch and a remake of the classic *FPS System Shock* by Night Dive Studios.

Kickstarter and Indiegogo are obviously the two top crowdfunding platforms for newcomers in the indie game world. However, Kickstarter has a stronger track record in amassing more funds for its video game campaigns. On the other hand, Indiegogo is more lenient about reaching your crowdfunding goals. Unlike Kickstarter, the platform has an option called *flexible funding*, which means you get to keep pledged funds even if the goal amount is not met. Another feature called InDemand allows the public donate to your campaign even after the campaign end date. This type of flexibility is exactly what good crowdfunding is all about.

Kickstarter is a bigger platform overall but not quite as flexible. Indiegogo's terms of service are not as strict as those of Kickstarter, allowing for political, religious, and environmental campaigns. In addition to for-profit crowdfunding, Indiegogo offers a platform for charitable purposes called Generosity.com.

Gambitious (gambitious.com)

Seeing the light of day in 2011, Gambitious is a Dutch video game publisher and a crowdfunding platform. The company offers developers the support of accredited investors in exchange for game revenue shares. Gambitious and their investors had their break with *Train Fever* by Urban Games in 2014, a business simulation game, which has sold more than 140,000 copies so far. Starting out with an investment option first, the company has since expanded into more open types of crowdfunding.

Like Fig, Gambitious is a curated platform, set on correcting the overpopulated world of crowdfunding. There don't seem to be any limitations as to the genre of supported video games at Gambitious. The company has had success with every game it has funded, with four of the first six titles delivering profits in the first month following release. Because of the selective nature of Gambitious, it may be a platform for developers with previous successes in the video game industry or a game with a killer concept. But if you get your foot in the Gambitious door, you can probably expect a lot of dedication and resources for your efforts.

CHAPTER 8

■ ■ ■

Knowing Your Old-School Games

The challenge of history is to recover the past and introduce it to the present.

—David Thelen, historian

In this chapter you'll take a detailed look at some of the most successful and historically significant gaming computers and consoles in chronological order of release. Each system will be presented with its biggest selling points at the time of its entry into the market. I'll focus on the early days of gaming, during which history was made and pioneers ruled the day, specifically, the exciting and dramatic era that spanned from 1977 to 2001.

In 1977 the Atari 2600 was introduced. During its 15-year production run, the console became the epitome of the 8-bit era and thus a building block for the ensuing 16-bit era—and beyond. The 2600 even went on to survive the Great Video Game Crash of 1983, an industry disaster of monumental proportions.

In 2001 Microsoft's Xbox was released to great acclaim. This heralded both the beginning of Microsoft's multibillion-dollar *Halo* franchise and the giant's entry into the console market with a technologically superior product.

The platforms presented in this chapter were primarily chosen for their historical importance. Some bias was admittedly present in choosing which systems to showcase. This bias extends to the selection of important games for each platform as well. And although all of these systems had a ton of accessories made for them in the form of light guns, steering wheels, and other such exotic devices, I won't be focusing on any of these gadgets. Also, for the sake of brevity I won't cover portable game consoles.

The games for these systems have in most cases sold millions or even hundreds of millions of copies on a global scale. These older platforms have all obviously contributed to the video game mechanics and aesthetics we enjoy today. Also, some of these gaming platforms continue to live on in current times, either as game franchises originating on them or as actual manufactured hardware as in the case of some of the Sega and Nintendo consoles.

A successful entrepreneur focuses not only on the present or the future; they are familiar with past innovation. Please try each one of the important games listed in this chapter, preferably on the original hardware (although free emulation software is plentiful). Let the past inspire your present. What worked in the past still works today.

© Robert Ciesla 2017
R. Ciesla, *Mostly Codeless Game Development*, DOI 10.1007/978-1-4842-2970-5_8

1977

Atari 2600

- Sold more than 30 million units.

- Best-selling game for the system: *Pac-Man* from 1982. Sold more than 7 million copies.

As all those generic and simplistic *Pong* consoles faded into obscurity, 1977 saw Atari launch one of the most successful gaming systems to date. For one, the system had impressive visuals for the times, and the cartridge-based delivery format was fast-loading and durable. Also, the controller that shipped with the 2600, the Atari Joystick, became a somewhat revered piece of industrial design.

The Atari 2600 Jr. was released in 1986 as a budget version of the original (see Figure 8-1).

Figure 8-1. *The Atari 2600 Jr.*

Spanning three decades, the 2600 had a software library of about 600 games and continues to live even in 2017 in the so-called home-grown segment. Many a games enthusiast is working on an Atari 2600 title as you read this, some of them quite impressive in both technical and gameplay-related terms.

Like any system, the 2600 had to have both huge successes and massive failures during such a long run. Those iconic, timeless classics are what made the machine thrive: *Pac-Man, Space Invaders, Missile Command*, and one of my favorite games of all time, *H.E.R.O.* by Activision. Even in the 1990s, the little Atari wonder churned out decent titles, including *Klax, Pick 'n Pile,* and *Xenophobe*.

Of course, there is the little disaster called *E.T.* for the 2600, a game some consider one of the worst ever made. Another one called *A-Team* actually made your 2600 cry a little. These titles demonstrated the power of licensed games. Developers even then knew a title from popular culture sells, even if you stick it on a reprehensible product. Naturally, in modern times, most developers abhor such a practice.

Here are some important games:

- *H.E.R.O.* (1984) by Activision
- *Pitfall 2: The Lost Caverns* (1984) by Activision
- *Solaris* (1983) by Atari
- *Pitfall!* (1982) by Activision
- *River Raid* (1982) by Activision

This is the worst game on the system and perhaps the entire galaxy (as per popular opinion):

- *E.T.* (1982) by Atari

1982

Atari 5200

- Sold a meager 1 million units

While its predecessor, the 2600, enjoyed a lengthy 15-year commercial life span, the Atari 5200 went on for just two (see Figure 8-2). In a word, the Atari 5200 was a flop. The reasons for this were numerous: poor controllers, bulky externals, and games that didn't utilize new hardware to its full being perhaps the biggest culprits. Discontinued in 1984, the 5200 nonetheless provided the video game community with some valuable lessons. Of these, the biggest is without a doubt this: make sure your products have zero controller issues. This goes for both hardware manufacturers and game developers at any level.

Figure 8-2. *Atari 5200*

Instead of originality, Atari opted to encourage predictability with 5,200 titles. The system received (only slightly) visually updated versions of arcade and Atari 2600 classics. These included titles like *Breakout, Defender,* and *H.E.R.O.* Again, many of these games failed to impress audiences. The graphics chip wasn't revolutionary compared to the 2600, but it was much more capable. Another lesson this failed system taught us is this: make sure you make the most of available hardware.

Here are some important games:

- *Ballblazer* (1986) by Lucasfilm Games

- *Rescue on Fractalus* (1984) by Lucasfilm Games/Atari

- *Robotron: 2084* (1983) by Atari

- *Frogger* (1983) by Sega

- *Zaxxon* (1982) by Sega

Commodore 64

- Sold more than 20 million units.

- Best-selling game for the system: *The Last Ninja 2* from 1988. Sold more than 5.5 million copies.

The Commodore 64 is a much-loved computer that dominated the markets during the 1980s in America and abroad (see Figure 8-3). A versatile beast, the Commodore 64 used at least three types of data formats for storage. You had floppy disks, cartridges, and—of course—cassettes to load your software from. The tape-based format was notorious for taking an eon to load a game (as in, say, 20 minutes) only for a corrupted screen to appear where the game should've been. Back to square one. Good times.

Figure 8-3. *Commodore 64*

It can be safely said that no other computer system had as big of an influence on the entire home computer game scene as the Commodore 64. Dozens of trends can be traced on the machine. One of these has to do with the unique sound generation chip in the Commodore 64, or the *sound interface device* (SID) as it's more commonly known. Providing three simultaneous voices and a ton of different tones, the chip is a surprisingly capable one. That chic "8-bit sound" still prevalent in many new indie games is probably inspired by the SID music in thousands of Commodore 64 games played by electronic musicians in their youth.

The Commodore 64 era lasted from 1982 to around 1993. That's more than a decade of great, memorable games and superior 8-bit aesthetics. Best suited for arcade games, the Commodore 64 struggled with 3D games, but some attempts were made in that style.

There was an element of stubbornness with many Commodore 64 developers. They simply refused to yield in front of seemingly unsurpassable technical obstacles.

One of the most ambitious 3D titles for the system was *Elite* by Ian Bell and David Braben in 1984. A conversion from the BBC Micro computer version, the C64 Elite was a space shooter and stock market simulation rolled into one. Players would roam a black-and-white wireframe galaxy in search for goods, trade them for profit, and fire a few lasers along the way. A massive hit on all systems, *Elite* went on to spawn several sequels. The latest, the highly acclaimed *Elite Dangerous*, was released for modern platforms in 2014.

Here are some important games:

- *Outrun Europa* (1991) by U.S. Gold

- *Turrican* (1989) by Rainbow Arts

- *Paradroid* (1987) by Hewson

- *Elite* (1984) by Ian Bell and David Braben

- *Archon* (1983) by Electronic Arts

1983
Nintendo Entertainment System (NES)

- Sold more than 61 million units.

- Best-selling game for the system: *Super Mario Bros* from 1985. Sold more than 40 million copies.

The Nintendo Entertainment System is an iconic piece of hardware with an amazing library of games (see Figure 8-4). It is quite simply the Stratocaster guitar of game consoles. Many things were overlooked with the unit, such as the oft-flickering sprites, a garish palette of color, a rather feeble sound generator, and the most pain-inducing controller pad of all time (with its razor-sharp edges and pollex-destroying ergonomics). What pushed the NES out of the junkyard of mediocre electronics was an Italian plumber, one Mario, and the numerous titles based on his escapades. The success of the *Mario Bros* franchise alone made Nintendo a household name. Running and jumping had never been as fun.

Figure 8-4. Nintendo Entertainment System

The Mario story is an important one for several reasons. First, the level of violence in the games is negligible. Second, perhaps *Tetris* aside, *Super Mario Bros* is a series of games that take the basic mechanics of gameplay very seriously. The graphics, while decent, are functional at best. Instead, the emphasis is on fluid controls and a greater degree of flexibility in the era of rigid, maze-like game mechanics.

Here are some important games:

- *Contra* (1988) by Konami

- *Super Mario Bros 2* (1988) by Kensune Tanabe and Shigeru Miyamoto

- *Megaman* (1987) by Capcom

- *The Legend of Zelda* (1986) by Shigeru Miyamoto and Takashi Tezuka

- *Super Mario Bros* (1985) by Shigeru Miyamoto

The Great Video Game Crash of 1983

Pretty much the Black Tuesday of the video game industry, the Great Video Game Crash of 1983 hit several console platforms hard. The most affected brands included Atari, ColecoVision, and Odyssey. A sharp decline in revenue began in 1983, reaching its low in 1985, a two-year period of time during which the scene permanently changed. The market was simply over-saturated with both consoles and their games, and there were fewer and fewer hit products. Also, some stiff competition began between gaming consoles and personal computers. The latter stepped on the former's territory, providing not only business applications but games as well. The then-current consoles were simply becoming obsolete. As a result, revenues fell from $3.1 billion in 1983 to a mere $100 million in 1985. Tons of unsold game cartridges were dumped in deserts, and more and more customers walked home with a hip PC under their arm.

Many console brands went bankrupt during these dark years. ColecoVision never recovered and folded in 1985. Yet there were strong survivors. For Atari, one of the biggest lifeboats during the storm was in its line of personal computers: the Atari 400 and 800 in particular. Nintendo pulled through mostly on the strength of its game franchises such as *Super Mario* and *Donkey Kong*.

1985
Commodore Amiga

- Sold approximately 5 million units.

- Best-selling game for the system: *Lemmings* from 1990. Sold more than half a million copies.

Launching Commodore's 16-bit era, the Amiga range was an audiovisually sophisticated piece of hardware, favored by creative people and gamers alike. Notable users included Andy Warhol, who loved demonstrating the visual power of the machine. Graphical qualities aside, the Amiga line was a great computer for sound production and desktop publishing. Being easy to expand, the Amiga could pretty much do it all.

The line started out with the Amiga 1000 in 1985. However, the most popular 16-bit Commodore turned out to be the more compact Amiga 500, released in 1987 (see Figure 8-5). After a few more models, such as the abhorrent Amiga 600 and the rather wonderful Amiga 1200 (which sadly entered the game far too late to make a difference), Commodore folded in 1994. The company's last-ditch effort was the Commodore CD32, a CD-based game console. Very much up to the task even considering the competition from Sega and Nintendo, the console was based on the last-generation Amigas but unfortunately failed to reinvigorate the Commodore brand.

Figure 8-5. *The Amiga 500 Plus from 1991*

While never selling by the dozens of millions, the Amiga line was nonetheless a popular platform over the course of its life. The secret to its success was both in its (for the time) superior hardware as well as in the multitude of uses it provided. From a games machine to a more or less serious audio-recording workstation, the Amiga handled most tasks with ease, especially after some hardware upgrades.

Some of the best 2D games of the 1990s came out on the Amiga platform. The hardware was capable of relatively fast 3D as well, but a main bulk of the game software came strictly in two dimensions. The Amigas did more for pixel art than any other system. A color palette of 16 was often preferred by graphics people operating the hardware. This, combined with a rather fine resolution of 320×256 pixels (in the European models), led to the development of some beautiful hand-drawn antialiasing and dithering techniques. Software houses such as Psygnosis and The Bitmap Brothers utilized every speck of the Amiga's audiovisual prowess, constantly pushing the envelope. Also, one of the most successful puzzle game franchises of all time, *Lemmings,* started its life as a Psygnosis game on the Amiga. The green-haired simpletons eventually made it to most systems of the era, including the Sega Genesis, Super Nintendo, and the PC Engine. The latest *Lemmings* game appeared on the PlayStation Vita portable console in 2014.

Here are some important games:

- *Turrican II* (1991) by Rainbow Arts

- *Lemmings* (1991) by Psygnosis

- *Paradroid 90* (1990) by Graftgold

- *Xenon 2 Megablast* (1989) by Bitmap Brothers

- *Starglider 2* (1988) by Argonaut Software

Atari ST

- Sold approximately 3 million units.

- Best-selling game for the system: *Lemmings* from 1990. Sold more than half a million copies.

The Atari ST series of computers went neck and neck with its main competitor, the Commodore Amiga, getting introduced and perishing at the same time (see Figure 8-6). The hardware was quite similar, with both systems having a Motorola CPU. Both platforms had strong followings among hobbyists as well as some segments of the creative industry. The main difference between the STs and Amigas was in the audiovisual capabilities, with the Commodore offering more powerful audio and video chips.

Figure 8-6. *The Atari 1040ST. Image © Bill Bertram 2006. Used under CC-BY-2.5 license.*

Although the Atari ST had pretty much an obsolete sound generator (dating from 1978 no less), the machine came with two MIDI ports out of the box. MIDI was, and is, a very desirable technology among musicians. In 1985 it was pretty much unheard of to have this functionality in a home computer without expensive upgrades. Many ST models still work relatively well for music creation purposes. In fact, the Atari MIDI controller is considered one of the most reliable even today and prized by many musicians.

The ST fared well in the games department, too. One of the most iconic role-player games (RPGs) of all time, *Dungeon Master,* debuted on the system in 1987. It's estimated this game alone sold more than 100,000 copies during its run.

Soon after its release, games in all genres, from flight simulators to simple arcade games, began to appear on the ST in earnest. Eventually the games library for the system reached well into the thousands, making the ST a veritable games machine.

Here are some important games:

- *Frontier: Elite 2* (1993) by Gametek/Konami

- *Midwinter 2: Flames of Freedom* (1991) by Microprose

- *Gauntlet 2* (1988) by U.S. Gold

- *Falcon* (1988) by Spectrum Holobyte

- *Dungeon Master* (1987) by FTL

1986

Sega Master System

- Sold more than 18 million units and counting, thanks to Brazilian Sega fans.

- Best-selling game for the system: *Sonic the Hedgehog* from 1991. Sold more than 6 million copies.

Relatively late in the game, Sega introduced the Master System to America in 1986 (see Figure 8-7). An 8-bit console, it was naturally created to butt heads with the NES. The graphics hardware, for one, was superior compared to the competition. You simply won't find as many games with feeble sound and flickering sprites in the Master System library.

Figure 8-7. *Sega Master System*

Bundled with the modest shooter *Safari Hunt* and the far better racing game *Hang-On*, the Master System was released to modest acclaim. However, Sega did manage to find more success with its 8-bit platform a couple of years later. Conversions of popular arcade games, such as *R-Type* and *Space Harrier*, did contribute to the Master System eventually becoming a console to be reckoned with. The system's technical edge made sure these conversions were usually better than the ones Nintendo came up with.

Most people, whether into video games or not, know exactly to whom Super Mario refers to. The same can't be said for Alex Kidd, can it? Designed to be the Master System's Mario, the *Alex Kidd* series of games were fine run 'n' jumpers. They did everything except deliver Sega a mascot. To fill the mascot void, Sega released the *Wonderboy* series of games for the platform. A popular enough franchise on its own merit, *Wonderboy*, too, failed to become a household name.

The Master System received a massive shot in the arm in 1991 in the form of *Sonic the Hedgehog*. The franchise is still going strong in 2017 with new games appearing every so often on newer platforms, including in the mobile world. Sonic, a blue anthropomorphic hedgehog, also makes for some great fan merchandise and spin-offs. However, even a strong, memorable character may not be enough to stay in the lead in the video game industry. You often also need a technological gimmick, and in Sonic's case it was the then unheard of speed of the proceedings, combined with some smooth scrolling, even on these older systems. Sega bounced back, big time, and on to new heights. The Sonic franchise is its definitive contribution to game development strategy.

The Sega Master System was officially scrapped in 1992. Interestingly, the console continues to be commercially viable in 2017, perhaps now more than ever. The platform is still profitable in Brazil, a fairly large market of more than 200 million potential customers. Manufactured by *Tectoy*, the Brazilian Master System comes bundled with more than 100 games, making for a cheap console with an instant library of fine titles. The annual sales of this "new" Master System were estimated at around 100,000 in 2015, making it about as popular as PlayStation 4.

Here are some important games:

- *Sonic the Hedgehog* (1991) by Naoto Ōshima, Yūji Naka, and Hirokazu Yasuhara

- *Operation Wolf* (1990) by Taito

- *Wonderboy III: The Dragon's Trap* (1989) by Westone

- *California Games* (1989) by Sega

- *Alex Kidd in Miracle World* (1987) by Kotaro Hayashida

Atari 7800

- Sold approximately 3.5 million units

A successor to the failed 5200 and the last third-generation Atari console, the 7800 had some serious potential (see Figure 8-8). As was the case for the Sega Master System, the graphics chip in the Atari 7800 was superior to the one in the NES, the market leader at the time. Originally slated to be released in 1984, the 7800 was shelved for two years because of changes in ownership. New CEO Jack Tramiel wanted to carefully re-assess all Atari hardware prior to release.

Figure 8-8. *The Atari 7800. © Adam Jenkins 2010. Used under CC-BY-2.0 license.*

Wisely, Atari decided to capitalize on the (back then) ongoing success of its 1977 console, the 2600. In addition to supporting that platform on its own merit, Atari also made the 7800 nearly 100 percent compatible with 2600 game cartridges. This guaranteed a massive library of hundreds of titles for the new console at launch.

Unlike its predecessor, the 5200, the Atari 7800 utilized its enhanced visual capabilities to their fullest in many titles. The only technical flaw with the Atari 7800 was in its sound capabilities. The units used the same audio chip as the original Atari 2600, which even by the standards of 1986 was inadequate. In many cases, the 7800 sound is best enjoyed silent.

Despite the hardware's potential, the 7800 sadly never caught on as the next big Atari machine. The sales were rather lukewarm, with fewer than 4 million units sold, despite the decent games library. The 7800 will mostly be remembered as Atari's reaction to the failure that was the 5200.

Here are some important games:

- *Midnight Mutants* (1990) by Atari

- *Ninja Golf* (1990) by BlueSky Software

- *Alien Brigade* (1990) by Atari

- *Tower Toppler/Nebulus* (1988) by Atari

- *Pole Position II* (1984) by Atari (the game sat on the shelf for two years prior to release)

1987
PC Engine (Turbografx-16) by NEC Corporation

- Sold approximately 5.8 million units

The mighty PC Engine was a unique 8-bit console with a lot going for it (see Figure 8-9). Released during the 16-bit era, the platform was able to compete directly with more modern hardware. Part of this was because of the hybrid nature of its inner workings. While the CPU in the unit was 8-bit, PC Engine had not one but *two* 16-bit graphics processing units. For comparison, the Sega Master System, a fellow 8-bit console, could muster a maximum of 32 colors on-screen at once, while PC Engine could output an impressive 482 colors. This was rather unheard of back in the day and resulted in a console that could deliver very accurate ports of arcade games onto the little screens at home.

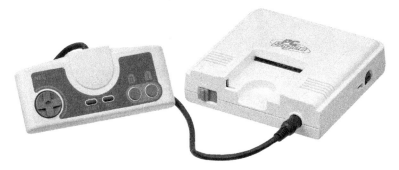

Figure 8-9. *PC Engine*

The audio capabilities of PC Engine were on par with the graphics chips in the console, meaning they were vastly superior to both NES and the Master System. The console was capable of generating both impressive synthesized and sampled audio like a beast, strengthening its technical edge over the other 8-bit consoles. Unfortunately, none of this technological prestige helped challenge the sales of either NES or Sega's Master System, which combined went on to sell some 79 million units. PC Engine ended up shipping a mere 5.8 million consoles. The console did manage to gather an impressive games library for itself.

Here are some important games:

- *Air Zonk* (1992) by Red Company/Hudson Soft
- *Parasol Stars* (1991) by Working Designs
- *Bomberman* (1990) by Hudson Soft
- *Bonk's Adventure* (1989) by Hudson Soft
- *Military Madness* (1989) by Hudson Soft

1988
Sega Genesis (Megadrive)

- Sold more than 35 million units—and counting.

- Best-selling game for the system: *Sonic the Hedgehog* from 1991. Sold more than 15 million copies.

Sleek, sexy, and very successful, Sega Genesis is more than a game console: it's a central piece of pop culture of the 1990s (see Figure 8-10). Many a jaw dropped to the floor as words like *radical* and *mega* were uttered by gamers in the throes of puberty. Every single 1990s kid either knew someone who had a Genesis or owned one themselves. For an audience used to blocky sprites and garish colors, Genesis provided some amazing graphics.

Figure 8-10. *Sega Genesis*

The Genesis wasn't quite the hit in Japan the executives had hoped for. The system fared much better in North America and Europe. Also, in 1991 the Genesis got a considerable global sales boost from Sega introducing *Sonic the Hedgehog* to the world. Of course, Sonic wasn't the only reason people love these consoles. The overall quality of games was high on the Genesis. Many popular Genesis games have been converted to Windows to be sold on platforms like Steam.

Like the Master System, the Genesis is still being manufactured in Brazil. Tectoy is introducing a new version of the console in the summer of 2017 with a couple of dozen built-in games as well as a cartridge slot and support for SD memory cards. Brazilians sure love their Sega.

Here are some important games:

- *Comix Zone* (1995) by Sega

- *Virtua Racing* (1994) by Sega

- *Sonic the Hedgehog* (1991) by Sega

- *Road Rash* (1991) by Electronic Arts

- *Golden Axe* (1989) by Sega

1990
Super Nintendo

- Sold close to 50 million units.

- Best-selling game for the system: *Super Mario World* from 1990.
  Sold more than 20 million copies.

The NES made Nintendo a household name. The Super Nintendo (i.e., the SNES)
solidified Nintendo as a market leader (see Figure 8-11). The hardware was very
impressive for the time, capable of producing games indistinguishable from their arcade
counterparts. The SNES thrived for 13 years, being manufactured from 1990 all the way
to 2003 in many parts of the world. Nintendo had all the bases covered: a loyal following,
some amazing audiovisuals, and plenty of top-notch games. The console was in direct
competition with both the Sega Genesis and PC Engine by NEC. While all three systems
did well, it was Nintendo that won in the sales game, with some 50 million customers.

Figure 8-11. *Super Nintendo*

Three-dimensional games were in their infancy in 1990. The SNES, however, wiped
the floor with its competition in this category. The hardware was capable of a drawing
process called Mode 7, which allowed for smooth (if rudimentary) 3D surface scaling.
Games utilizing this technique included the popular racers *Super Mario Kart* and *F-Zero*,
as well as the arcade flight simulator *Pilotwings*. Mode 7 was hyped at the time of the
release of the console and for a good reason. It provided visuals unheard of in any home
gaming system at the time.

A major factor in the long shelf life of the SNES was that it provided the means to
expand the hardware of the console with extra chips built into specific game cartridges.
The most popular chip upgrade for the SNES was undoubtedly Super FX, built into
cartridges like the popular 3D shooters *Star Fox* and *Vortex*. Super FX enabled decent
polygon-based 3D graphics and particle effects for the SNES and, again, helped keep the
console relevant well into the new millennium. Even the mother of all FPS games, *Doom*,
got a decent SNES port thanks to coming on a cartridge featuring the Super FX 2 chip, a
greatly improved model from 1995.

Here are some important games:

- *Yoshi's Island* (1995) by Nintendo

- *Super Mario Kart* (1992) by Shigeru Miyamoto

- *Street Fighter 2* (1991) by Yoshiki Otamoto

- *Pilot Wings* (1990) by Bandai/Nintendo

- *Super Mario World* (1990) by Nintendo

1994
Sony PlayStation (PS1 or PSX)

- Sold more than 102 million units.

- Best-selling game for the system: *Gran Turismo* from 1997. Sold close to 11 million copies.

Sony PlayStation was the first console to sell more than 100 million units (see Figure 8-12). At the time of its release in 1994, it came with some pretty advanced hardware capable of some fine 3D graphics. Part of the PS1 success story was in how Sony handled its relationship with third-party developers. Instead of focusing mostly on in-house games development like Sega and Nintendo, Sony offered its APIs for any programmers at large. Also, the dual analog controller was a refreshingly bold affair, offering two control sticks in addition to the traditional configuration of a D-pad and four buttons.

Figure 8-12. Sony PlayStation

Although a huge success, the PS1 had its share of issues. One of the major ones was overheating. Another issue was a graphical one; the PS1 is not known for fantastic texture mapping. Often textures in PS1 titles appear warped. This is because the console used *affine texture mapping*, which is a fast but inaccurate way of mapping textures.

The PS1 had an impressive life span from 1994 to 2005. Not only that, it made Sony a market leader in the game console world. All PlayStation models have garnered considerable worldwide success.

Here are some important games:

- *Silent Hill* (1999) by Konami

- *Driver* (1999) by GT Interactive Software

- *Tekken 3* (1998) by Namco

- *Gran Turismo* (1997) by Sony

- *Wipeout* (1995) by Psygnosis

2000
PlayStation 2 by Sony

- Sold more than 150 million units.

- Best-selling game for the system: Gran*d Theft Auto: San Andreas* from 2004. Sold more than 17 million copies.

After the massive success of PlayStation, Sony proceeded to make game console history with PlayStation 2 (see Figure 8-13). Moving well more than 150 million units, PS2 became the best-selling game console of all time. The total number of games sold for the system is a staggering 1.5 billion. During its run from 2000 to 2012, PS2 and its impressive games library influenced untold numbers of budding games developers.

Figure 8-13. *Two main editions of PS2: regular (left) and slim*

By 1999 the original PlayStation had begun to show its age, mostly because of low-resolution games with graphical glitches, especially in 3D titles. The competition was getting stiff: the average desktop PC was becoming a major gaming platform thanks to its modular design and a steady stream of powerful 3D video cards. Sony took on the challenge by including the Emotion Engine chip in PS2, a rather capable piece of hardware. It offered high-resolution graphics with hardly any "glitching" of textures.

Sony also made sure PS2 could run a majority of PS1 games, adding to its appeal. Not only that, but many games running on PS2 from the previous console had noticeable graphical improvements thanks to improved texture filtering. The console also offered subscription-free online multiplayer on titles such as *Final Fantasy X* and *FlatOut*.

Here are some important games:

- *Tekken 5* (2005) by Namco

- *God of War* (2005) by Sony

- *Shadow Of The Colossus* (2005) by SCE/Sony

- *Gran Turismo 4* (2004) by Polyphony Digital/Sony

- *Soul Calibur 2* (2003) by Namco

2001

Gamecube by Nintendo

- Sold more than 21 million units.

- Best-selling game for the system: *Super Smash Bros Melee* from 2001. Sold more than 7 million copies.

The turn of the millennium wasn't an easy time for Nintendo. In a market dominated by two generations of Sony PlayStations, the Mario franchise makers began to lag behind in sales and innovation. With Gamecube, Nintendo focused on creating a developer-friendly system (see Figure 8-14). From a programmer's standpoint, it was easier to harness the impressive graphical prowess of the platform than it was on the main competitor, PS2. Also, the CPU of the Gamecube was simply more powerful to begin with. The last technological cherry on top in favor of the Nintendo machine was a superior audio chip.

Figure 8-14. *Gamecube*

As was to be expected, the Gamecube built on strong franchises for its games library. Titles like *Super Mario Sunshine* went on to solidify these already well-received franchises. In addition, Nintendo came up with two new, wildly successful series of games in the form of *Animal Crossing* and *Pikmin.* Unfortunately, not even the combination of a strong hardware platform and a killer games library could do enough to thwart PS2 from the position of the console market leader. Gamecube ended up being somewhat of a flop.

Here are some important games:

- *F-Zero GX* (2003) by Nintendo

- *The Legend of Zelda: The Wind Waker* (2002) by Nintendo

- *Animal Crossing* (2001) by Nintendo

- *Super Smash Bros Melee* (2001) by Nintendo

- *Star Wars Rogue Squadron II* (2001) by Factor 5/Lucasarts

Xbox by Microsoft

- Sold more than 24 million units.

- Best-selling game for the system: *Halo 2* from 2004. Sold more than 8 million copies.

The Xbox made Microsoft hip again (Figure 8-15). Instead of being "that Windows business," Microsoft became a veritable competitor to the likes of Sony and Nintendo on the console market. Released in 2001, the Xbox had fierce competition in the form of PlayStation 2 and Gamecube. Thanks to the best graphics chips at the time, Microsoft's offering became very popular very fast. Not even the clunky, heavy chassis of the console would hurt its popularity.

Figure 8-15. *Xbox*

In addition to great technical specifications, the Xbox launched with a great franchise. The big-budget first-person shooter *Halo* became a multimillion-dollar seller for the system and went on to spawn several successful sequels on multiple platforms. *Project Gotham Racing* was another franchise builder released with the Xbox. The racer had outstanding visuals for the time and went on to spawn three sequels, all of which have been favorably received. A console is only as strong as its games, and the Xbox had a great line-up for the time.

As the Xbox matured, several other great titles were introduced for the system. *Outrun,* a highly successful arcade cabinet driving game from 1986, got a brilliant sequel in 2003. *Outrun 2* was ported to Xbox in 2004 by Sumo Digital and remains one of the best arcade racers of all time. Halo, too, got an impressive sequel the same year. *Halo 2* went on to become a best-selling game on Xbox.

Here are some important games:

- *Outrun 2006: Coast 2 Coast* (2006) by Sumo Digital

- *Elder Scrolls III: Morrowind* (2002) by Ubisoft

- *MechAssault* (2002) by Day 1 Studios/Microsoft

- *Project Gotham Racing* (2001) by Microsoft

- *Halo* (2001) by Bungie

The Homebrew Market

Often the fandom of a gaming system doesn't end when the system is taken off the shelf. Even decades after the third-party production of games grinds to a halt, some hobbyists insist on keeping the hardware alive on some level. So-called homebrew games are definitely a thing. All of the platforms featured in this chapter are part of this scene. In fact, even the most obscure gaming systems have some kind of homebrew crowd out there for them. Many homebrew titles dig deep into the sometimes primitive hardware to pull something magnificent out, which can be attributed to both the skill of the programmer and the lack of deadlines. To see what old hardware is really capable of, you should get acquainted with the homebrew scene.

179

While most of these projects are offered as free online downloads, some are delivered as boutique items with high-quality packaging on either cartridges, tapes, floppy disks, or other media compatible with the original system.

The Atari 2600 (from 1977) is still a semisupported system. Since 1995, three years after Atari dropped the platform, more than 100 new games have been released as homebrews. The 2600 is notoriously hard to program, but some coders really love the challenge. Popular newer releases for the fossilized Atari include the innovative shoot-'em-ups *Oystron* by Piero Cavina and *Thrust* by XYPE. Even an understandably simplistic conversion of *Halo* found its way to the Atari 2600 in 2010. *Halo 2600* was programmed by Ed Fries, a former vice president of game publishing at Microsoft no less.

One of the most prolific homebrew scenes revolves around the Commodore 64. The system has seen hundreds of new games since its demise in the early 1990s. No special hardware is needed to develop for the Commodore 64 after all. Brands such as Psytronik and Protovision continue to release an occasional game, all of which are very professional and polished within the technical limitations of the hardware. Back in the day these titles would've been among the best commercial games out there. Not content with merely creating new Commodore 64 software, Protovision is manufacturing hardware such as four-player joystick adapters and network cards for the computer. The dedication in the scene is immense.

Newer gaming platforms have their fair share of homebrews as well. Sony encouraged PlayStation-related hobbyism during the console's first run. This was done in the form of a development system called Net Yaroze, released by Sony in 1997 with a price of $750. Consisting of a special-edition PlayStation console and a whole host of assorted accessories, the system allowed motivated gamers to have a go at games development. By connecting the system to a desktop PC, one could in theory come up with the next big hit game for the console. Sony did cripple the system so that Yaroze developers couldn't actually distribute their games on physical media. Distribution on CD-ROMs was reserved for those with the official developer license. So, while no commercially successful titles actually emerged from the bedrooms of Net Yaroze enthusiasts, quite a few of these games were in fact distributed on the cover of magazines dedicated to the PlayStation. The handful of universities teaching courses in games design at the time utilized the system as a learning tool, too.

Coding a game on a Net Yaroze system is not an easy feat. Only a handful of coders persevered to actually produce a commercially viable title. One such title, *Devil Dice,* was picked up by Sony itself. A brilliant puzzle game by developers Shift, Sony couldn't say no to providing distribution for the title. *Devil Dice* went on to sell a million or so copies. Other impressive Yaroze titles include the enjoyable top-down sports simulation *Total Soccer* by Charles Chapman and *Blitter Boy* by Chris Chadwick, a delightful arena shooter with some eloquent production values.

CHAPTER 9

■ ■ ■

Game Developer's Battle Station

Before you install any software, you'll need the right hardware for it to work on. I'll now go through the components in modern computer systems and what they mean to the indie developer.

Resources

The term *resources* refers to the total assets a computer system has at its disposal. The computer consists of several different components, which combine to form its overall processing ability. These components include the central processing unit (CPU), random access memory (RAM), video card, and hard drive(s).

Modern game software is probably the most resource-hungry type of program available, aside from high-definition video processing. When designing games, you want to make sure you require only the minimum amount of resources from the buyer's hardware. Cut down on eye candy whenever you can without looking amateurish. Either do it well or don't do it at all.

CPU

CPU stands for *central processing unit*. This is the brains of your computer and in general a good indicator of the swiftness of the system. It's that tiny, well-ventilated silicone chip inside your hardware with a price range of $30 to $1,000. As of 2017, there are two contenders for the processor crown: Intel and AMD. While AMD's offerings are usually more cost-effective, they are generally the less powerful of the two brands. Any midrange Intel CPU (see Figure 9-1) provides a good dose of efficiency for your game-making needs without costing you any limbs.

In the past CPU speed was presented in megahertz (MHz) or one million cycles per second. Many processors of yesteryear rarely reached past the one-to-two megahertz range (see Figure 9-2). Today CPU speed is usually specified in gigahertz (GHz) or one billion cycles per second. The more gigahertz a CPU has, the faster it usually runs anything you throw at it. For example, a 2.66GHz CPU provides a faster system than a 1.66GHz one.

© Robert Ciesla 2017

R. Ciesla, *Mostly Codeless Game Development*, DOI 10.1007/978-1-4842-2970-5_9

Figure 9-1. *A modern Intel CPU*

Figure 9-2. *The CPU of a primordial Commodore 64 computer. Photographed by Konstantin Lanzet.*

CPUs and Cores

One other factor worth considering is the core count of a CPU. Most CPUs since 2005 or so have been multicore processors, meaning they contain two or more separate processors within one physical unit. Dual cores, quad cores, and even eight cores are all the rage nowadays. The more the merrier, but all that core multiplication tends to hurt one's wallet. Also, not all software supports more than one processor. Most, if not all, modern operating systems do. The same can't be said for all (or even most) game development toolkits. If a toolkit's blurb mentions "multicore" or "*n*-core" support, it benefits from more than one CPU core, which is the way to go.

■ **Scientific fun fact**   one of the most successful home computers ever, the Commodore 64 from 1982 had an impressive 1MHz CPU. This is roughly 0.001GHz.

Hard Drive

A hard drive is a block of metal inside a computer where data is more or less permanently stored, unless disaster strikes in the form of fire, flood, or alien invasion. There are roughly two types of hard drives: *mechanical* and *solid-state disk* (SSD). Mechanical drives have moving parts in them (i.e., spinning magnetic discs), while SSDs don't. As a result, SSD technology is silent—and cool (not cool as in hipster tats, but cool as in ice; not Vanilla Ice, rather, ice as in frozen water).

The amount of data a disk stores is usually indicated in gigabytes (GB). Rare is even a basic computer in 2017 with less than 320GB of hard disk space. For game developers' needs, a 500GB drive is usually a minimum. It all depends how resource heavy you intend to go.

Mechanical drives are still largely in use because of their good price-to-performance ratio. An SSD drive often costs nearly twice the amount of moolah compared to a traditional disk of the same size.

Gigabytes and Megabytes

A gigabyte is one of the most common units of measurement in digital information. It can specify anything from the amount of information stored on a computer to the size of a video file on a smartphone. One gigabyte is roughly one billion bytes worth of data. A *megabyte* is simply a smaller unit, equating to a mere one million bytes of data. A single *byte* consists of eight *bits*. A bit is the smallest unit of measurement in any digital system, and it's either a 1 or a 0.

A modern video game requires anything between 2GB and 10GB of free space on a computer. In the 1990s most games needed much less than 1GB of such space, thanks to incorporating less audiovisual data. Requirements were usually specified in megabytes back in the day.

- The amount of data storable available on a modern computer ranges from 250GB to 2000GB.

- The total amount of data available on a standard DVD is 4.7GB.

- Compact discs hold 700MB of data (or 0.7GB).

- A single high-quality digital photo is roughly 5MB to 10MB (or 0.005GB to 0.01GB) in size.

Random Access Memory (RAM)

Random access memory is a temporary storage area for your computer (or other device). Its contents are erased as soon as you switch the system off. The more RAM you have, the smoother your system will run. Also, more RAM equals the ability to run several software packages simultaneously without much in the way of slowdowns. Think Firefox, Photoshop, iTunes, and your favorite games engine all starting up and running at the same time without a single hiccup. Having 16GB of RAM (or greater) will help with such an endeavor. These days, at least in theory, a single gigabyte of RAM is usually enough for basic operation, such as getting online or playing visually less intense games.

Video Card

Also called the *graphics processing unit* (GPU) or a *graphics card*, a video card handles all those complicated operations to provide the user with a graphical display. There are many different GPUs on the market; some are able to handle a complicated 3D game with ease, and others struggle with YouTube. As a developer using software on a Windows PC or a Mac, switching video cards is often plausible, and you should get a card that sits somewhere between the aforementioned extremes.

Just like the computer itself, a video card has some built-in RAM in it. The amount of graphics memory varies from as low as, say, 16MB (which translates to 0.016GB) to well over 2GB. The more video card memory is present, the higher the display resolutions your system can use. Also, some high-detail settings in games may require large amounts of video card RAM to display correctly. However, the GPU memory amount does not usually affect the unit's visual processing prowess.

In physical terms, a *dedicated* (or *discreet*) video card is a replaceable component in the system. That is, it's a card you can pull out and sell on eBay and upgrade to a better one. *Integrated video* refers to a nonreplaceable system of chips within your computer. These types of chips are the kind that allow one to go online—and not much else.

So, a dedicated video card is almost always much more powerful than integrated video. You should get a computer that has a decent dedicated card in it right from the get-go. Video card prices range from $30 to $300 and more. Also, there's nothing wrong with an older and/or secondhand GPU. They aren't toothbrushes, for goodness sake. A geriatric, diaper-wearing GPU from, say, 1999 is fine as long as its specs are still usable for your developmental plans.

When taking a look at video card specs, examine bandwidth carefully.

- Cards with at least 20 gigabytes per second (GBps) of bandwidth are adequate for most 2D needs. Examples: Radeon 9800, Geforce GT 530.

- 60GBps or more means the video card in question is ready for serious 3D development. Examples: Radeon 4850, Geforce GTX 750.

Your Hardware Needs as an Indie Developer

Basically, there are only two sensible options for your development system. You'll take a closer look at them next.

Option 1: Windows 7/8/10 PC

$500 to $800
Windows 7/8/8.1/10 in 64-bit

Most of today's game development software runs on Windows. The most elegant solution is therefore to stick to a midrange, branded or custom-built PC running this type of operating system. The lower-end PCs below $400 or so tend to last a few months at a time and are not a wise investment. As a developer, you'll be doing more than firing up Firefox.

Unlike with Apple products, there's not much point in going to the secondhand market for these types of PCs. Midrange Windows machines, which is what I'm talking about, really need that warranty. Let's face it: they are somewhat flimsy and generally aren't built to last longer than a couple of years. Again, make sure the video card in your battle station is not integrated.

Here are the recommended minimum hardware specs:

- Dual-core CPU, clocked at 2.66GHz or faster

- AMD 4850 or Nvidia GT 650M or equivalent video card (100Gbps bandwidth)

- 8GB of RAM

- A 7200 rpm 500GB hard drive

Option 2: iMac (Previous Generation), Mac Pro, or Mac Mini

$300 to $900 secondhand/$500 to $2,000 new
Mac OS X El Capitan or newer running Windows 7/8/10 on Bootcamp

You'd think the Mac is not really one for the hardcore gamer, let alone the serious games developer. You got a lot of nerve. Also, you'd be wrong. These machines are extremely durable and do handle most things you can throw at them. Macs can also have Windows running on them via the included Bootcamp software. Over the years I've owned almost a dozen Apple computers, from a modest Power Mac G3 to a late 2012 iMac, most of them acquired secondhand. None of them failed on me. None had hardware-related issues.

There's no need to go for the $5,000 Mac Pros from 2015. iMacs, Mac minis, and Mac Pros from 2009 or so onward are still a decent catch for the budding games developer. If the specs are adequate, go get yourself a Mac from the secondhand market.

Here are the recommended minimum hardware specs:

- Intel Core 2 Duo or i5 CPU, clocked at 2.66GHz or faster

- AMD 4850 or Nvidia GT 650M or equivalent video card (100Gbps bandwidth)

- 8GB of RAM

- A 7200 rpm 500GB hard drive

Bootcamp: Windows on a Mac

Most game development software is on Windows. So, why go Mac? Here's the kicker. Bootcamp is a free utility included with every version of Mac OS X since 2006. This software allows you to run a legitimate version of Windows on your Mac without too much of a hassle. With Bootcamp, your Mac essentially has two rock-solid operating systems. You do need a license for Windows, though (i.e., a legitimate Windows install DVD), which needs to be purchased separately.

After Bootcamp is installed, you can choose between Mac OS X and Windows at each bootup of your Mac. This unlocks all Windows-based software for your Mac.

Learn more about Bootcamp at `www.apple.com/support/bootcamp/`.

The Ecological Imperative

Mac OS is a great operating system, even in its earlier iterations. In fact, part of the Soiree Games machinery runs on OS X 10.4.11 Tiger (from 2009) and OS X 10.5.8 Leopard (from 2010). We have both a backup server and a 2D graphics development system running on these old operating systems.

Up until 2005, Apple utilized IBM's PowerPC processors for the whole Mac series of computers. When buying secondhand Macs, make sure the CPU type is Intel, if you intend to develop competitive games for current-generation crowds. PowerPC games development, while interesting, has very little money in it in 2017 and beyond. One notable PowerPC developer still selling software for the platform is Ambrosia Software.

Older operating systems can handle most 2D and even some 3D object design with ease. Think earlier versions of Photoshop and Blender; there's no need to ditch that Power Mac from 1999 just yet, my friend. That would be most unecological, for one.

For about $30 to $40 you do get a decent computer. Go for a Power Mac G4 or G5. Heck, even go G3 if you dare. Donate your old computers to your graphic and audio artists; they will love them. After all, the audiovisual output from these older systems is pretty much future-proof; you get the same, relevant JPEG, PNG, WAV formats (and many others) out of them. While PowerPC machinery may not be powerful enough for your primary development computer needs, there are plenty of tasks the ecological developer can relegate onto these old-school systems.

Of course, the same applies on the Windows side of things. Don't throw away that Pentium 4 just yet. It probably has quite a bit of mileage left in some creative tasks crucial to games development. Think graphics, audio, or testing. Even a Pentium 3 from the Proterozoic era[1] is up for all that, and more. So, reinstall that Windows XP (just don't go online) and get some work done.

A Few Words on Displays

As for your display needs, a Full HD–capable monitor is enough when it comes to resolution (1920×1080 pixels). Anything between 21 inches and 24 inches of screen estate is usually fine.

■ ■ ■

## CHAPTER 10

A Game Maker's Lexicon: Level 2

This chapter aims to further educate you about some concepts crucial to video game making. While this chapter is optional, it is recommended reading for everyone. Remember, the more understanding you have of these concepts, the more fluently you can communicate with people in the industry.

Tread on without fear. Because this is a beginner's book, actual lines of programming code will be kept to a minimum in this chapter as well.

Digital Units of Measurement

There are four important expressions related to units of measurement in the digital world (see Table 10-1). It's quite easy to get them confused. Basically, you can thank various lobbying groups for this.

Table 10-1. *A Comparison of Different File Size Units*

Unit	Abbreviation	Unit in Bytes	First Known Use
Gibibyte	GiB	1,073,741,824	1998
Gigabyte	GB	1,000,000,000	1975
Mebibyte	MiB	1,048,576	1998
Megabyte	MB	1,000,000	1965

32-Bit/64-Bit Architecture

To simplify, *bit architecture* refers to the amount of random access memory (RAM) a central processing unit (CPU) can access. A 32-bit CPU can utilize a maximum of 4GB of RAM. If you want more RAM in your system, you need to go 64-bit. More RAM equals (among other things) less hard disk access, which in turn leads to having a faster system. As 64-bit devices can move twice the amount of data than their 32-bit counterparts per second, some gains in speed are to be expected. However, these mostly apply to multitasking situations or dealing with large data sources such as video files.

© Robert Ciesla 2017
R. Ciesla, *Mostly Codeless Game Development*, DOI 10.1007/978-1-4842-2970-5_10

Most CPUs gained 64-bit capabilities around 2004 to 2005. Some examples include Intel Core 2 processors; the Intel i3, i5, and i7 families; and AMDs Phenom and Athlon processors.

Now, to sum up:

- A 64-bit processor performs best with 64-bit software (think Windows 64-bit editions).

- A 32-bit processor is *not* compatible with 64-bit software.

- A 64-bit processor *is* compatible with both 64-bit and 32-bit software.

For a game developer's system, any 64-bit CPU paired with a 64-bit edition of Windows 7 or 8 should suffice. Also go for 8GB of RAM; it's a good compromise of having a speedy system and emulating the average user's machinery. Don't invest in a $5,000 system; the average gamer certainly won't. But if you do, why not invest in an average PC, as well, for testing purposes?

Hard Drives Revisited

Mechanical drive speed is measured in rotations per minute (rpm). Generally speaking, there are three speed standards available without extra hardware. They're rated at 5400 rpm, 7200 rpm, and 10000 rpm. While some geeks with large glasses may insist "a 7200 rpm drive is not any faster than a 5400 rpm one," I beg to differ. Please, make sure your disks go to at least 7200 rpm. This will cut precious seconds, hours, and ultimately days from your development time. If possible, get a Western Digital Velociraptor—if you have the money. They go to 10000 rpm.

Solid-state drive (SSD) performance, while initially very impressive, tends to deteriorate the more data the drive accesses. You might experience a gradual reduction in disk performance as the months go by. Therefore, I recommend you stick to the cheaper mechanical drives—and always back up your data on at least two separate external drives. However, it's worth keeping in mind that since SSD drives have no moving parts, they're more durable against physical damage.

Potential Mac buyers watch out. Does that older iMac/Mac mini appear enticing with good features and a reasonable price tag? It probably has a 5400 rpm drive. Check out all the specs with vigor, especially if you go secondhand. Oh, and, some early Macbook Airs had a lovely hard drive spinning data at 4200 rpm. Needless to say, do not acquire these devices.

Advanced Visual Terminology

In this section, you'll find the meanings of some common computer graphics–related terms. Also discussed are some common visual processing effects. Most of the time you don't have to actually program any of these techniques into your games. The game-making software takes care of that.

The terms are described here to give you some basic insight into their workings and the effects they have on your projects and games in general.

Antialiasing (AA)

This is a technique to reduce the jagged edges in digital graphics. There are new, fancy techniques out every month, it seems. As of 2017, a 3D game without some form of constant antialiasing is a rare sight. Some 2D games forsake the antialiased look for the most part to create an old-school vibe. Sometimes jagged edges are all you need.

Hand-drawn antialiasing has been a common technique in 2D game graphics since the 1980s. These days AA usually refers to an automated feature in a 2D or 3D environment, calculated in real time by one's video card. You may be able to speed up your game by toning down or switching off AA entirely.

Some forms of antialiasing eat up a lot of graphics processing unit (GPU) power and are best avoided. These hungry varieties include *super-sampling antialiasing* (SSAA) and *multisample antialiasing* (MSAA).

Billboard

A *billboard* is a texture that always faces the player right in the eye. This usually means any type of user interfaces in 3D games, such as score and health displays. Think of billboards as 2D elements in a 3D world.

Cel Shading

Also known as *toon shading,* this technique refers to a cartoony rendering method of 3D graphics. Think comic books and animated movies. There's less detail and realism at play, so cel shading is easier on the video card than more photorealistic types of rendering. Dozens of developers prefer the aesthetics of cel shaded graphics. The successful *Borderlands* franchise, for one, relies on this technique for its visuals.

Clipping Plane

In essence, *clipping* refers to the discarding of some visual data. What is not needed to be drawn gets clipped, at least in any decently optimized project. Every act of drawing something on-screen takes a toll on a computer's resources after all.

A *clipping plane* refers to the invisible border crossing that hides any visual objects, including scenery. In a 2D context, a clipping plane usually refers to the edges of the visible screen. There's no reason to draw what the user doesn't see. In 3D a clipping plane also operates on the *z*-axis or depth level. Usually, the clipping plane operates in tandem with fog.

Fog

In a computer graphics–related context, *fog* refers to the technique of blending 3D objects into the same color hue and fading them out as they move away into the distance. Not only does digital fog add to the atmosphere of the proceedings, but it's also an efficient way of disguising the clipping plane. While not usually a very realistic representation of actual atmospheric conditions, digital fog is a cheap and well-established technique used in video games since the late 1990s. Some type of fog is pretty much a necessity to maximize the frame rate in most 3D video games.

Viewing Frustum

In geometry parlance, a *frustum* means a cone or pyramid shape with part of the top sliced off. When it comes to computer graphics, a *viewing frustum* is a 3D volume that specifies which objects are visible. Only objects inside the frustum are rendered. Think of it as a virtual camera. Now, *view frustum culling* refers to the process of cutting specific objects off the rendering queue. Again, either these objects are not inside the frustum or they are occluded by other objects and thus not in need of being rendered. Remember, the less that is rendered, the smoother the proceedings are in general. Only the smallest of 3D worlds don't need frustum culling of any kind (think 3D puzzle games).

There are basically two types of projection in viewing frustums.

- *Perspective projection (see Figure 10-1)*: The frustum is in the shape of a pyramid with part of the top missing. This is the most common type of frustum in 3D video games. Like actual cameras, this type of projection works on the concept of a *focal point.*

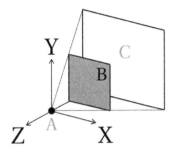

Figure 10-1. *A viewing frustum using perspective projection*

- *Orthographic projection (see Figure 10-2)*: The frustum is in the shape of a rectangle. This results in imagery that is most suited for side-viewed (pseudo) 2D games, such as platformers or other arcade games. Objects don't change size in relation to the virtual horizon, because there is no such horizon in an orthographic projection in the first place.

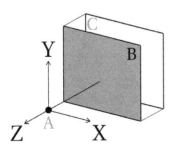

Figure 10-2. *A viewing frustum using orthographic projection*

Let's break down the main components of the viewing frustum. These basic components include the *camera* (A), the *near plane* (B), and the *far plane* (C). Graphics rendering is done between the two planes (i.e., inside the frustum). Any objects outside of this space should exist only as variables.

Z-buffer

Z-buffer refers to an algorithm that makes sure the perspective system in a 3D environment is kept as realistic as possible. This means making sure objects designated as belonging in the background aren't blocking the ones placed in front of them, no matter what the viewing angle is. The Z-buffer is part of any working viewing frustum.

Shader Languages

Shaders are a relatively complicated topic and one that you are not required to master. While not necessary for a compelling gaming experience, visual effects in the form of these shader programs can be used to enhance the production values in a game and also to offload visual effects onto the video card. Like discussed in earlier chapters, this offloading process usually speeds up the overall execution of the game since video cards are specialized pieces of hardware capable of some very serious data crunching.

Shaders can be written in several languages. The most common languages in use today are the two main variations of the OpenGL Shading Languages (GLSL and GLSL ES) and Microsoft's High-Level Shading Language (HLSL). All of these shader languages are based on the C language syntax.

Like the name suggests, both GLSL and GLSL ES are part of the universally supported OpenGL API. GLSL is meant for desktop computers, while GLSL ES works best on projects for mobile devices, such as smartphones.

HLSL is a proprietary Microsoft technology running off of the DirectX platform. This shader language was made available in DirectX version 8.0 and remains popular.

Different game engines support different shader languages. GameMaker Studio, for one, supports GLSL, GLSL ES, and HLSL for your shaders. Some platforms support only a specific type of shader dialect. For example, Microsoft's HLSL shaders do not run well (or at all) on other than Windows or Xbox devices as the language relies on the DirectX API.

Now, a shader program can be split into different elements. Let's take a look at these building blocks next.

Pixel Shaders (Fragment Shader)

A technique for 2D projects, *pixel shaders* (also called *fragment shaders*) simply alter the color and other properties of pixels (sometimes called *fragments* in this context).

Vertex Shaders

Vertex shaders act on 3D models and geometry, altering their color and other attributes. Remember, 3D objects are comprised of vertices. These shaders cannot create new vertices or even any kind of visual primitive shapes. Vertex shaders are used solely to modify existing graphical data.

Geometry Shaders

These types of shader programs are capable of drawing new graphical primitives such as triangles and lines. Geometry shaders can add detail to a scene, such as deeper, more realistic shadows.

How to Implement Shaders

The actual implementation of shader effects varies from game engine to game engine. In some tools, the process is made easy. Clickteam's Fusion, for one, offers shader implementation with a few mouse clicks; no coding is needed. In GameMaker Studio, you are required to enter both a fragment and vertex shader code for every effect in a dedicated shader code editor. Then, you integrate this code into the draw event of your project using a few specific commands in GML (the GameMaker scripting language). It sounds complicated, but as soon as you've achieved it once, you can simply copy and paste the necessary objects in your projects, make a few changes here and there, and focus on writing the actual shader code.

Texture

You can think of a texture as an image file that in turn is a series of pixels arranged to form a functional picture (see Figure 10-3). Textures in a 3D context are the "paint" slapped on 3D objects. For most purposes, textures need to be in a 1:1 aspect ratio (e.g., 1024×1024 or 2048×2048 pixels in size).

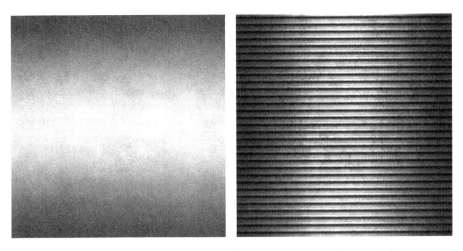

Figure 10-3. *Typical textures depicting metallic surfaces.* © http://jojo-ojoj. *deviantart.com/ used under CC-BY-3.0.*

Texture Atlas

Also known as a *sprite sheet,* a *texture atlas* is a single large image file containing all or most of a game's sprites (see Figure 10-4). Basically every object you see moving around in a video game is taken from texture atlases particular to that game. Texture atlases are used both in 2D and 3D contexts. Larger projects usually include several texture atlases for different levels in the game and other uses.

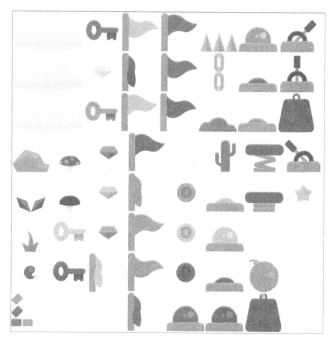

Figure 10-4. *A small texture atlas containing keys, flags, a cactus, and other game-related graphics*

While not a necessary approach for manipulating in-game visual data, the use of texture atlases is a popular approach for modern graphics hardware. It's more efficient for the video card to access specific regions from a single large image file than to constantly access different individual sprite files.

Texture Mapping

This is a method of wrapping textures (i.e., images) around a 3D model. Think of it as a coat of paint being applied on a three-dimensional object. There are all sorts of math involved in this, but we don't need to go there. This process is more user-friendly than that in today's computer graphics software.

Note that a texture is laid on top of an object using UV coordinates, which are a texture's coordinates on top of the 3D object. What do the *U* and *V* stand for? Nothing at all. It's just a well-established notation. Think of U as X and V as Y in the context of positioning textures.

Now, there are actually many kinds of texture mapping going on in a typical 3D video game, in addition to the technique of slapping on a coat of paint on an object. Think of all of these techniques as additional layers of visual information, each contributing something to the finished look of a 3D model.

Bump Mapping

Simple *bump mapping* is an older method used to add surface detail to a 3D object, such as blemishes on human characters, without much in the way of simulating reflective surfaces.

Normal Mapping

A *normal map* is usually a purple and blue texture that works as an advanced type of bump mapping. Normal maps create the illusion of light reflecting off a surface without adding actual polygons (i.e., detail) to a model. A normal map will add realistic sheen and depth to any object for most viewing angles.

Environment Mapping

The term *environment mapping* refers to the method of simulating a reflective surface on a 3D model, in particular one that reflects a predetermined texture image. Think of the windows of a car reflecting a texture of some 3D surroundings in a driving game. Also called *reflective mapping*, this technique is seldom scientifically accurate but pleasing nonetheless for the average gamer. Environment mapping is often used in combination with normal mapping for more realistic results.

Environment mapping can be split into specific techniques. The two most common varieties are briefly discussed next:

- *Sphere mapping*: The surface consists of a spherical wall (a kind of a disco ball if you will) surrounding the objects in the scene, reflecting off of them where necessary. Sphere mapping is easy on the resources (especially video card RAM), but it doesn't provide the most detailed simulation of reflective surfaces.

- *Cube mapping*: This is a more advanced form of environment mapping that uses six faces of a cube to portray a scene, which will then be reflected on objects. Cube mapping uses a larger texture than sphere mapping, which means more memory usage. However, the end result is more detailed.

Interpolation

This term refers to the process of determining the in-between values from two or more values. For example, the interpolated values of 0 and 3 would be 1 and 2. Interpolation is used in all types of texture mapping and filtering.

Texture Filtering

Texture filtering is a type of antialiasing (remember that one?) for 3D surfaces. There are mostly three types of filtering used in games these days. You'll meet the three contestants now, in order of resource intensity.

Bilinear Filtering

This is an older method used to smooth textures when displayed larger or smaller than they actually are. Most of the time, when drawing a textured shape on the screen, the texture is not displayed exactly as it is stored without distortion. This is where bilinear filtering comes in, performing corrective action where needed. Rare is the system in 2017 that doesn't run bilinear well.

Trilinear Filtering

Trilinear filtering is an extension of the bilinear filtering method. It is less blurry but takes more resources, although this was only a problem in early millennial times; current-generation video cards can tackle this type of filtering with ease.

Anisotropic Filtering (AF)

This is texture filtering method that eliminates some of the blurriness apparent in older filtering methods. AF is somewhat resource intensive. Low-spec video cards may struggle with this technique even today. Use this with caution, and never force it.

Mipmaps

Mipmaps are textures stored at various sizes. Take a brick wall. Think up-close, medium distance, and far in the horizon types of scenarios in a game. Instead of resizing one texture fully in real time (based on the distance of the player from the brick wall), special prestored texture maps are taken from a mipmap file and displayed instead. Using mipmaps usually means the graphics run faster.

The highest-resolution texture is first in the image file. Each following texture in the mipmap set is smaller in height and width by a power of 2. Now, let's say the maximum resolution mipmap of an imaginary brick wall is 512 pixels by 512 pixels. So, the next texture is 256 by 256 pixels, followed by one that is 128 by 128 pixels, and so on. A mipmap file contains eight textures, with the biggest texture on the left gradually halved when moving to the right.

Note that the abbreviation comes from Latin *multum in parvo*. Roughly translated, it means "a great amount in a small space."

Transform and Lighting (T&L)

Transformation is the technique of producing a two-dimensional representation from visual material that is three-dimensional in its properties. *Lighting* simply refers to the application of simulated lighting conditions on textures, such as rendering the reflections of a streetlamp in a 3D game onto a representation of a brick wall. In essence, T&L is the task of calculating geometry in a computer context.

Until 1999 or so, T&L was performed on the CPUs of computers. Since the advent of 3D video cards, the process has moved onto the video hardware side of things, which allows for much more complicated scenes. The first video card to support hardware T&L was the Nvidia Geforce 256 from late 1999.

Raytracing

This is a computationally intense technique of simulating the behavior of light in a digital context. Raytracing produces very realistic images where most kinds of real-world optical effects are accurately simulated. The resulting images can be almost indistinguishable from actual photography.

The technique is rarely used in real-time applications, such as video games, unless it's in a prerendered sequence, such as an introductory video. Most computers today are not capable of creating a smoothly running interactive raytraced scene, at least one of a more complicated nature.

Bloom (Glow)

This is a visual effect that simulates over-exposure in film cameras. Quite simply, bloom makes objects or entire scenes glow. Over-use of bloom is quite common in modern video games. Bloom should have realistic light sources in a scene. A tiny candle glowing like a nuclear reactor isn't a realistic approach and might look comical.

Depth of Field (DOF)

This is another effect that aims to emulate the way cameras work. You may have noticed how cameras can be made to focus on specific parts in a view. The background is blurry, while the area of focus is not. This is known as *depth of field*. It can be quite cinematic and thus desirable in video games, especially in those of the 3D variety.

Gradient Noise

In a visual context, a little noise can be a great thing. In fact, mathematical noise is used to create realistic terrain for video games and movies all the time. *Gradient noise* refers to algorithms that output visual procedural content (i.e., noise maps), which can then be interpreted in various creative ways depending on the context (see Figure 10-5). The aforementioned terrains are made by a combination of gradient noise and the interpretation of this noise in a 3D world as *height maps*. The term *gradient* is used because these noise algorithms interpolate values between specific "hotspots" of the noise map. This approach allows for smooth transitions between these values and thus the pleasantly undulating, realistic terrain.

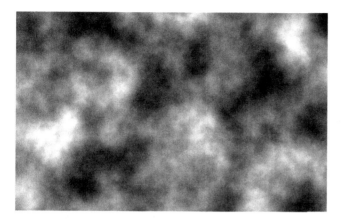

Figure 10-5. *A typical noise map used to create 3D terrain. Think of it as the top-down view of the terrain.*

There are many different gradient noise algorithms. Perhaps the most popular one is Perlin noise, named after its inventor Ken Perlin. You'll see this type of noise generation implemented in most 3D games and game engines.

Parallax Scrolling

This is a technique where two or more layers of background images move by the viewer at different speeds, some slower and some faster. This creates the illusion of depth. Parallax scrolling in video games was popularized in the 1980s and is still popular in 2D titles. In recent years the technique has been implemented on many a web site, as well.

Voxel

This term is short for *volume pixel* (see Figure 10-6). An alternative to using "traditional" polygons (i.e., vertices) in 3D graphics, voxels are a technique used to create terrains in several games from the 1990s and onward. In this context, a single voxel represents a very small part of a terrain, which makes the approach well-suited to destructible and modifiable terrain. Detailed voxel-terrains, however, are quite hungry for memory and can slow even a powerful computer to a halt. Luckily, using voxels for simple terrains works well and is acceptable among both gamers and developers. The "voxel look" of blocky, semi-retro aesthetics is considered quite hip by some indies. Having said that, I am not a fan of this look.

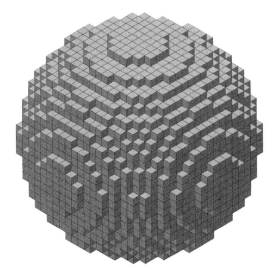

Figure 10-6. *A voxel-based sphere*

Some voxel-based games include Novalogic's *Comanche* series of helicopter simulators and more recently the indie hit *Minecraft*.

Delta Time (Δt)

Delta time refers to a technique that allows for frame rate independence in graphics-intense applications such as video games. With delta time, the proceedings at hand are kept running at a consistent rate, regardless of any slowdowns a computer might experience because of old hardware or other issues. The same goes for systems running excessively fast; delta time takes care of those as well, delivering a unified experience across all platforms.

Think of it this way: a frame rate–dependent (non-delta-timed) game would run twice as fast on a system doing 120 fps compared to a system running at 60 fps. With delta time in place, they would both deliver a game seemingly executing at the same speed. Now, if a third system could reach only 15 fps, with delta time the crummy old computer, too, would deliver a somewhat playable experience. All the in-game events would take place concurrently with the other systems in real-world time, if only appearing less smooth. Object movement per frame would just have to be multiplied by 4 to compensate for the lack of frames per second to reach the updated state of an optimal 60 fps system.

In addition, in the context of multiplayer online games, delta time keeps all participating devices with different network speeds on a level playing field. A delta time approach provides a synchronized experience for all connected devices regardless of differences in hardware and Internet bandwidth.

Finite State Machine (FSM)

In short, a *finite state machine* is the means of simplifying the inner workings of a software program to specific *states* that are activated at meaningful points during the user experience. Instead of telling a computer to move a character left by 20 pixels, looking up at the sky, smiling, playing a sound effect, and right levitating by 7 pixels, the programmer can create a process called, say, "State Four: A Happy Guy Levitates," by creating such a state within the development software's finite state machine. From a user's viewpoint, you get the whole aforementioned shebang actually on-screen, of course. From the programmer's viewpoint, you work in simplified *states* rather than thousands of lines of code each time you want a certain spectacle on-screen.

So, a finite state machine can be used both as a simplifying tool and an effective means of documenting a software program to all members of a team, current and future. Also, I've yet to hear of a single programming language that didn't support some type of finite state machine. There are implementations for all living languages, including GameMaker's GML.

Working in simple arcade games, a finite state machine might sound overkill, but if you take it on once, it will forever change the way you see code. Know-how in finite state machines gives you confidence to tackle large, complex projects—and to present such projects in understandable terms.

UML and FSM, Best Buddies

Unified Modeling Language (UML) is an outwardly simple general-purpose visual modeling language commonly used in software engineering. The charts it produces are helpful in representing information in a succinct and understandable manner. Think of UML as a meta-language to make software blueprints with.

Small and large teams alike will benefit from using UML. Using UML facilitates the use of the finite state machine approach greatly as you can visualize each state with ease.

Here is a list of implementable FSMs:

- *Zero Engine by Ace*: A game development engine designed to aid in the process of making 2D games quickly and easily (in essence, a game engine within a game engine).

  For GameMaker.

  http://gmc.yoyogames.com/index.php?showtopic=454506.

- *Deterministic Finite State Machine framework based on Game Programming Gems 1 by Eric Dybsend*: For Unity. http://wiki.unity3d.com/index.php?title=Finite_State_Machine.

Machinima

This term *machinima* refers to the use of computer graphics, usually visuals from a specific video game engine, to create noninteractive content. In essence, it's digital puppetry with premade assets. Most often, machinima is a type of art indulged in by fans of video games.

The practice was perhaps best established in 1993 with Id Software's *Doom*, which allowed players to record sequences of gameplay. Since then, entire series of machinima have emerged. The first major machinima film sequence was *The Diary of a Camper*, released in 1996 and based on the *Quake* engine. Created by Rangers, a gaming clan, the video is a mere minute-and-a-half long (and may or may not make much sense to modern casual gamers). Nonetheless, it's considered a milestone of machinima.

The term was coined in 2000 by Hugh Hancock who launched a web site simply called Machinima.com dedicated to the art form. In addition to *Doom* and *Quake*, popular game assets used for machinima films include those found in *Halo* and *The Sims*.

The Golden Age of Arcade Video Games

This is generally considered the period of time between 1978 and 1983, when coin-operated arcade cabinets became popular attractions around the world. Many evergreen games were introduced during this time including *Space Invaders, Robotron 2084, Asteroids,* and *Missile Command.*

Grinding

This is the process of a player performing repetitive tasks (such as slaying a set number of enemies or traveling between two points almost endlessly) to attain rewards of some kind in a game. These might include specific items or character skills. Grinding is a popular mechanic in many free-to-play games, where the ensuing frustration is used to manipulate players into paying actual money to bypass the grinding process and get to the rewards faster.

Konami Code

This term refers to a controller button combination introduced in the popular NES shoot-'em-up *Gradius* in 1986. Entering the code enables a cheat mode for the game. It has been since used in dozens of video games for varying purposes. As for the code, it's simply *up, up, down, down, left, right, left, right, B-button,* and *A-button* on the D-pad.

More on Programming

In Chapter 3 you learned what programming is all about. Let's now take a deeper look at some fundamental concepts of programming. Some concepts will be familiar, but repetition rarely hurts the beginner in these matters. I'll approach the curriculum from a more or less universal standpoint, as most programming languages follow this set of logic.

There are many types of programming tasks with numerous approaches and related concepts. For the purposes of this book, I'll narrow these to three core concepts. Understanding them will help you write and decipher code in the programming language of your choosing.

- Variables and operators (i.e., data organization)

- Data structures (i.e., variable arrays and lists)

- Flow control (i.e., flow control statements)

Variables and Operators

As mentioned in Chapter 3, a variable is an arbitrary, often user-defined, label for a storage location of meaningful data. Every piece of software includes several variables, from spaceship coordinates to the name of player 1, and more.

The first step to using variables is to define what type of values they will accept. Variables come in many varieties as different types of data need to be stored in different ways (see Table 10-2). Some simple programming languages don't require you to define the variable type, but most do.

Table 10-2. *A Comparison of Variable Definitions in Common Programming Languages*

Language	Variable Type	Variable Type Name	Example Definition(s)
Generic C++	Character (single alphanumeric)	char	char example='a';
	String (text variable)	char *	char *name="Joe";
	Boolean (true or false, 1 or 0)	bool	bool happy=true;
	Numeric integer (for values between -32768 and 32768)	int	int level=4;

GML (GameMaker)	Any type	var	var level=5;
			var myname="Joe";
			var happy=true;

Java	Character (single alphanumeric)	char	char example='a';
	String	String	String name="Joe";
	Boolean	boolean	boolean happy=true;
	Numeric integer	Int	int level=4;
Python	Any type	n/a	level=5; name="Joe";

Why have different types of variables in the first place? Why can't you just have a general-purpose variable for all uses? Simply put, that would be a waste of resources. Not all information in a program needs to have a ton of bits reserved for it. Many smaller operations within a software project need only a couple of bits to get the job done. Why reserve dozens of bits to a variable that exists only to, say, store a player's initials?

Note that in many languages, a semicolon (;) must be added after each code statement. This is implemented simply to separate major statement elements. In this context, the semicolon is referred to as a *statement terminator*.

Just defining variables isn't enough. You also need some *operators* (see Table 10-3) to do something useful with them, such as simple arithmetic or comparisons.

Table 10-3. Typical Variable Operators

Symbol	Operator Name	Examples of Use in Most Languages

-
--
-=
	Subtraction
	Decrement
	Compound subtraction
		`a=a-1; // decrease value of variable`
		`"a" by one`
		`--a; // same as above`
		`a-=5; // subtract 5 from "a"`

+
++
+=
	Addition
	Increment
	Compound addition
		`a=a+1;`
		`++a;`
		`a+=8; // add 8 to "a"`

*
*=
	Multiplication
	Multiplication compound
		`a=a*2; // double the value of "a"`
		`a*=2; // same as above`

/
/=
	Division
	Compound division
		`a=a/4; // divide "a" by four`
		`a/=4; // same as above`

%	Modulo (remainder)	`a = 20 % 8; // the value of "a" will`
		`be 4`

<
>
==
!=
>=
<=
	Less than
	Greater than
	Equal to
	Not equal to
	Greater than or equal
	Less than or equal
		`if (a>b)...`
		`if (b>a)...`
		`if (b==a)...`
		`if (b!=a) // if b does NOT equal a`
		`if (a>=b) // if a is greater or equal`
		`to b`
		`if (a<=b) // if a is less or equal`
		`to b`

&&
||
!
	Logical AND
	Logical OR
	Logical negation (NOT)
		`if (a==b && b==c) // if a equals b`
		`AND b equals c`
		`if (a==b || b==c) // if a equals b OR`
		`b equals c`
		`if (!`

In general, it's a good programming practice to use compound operators whenever possible. Also, you should use multiplication to divide values (`a*=0.5` is faster for the CPU to process than `a/=2`).

Data Structures

A data structure is simply a group of variables and in some cases methods/procedures. They are often useful to organize large amounts of data into easily accessible structures. Most major programming languages support several types of data structures (see Table 10-4).

Table 10-4. *A Comparison of Different Common Data Structures*

Data Structure Type	Usage	Example
1D array	Storing large amounts of simple data	Creating a list of character names (Bob, Mackenzie, Becket)
2D array	Storing data benefiting from having both row and column attributes (e.g., grids)	Storing the coordinates of pieces on a chess board with an 8×8 two-dimensional array
Class	Providing more complex "blueprints" for objects in object-oriented programming, including both variables and methods	A class called Cars is used to store data with top speed, color, and license number for all cars
3D array	Solving 3D problems	Storing three-dimensional locations or choices in a game
Linked list	Optimizing a project for minimal memory (RAM) usage instead of speed	Storing large data sets of indeterminate size

Because arrays and linked lists can sometimes get confusing, I'll now discuss the differences between the two. First, linked lists are preferred if you're not sure how many elements your data structure will include. Re-declaring an array's size can get cumbersome. Also, linked lists allow for more flexible insertion of new elements, unlike arrays that only let you add elements after the most recent one. On the other hand, arrays allow for random access of a data element, which is not possible with linked lists.

Flow Control

Think of any game program as a script that the computer is reading from top to bottom. At first, variables are declared and initialized. Then the player probably views the title screen, interacts with it, and enters the game itself. The player is then entering the main loop (or *game loop*) of the program. At this point in the "script," a specific set of steps are repeated until the player dies or decides to spontaneously quit. These steps usually include drawing the graphics, checking for collisions, and observing the player's interaction with the program and acting accordingly.

Now, there are basic flow control elements in every programming language (see Table 10-5). For the most part, the commands are identical in every modern language.

Table 10-5. *Five Most Common Flow Control Commands*

Type	Usage	Example
If	Examine status of variables or functions.	`if (age==99) printf("Hello spring chicken!");`
Then	Direct the flow of the program. Usually needed only in older languages or BASIC (see the example).	`IF AGE<100 THEN PRINT "YOU ARE STILL YOUNG"`
Else	Alternative flow direction if the condition or conditions are not met.	`if (old==true) printf("You are old"); else printf("You are not that old");`
While	Repeat part of the program as long as specific conditions are met.	`while (age==100) { printf ("You are old!"); }`
Goto	Jump to a different label in the listing. This is pretty much a relic from the older days. These days you're expected to break out of a (`while`) loop structure instead.	`IF HEALTH<1 THEN GOTO 10 (BASIC)` `goto Gameover; (C++)`
Labels	Labels work in tandem with the goto command. They are usually defined with an arbitrary name followed by a colon (:) in most languages. Again, labels are not considered chic anymore.	`Gameover:` `...`

Pseudocode and Code Comments

Let's take a look at a simple game listing in *pseudocode*. While not actually an implementable programming language, pseudocode can be used to demonstrate flow control.

What is actual programming in the example is in the *code comments*. There is a way in most, if not all, programming languages to insert lines of text that the computer will not process in any way. These strings of text are solely for the programmers themselves—or their teams. Listing 10-1 shows a snippet of some rather silly C++ code in Listing 10-1 to demonstrate code commenting in action. The comments are presented here in bold.

Listing 10-1. C++ Code Demonstrating Correct Code Comment Usage

```
printf("Mackenzie, I need you to get on that plane\n") // A superior idea
right there.
printf("You know what, Bob, I think I shall.\n") /* She agrees. */
```

You see, most languages consider anything after a double slash (i.e., //) an "invisible" bunch of characters. In addition, a slash and asterisk (i.e., /*) work to the same effect, but do remember to close these types of comment segments with as asterisk and slash (i.e., */). The latter type of commenting can span several lines.

Now, hold on to your neckbeards and behold the pseudocode listing of a very basic *Flappy Bird* clone (see Listing 10-2).

Listing 10-2. A Pseudocode Listing of a Flappy Bird Clone

```
Beginning:
        set player x coordinate variable to left side of the screen
        set player y coordinate variable to middle of the screen
        set obstacle x coordinate variable to the right edge of the screen

/* start playing some theme music before entering the title screen -loop.
   we don't want to start playing the music every single frame update! */

play theme music

Title screen:
        draw title screen // drawing events are generally performed every
        frame update
                IF enter is pressed GOTO Game loop
                IF escape is pressed exit program
GOTO Title screen

Game loop:
        draw player
        draw obstacles
        reduce 5 pixels from obstacle x // move obstacle to the left by 5
        pixels at all times
                // below: if obstacle reaches left side of the screen re-
                   locate the obstacle
                // to the right edge of the screen
                IF obstacle x < 0 obstacle x = screen_width
        IF space bar is pressed // self-explanatory
                IF space bar is pressed THEN reduce 5 pixels from player y
                ELSE add 1 pixel to player y // if space bar not pressed,
                move player down
        IF player collides with obstacle GOTO Game over
GOTO Game loop

Game over:
        draw game over -screen
        IF escape is pressed THEN exit program
GOTO Game over
```

That concludes the example. Learn to think in pseudocode. Absorbing this way of thinking makes you a programmer.

Let's now see some actual code and repeat the example in some tasty generic C++ (see Listing 10-3). You will not input any detailed low-level commands. The code won't actually work from any programming IDE as some crucial functionality is missing. The listing is meant to demonstrate how the pseudocode translates into an actual programming language. Also, for reference, I'm working with a screen resolution of 1024×768 pixels.

Listing 10-3. A Partial Listing of a Flappy Bird Clone in Generic C++

```
// First, we define and initialize some variables
int player_x=20, player_y=384;
bool player_dead=false; /* player_dead is a boolean variable. it uses a
minimal amount of
                  resources (one bit) as it has two states: true or false */
int obstacle_x=1024;
/* in C++ and its derivatives, you define functions next. the actual code
for these functions will be placed after the main program part. we won't be
doing that in our example. the expression before each function ("bool" or
"void") refers to the RETURN VALUE of each function. in our example, each
function returns either a boolean value (false or true) or nothing at all
(void). not all functions need to return a variable. */

bool Space_Key_Pressed();
bool Escape_Pressed();
bool Check_Collisions();
void Draw_Things();
void Draw_Title();
void Play_Theme_Music();
void Draw_Gameover_Screen();

/* the main program part begins next. note: this is not the game loop,
rather it donates the end of the definition part in C++ and begins the
actual activities in a program */

int main(void) {

Play_Theme_Music(); // execute a function that plays some delightful theme music

while (!Space_Key_Pressed()) { /* repeat the title screen-loop as long as
the space key is not
                  pressed. notice no GOTO-statements are needed:
                  when space is
            pressed, this loop will no longer run and whatever is
            beneath it
            will take place next */
Draw_Title();
if(Escape_Pressed()) exit(0); /* if the player presses ESC, we quit the
whole program. Such
                  is the power of the exit-command in C++ */
}
```

```
/* below is the main game loop. it will repeat until the variable
"player_dead" returns a value of true */
while (player_dead==false) {
        Draw_Things();
        if(Space_Key_Pressed()) player_y-=5; else ++player_y;
        if(Check_Collisions()) player_dead=true; /* player and obstacle
        collide. This means the
                                  end of the current loop. */
        // Move the obstacle left..
        obstacle_x-=5;

        /* ..and bring it back to the right edge of the screen when it
        disappears off the left one */
        if(obstacle_x<0) obstacle_x=1024;
}

// once the player_dead-variable receives a value of "true", the section
below is reached.

while(!Escape_Pressed()) Draw_Gameover_Screen(); /* display game
over -screen until the player
                                                presses escape */
exit(0); // exit the program
}
```

More on Physics

To come across as less of a dolt when surrounded by any insufferable beta males, we'll now go through some elementary physics.

Newton's Laws of Motion

Sir Isaac Newton (1643 to 1727) formulated the basis for modern physics in his magnum opus, Philosphiae Naturalis Principia Mathematica (often simply referred to as Newton's Principia). His core findings can be summed into three laws of motion. As all digital physics engines are based on these laws, you might as well take a closer look at them.

- An object either remains at rest or continues to move at a constant velocity, unless acted upon by an external force.

- If a force acts on an object, it will cause an acceleration of that object (for bigger masses, a stronger force is needed).

- For every action there is an equal and opposite reaction.

Euler's Method

Not so fast! There's more physics goodness ahead of you. Leonhard Euler (1707 to 1783) was a Swiss scientist who expanded on Newton's work. His work is actually a big part of video game physics today.

In a computer context, the various properties in a physics simulation are sampled at specific intervals. Sampling them near-continuously would be optimal. Such an approach, however, is a tad too heavy on the hardware today.

This is where the Euler's method (i.e., Euler's integration) comes in. It simply refers to the technique of making predictions at set intervals when simulating the laws of physics. The approach is precise enough to sample relatively accurate data for computer physics without being too heavy on the resources. However, the various attributes involved (such as velocity and position of a mass) might act unpredictably. Some "glitching" is to be expected when using the Euler method in the game world.

Ragdoll

A *ragdoll* is a combination of physics bodies that, when put together, simulate a more or less realistic (usually human-like) character. This is used for death animations in both 2D and 3D games because ragdolling provides a relatively convincing collapse for dead characters. However, programmers frequently struggle to keep the collapsed ragdolls still as various unwanted twitching effects are both common and comical.

Rigid-Body Dynamics

A rigid body is a physics object that cannot be deformed. The object remains in static condition throughout the simulation, no matter what external forces are applied to it. These types of objects cannot exist in the real world, but they provide a decent amount of realism to video game characters and props.

Soft-Body Dynamics

This is a field in computer physics simulation that deals with malleable bodies. These include cloth, water, and other more elastic types of applications. This is a rather complex and resource-intense form of physics processing. Accurate soft-body dynamics therefore take a heavier toll on one's system. They are mostly fully simulated in more realistic games, such as the *BeamNG* driving simulator, although several titles use them for cosmetic purposes where collisions aren't a factor.

Physics Engines Rundown

Let's take a look at the most widely used physics systems in game engines today, as shown in Table 10-6. They are available for all major platforms, both on the desktop computer and on the console side of things.

Table 10-6. *Comparison of Popular Video Game Physics Engines*

Engine	License	Game Engine Support	Main Benefits
PhysX	Proprietary	Shoot-'Em-Up Kit, Unity	Offers hardware-accelerated output with a compatible Nvidia video card
Bullet	Open source	GameGuru, Blender	Optimization available for Nvidia, AMD, and PS3 hardware
Box2D	Open source	GameMaker Studio, Stencyl, Construct 2, Unity (2D)	High performance for large-scale 2D projects
Newton Game Dynamics	Open source	Leadwerks	Exceptionally stable skeletal simulation (ragdoll)

CHAPTER 11

The Mostly Codeless Challenge

You have done well so far, my friend. Only three things remain for you to do.

- Create a game for the platform of your choosing using the topics discussed in this book.

- Distribute your game through a well-established digital store, such as Steam.

- Sell at least 100 copies of this game at a competitive price.

If you manage all this, your video game developer potential has been unlocked. You are then on the right path. May you continue to make great games and have them sell way more than 100 copies each.

In any case, congratulations!

If you fail this challenge, simply reread the book and try, try again.

Sincerely,
Robert Ciesla
CEO, Soiree Games
Proud nerd

© Robert Ciesla 2017
R. Ciesla, *Mostly Codeless Game Development*, DOI 10.1007/978-1-4842-2970-5_11

Index

Get the eBook for only $5!

Why limit yourself?

With most of our titles available in both PDF and ePUB format, you can access your content wherever and however you wish—on your PC, phone, tablet, or reader.

Since you've purchased this print book, we are happy to offer you the eBook for just $5.

To learn more, go to http://www.apress.com/companion or contact support@apress.com.

Apress®

Printed in the United States
By Bookmasters